3 9153 00939150 1

DISCARD

The Presidency of
ANDREW
JOHNSON

AMERICAN PRESIDENCY SERIES

Donald R. McCoy, Clifford S. Griffin, Homer E. Socolofsky
General Editors

George Washington, Forrest McDonald
John Adams, Ralph Adams Brown
Thomas Jefferson, Forrest McDonald
James Madison, Robert Allen Rutland
John Quincy Adams, Mary W. M. Hargreaves
Andrew Jackson, Donald B. Cole
Martin Van Buren, Major L. Wilson
William Henry Harrison & John Tyler, Norma Lois Peterson
James K. Polk, Paul H. Bergeron
Zachary Taylor & Millard Fillmore, Elbert B. Smith
Franklin Pierce, Larry Gara
James Buchanan, Elbert B. Smith
Abraham Lincoln, Phillip Shaw Paludan
Andrew Johnson, Albert Castel
Rutherford B. Hayes, Ari Hoogenboom
James A. Garfield & Chester A. Arthur, Justus D. Doenecke
Grover Cleveland, Richard E. Welch, Jr.
Benjamin Harrison, Homer B. Socolofsky & Allan B. Spetter
William McKinley, Lewis L. Gould
Theodore Roosevelt, Lewis L. Gould
William Howard Taft, Paolo E. Coletta
Woodrow Wilson, Kendrick A. Clements
Warren G. Harding, Eugene P. Trani & David L. Wilson
Herbert C. Hoover, Martin L. Fausold
Harry S. Truman, Donald R. McCoy
Dwight D. Eisenhower, Chester J. Pach, Jr., & Elmo Richardson
John F. Kennedy, James N. Giglio
Lyndon B. Johnson, Vaughn Davis Bornet
James Earl Carter, Jr., Burton I. Kaufman

The Presidency of
ANDREW
JOHNSON

by
Albert Castel

UNIVERSITY PRESS OF KANSAS

© 1979 by the University Press of Kansas
All rights reserved

Published by the University Press of Kansas (Lawrence,
Kansas 66049), which was organized by the Kansas
Board of Regents and is operated and funded by Emporia
State University, Fort Hays State University,
Kansas State University, Pittsburg State University, the
University of Kansas, and Wichita State University

Library of Congress Cataloging-in-Publication Data

Castel, Albert E.
The Presidency of Andrew Johnson.

(American presidency series)
Includes index.
ISBN 0-7006-0190-2
1. United States—Politics and government—1865–1869.
2. Reconstruction. 3. Johnson, Andrew, Pres. U.S., 1808–1875.
4. Presidents—United States—Biography.
I. Title.   II. Series.
E666.C23   973.8'1'0924 [B]   70-11050

British Library Cataloguing in Publication Data is available.

Printed in the United States of America

10   9   8   7   6   5   4

The paper used in this publication meets the minimum requirements
of the American National Standard for Permanence of Paper
for Printed Library Materials Z39.48-1984.

Editors' Preface

The aim of the American Presidency Series is to present historians and the general reading public with interesting, scholarly assessments of the various presidential administrations. These interpretive surveys are intended to cover the broad ground between biographies, specialized monographs, and journalistic accounts. As such, each will be a comprehensive, synthetic work which will draw upon the best in pertinent secondary literature, yet leave room for the author's own analysis and interpretation.

Each volume in the series will deal with a separate presidential administration and will present the data essential to understanding the administration under consideration. Particularly, each book will treat the then current problems facing the United States and its people and how the president and his associates felt about, thought about, and worked to cope with these problems. Attention will be given to how the office developed and operated during the president's tenure. Equally important will be consideration of the vital relationships between the president, his staff, the executive officers, Congress, foreign representatives, the judiciary, state officials, the public, political parties, the press, and influential private citizens. The series will also be concerned with how this unique American institution—the presidency—was viewed by the presidents, and with what results.

All this will be set, insofar as possible, in the context not only of contemporary politics but also of economics, international relations, law, morals, public administration, religion, and thought. Such a broad approach is necessary to understanding, for a presidential administration is more than the elected and appointed officers composing it, since its work so often reflects the major problems, anxieties, and glories of the nation. In short, the authors in the series will strive to recount and evaluate the record of each administration and to identify its distinctiveness and relationships to the past, its own time, and the future.

Donald R. McCoy
Clifford S. Griffin
Homer E. Socolofsky

Preface

Anyone writing about the presidency of Andrew Johnson encounters three major problems. The first is balance. His administration coincided with the most crucial and dramatic phase of Reconstruction. Therefore historians have tended to concentrate, to the exclusion of practically everything else, upon his key role in that titanic event. This book inevitably has the same focus. But it also examines other important aspects of his presidency, in particular foreign, economic, and Indian policies. By so doing I have attempted at least to indicate that Andrew Johnson occasionally thought about matters other than Reconstruction and that not everything of importance that happened during his administration had to do with the South and the Negro.

The second problem is trying to understand Johnson's motives; he has always been an enigma. Much is known about what he did, little about why he did it. He received and filed thousands of letters but wrote few himself. He kept no diary and rarely confided in anyone. He was, however, both a politician and a president, and hence, he was a man who sought and exercised power.

This approach also helps in solving a third problem, which is trying to be objective about Johnson. Most historians either admire or despise him, depending on whether they consider his Reconstruction policies right or wrong. In this book I am concerned more with whether he was good at using power than with whether he used it for the "good." Were the goals he set for himself realistic? Did he employ effective means of endeavoring to attain them? And what were the pragmatic consequences of his successes and failures?

I am not so rash as to claim that I have achieved perfect objectivity about Johnson. Like all historians I am influenced by my times, biases, and ideological predisposition. The only advantages I have over previous historians who have dealt with Johnson's presidency are the advantages provided by over one hundred years of subsequent history and, above all, by the writings of those historians. How much or how little I have benefited from those advantages the reader will, of course, judge for himself.

The research and preparation of this book was greatly facilitated by the American Council of Learned Societies, which provided a grant-in-aid; by William C. Davis, David Herbert Donald, and Bell I. Wiley, who gave indirect but valued encouragement; by Professors Ernst Breisach, Alan Brown, Ross Gregory, and Howard Mowen of Western Michigan University, who kept that "weary load" light; and by the staffs of the following organizations: Waldo Library and the Regional History Collection, Western Michigan University; the Kansas State Historical Society; the United States Army Military History Institute, Carlisle Barracks, Pennsylvania; the New York Public Library; the Manuscript Division of the Library of Congress; the Ohio State Historical Society; the Graduate Library of the University of Michigan; and the Andrew Johnson Project of the University of Tennessee. I also wish to thank Mrs. Becky Ryder, secretary in the History Department at Western Michigan University, for her efficient typing of the manuscript; Larry Massie, assistant director of the Regional History Collection at Western Michigan University, for his aid and company in conducting research; and my daughter, Ann, for her services as research assistant and general factotum—services which (for her at least) were highlighted by the July 13, 1977, blackout in New York City. Finally, I wish to acknowledge Max and Hilde, my almost constant but not always silent companions while I wrote, and to express my gratitude to my wife whose help was, as ever, essential.

Albert Castel

Kalamazoo, Michigan
August 1978

Contents

1

★★★★★

ANDREW JOHNSON
BECOMES PRESIDENT

At ten o'clock on the night of April 14, 1865, Andrew Johnson, vice-president of the United States of America, lay asleep in suite 68 of the Kirkwood House on Pennsylvania Avenue, Washington, D.C. Then he heard a pounding on the door of the outer room, followed by a frantic but familiar voice shouting, "Governor Johnson, if you are in the room, I must see you!" He climbed out of bed, lighted a lamp, pulled on his trousers, and approached the door. "Farwell? Is that you?" he asked. "Yes. Let me in!" came the response.

He opened the door and Leonard J. Farwell, a former governor of Wisconsin and now inspector of inventions at the Patent Office, darted in. Farwell was a friend of Johnson's who had visited him earlier that evening and had invited Johnson to come along to a performance of *Our American Cousin* at Ford's Theater. Farwell slammed the door shut, locked it, and then gasped out his dreadful news: President Lincoln had been shot!

Farwell had witnessed the deed and had run the two-and-a-half blocks from the theater to the Kirkwood House to warn Johnson that his life was in danger. Of course Farwell did not know that George Atzerodt, to whom John Wilkes Booth had assigned the mission of murdering the vice-president, was at that moment wandering the streets of Washington in a drunken stupor; Atzerodt had lost his nerve after, that very morning, renting a room directly above Johnson's at the Kirkwood House.

Overwhelmed by shock, for a while Johnson and Farwell clung to each other, unable to speak. Then more men arrived, bringing additional and contradictory reports of the tragedy at Ford's Theater, plus news that Secretary of State William H. Seward had also been attacked. Johnson thereupon asked Farwell to ascertain personally the president's condition and that of Seward. About two hours later Farwell returned: Seward was badly wounded, Lincoln was dying.

Accompanied only by Farwell and an army officer, Johnson at once walked to the house across from Ford's to which Lincoln had been carried. For half an hour he stood in the little room where Lincoln lay slant-wise on a bed. Then Senator Charles Sumner of Massachusetts suggested that Johnson leave—his presence disturbed Mrs. Lincoln. He did so, returning to the Kirkwood House.

At 7:30 A.M. Major General Henry W. Halleck entered Johnson's suite and informed him that he was not to leave the hotel without a guard. At that moment church bells began tolling: Lincoln was dead. As soon as Johnson took the oath of office, he would be president of the United States.[1]

No man before or since rose from lower depths to reach the height of that office than did Andrew Johnson.[2] He was born in a two-room shack in Raleigh, North Carolina, on December 29, 1808. His parents, Jacob and Mary, were illiterate tavern servants. Early in 1812 Jacob Johnson died as the consequence of rescuing two wealthy townsmen from an icy stream; his reward was burial in an unmarked grave in the local potter's field.

Mary Johnson eked out an existence for herself, Andrew, and his older brother, William, by taking in washing and sewing. In 1814 she married a ne'er-do-well named Turner Daughtry who merely increased the family's destitution. "I have grappled," Andrew Johnson declared in later years, "with the gaunt and haggard monster called hunger."

In 1822 the Johnson boys became apprentices to James Selby, a Raleigh tailor. Andrew learned the tailor's trade and—thanks to a physician and a preacher who befriended him—the rudiments of reading. Then in June 1824, fearful of arrest for having thrown stones at the house of an old woman (along with two other apprentices), William and Andrew fled to South Carolina, where they supported themselves by tailoring. Meanwhile Selby posted a ten-dollar reward for the apprehension of Andrew, whom he described as having "a dark complexion, black hair, eyes, and habits."

In the fall of 1825 Andrew returned to Raleigh and offered to finish the remaining five years of his apprenticeship. Selby, however, refused either to take him back or to release him from service. Andrew thereupon went to Tennessee, worked as a tailor in Columbia, and decided to settle in that state. On his next visit to Raleigh, he persuaded his mother and step-father to move to Tennessee also. Late in the summer of 1826, their possessions piled into a two-wheeled cart pulled by a blind horse, they crossed the Great Smokies into eastern Tennessee.

For a while Andrew plied his trade in Rutledge, then in March 1827 he opened a shop in the mountain village of Greeneville. Two months later he married seventeen-year-old Eliza McCardle, the daughter of a recently deceased shoemaker. Although she had only an elementary education, Eliza taught her new husband to write and cipher. In time she also bore him three sons—Charles, Robert, and Andrew, Jr.—and two daughters—Martha and Mary.

Johnson was a good tailor. "My work never ripped or gave way," he later boasted. Before long he was doing well enough to hire several assistants. He also sought to better himself in other ways. When working he had people read to him, and in his spare time he read to himself or practiced writing. And he joined a debating society, walking four miles every Friday night to attend its meetings and then walking back.

From the debating society and less formal discussions with friends in his tailor shop it was an easy step into local politics. In 1829 Johnson became an alderman and two years later, mayor of Greeneville. Then in 1835 he went to the state legislature. But there he blundered: He opposed as unconstitutional a bond issue for the construction of roads. In doing so he ignored the fact that the Greeneville region badly needed better roads. Not so the hometown voters, however, who retired him from the legislature at the next election.

Johnson was elected again in 1839, having meanwhile reconsidered his constitutional scruples. The following year he proclaimed himself a member of the Democratic party, and as such he successfully ran for the United States House of Representatives in 1842. Henceforth he continued to own the tailor shop, but he no longer worked there. He was now and forever a professional politician.

Johnson served five consecutive terms in the House. During this time his only noteworthy positive activity was to sponsor a homestead bill which eventually passed the House but failed in the Senate, mainly because of opposition from his fellow Southerners. Otherwise, according to Ralph W. Haskins, who has made the most thorough study of Johnson's congressional career, "His record in the House of Representatives reveals him as a dissenter often petty in dissent, a blunt man of principle to whom compromise was almost invariably the wrong solution, and a verbal bludgeonist who now and then showed a trace of the demagogue."[3]

In 1852 the Whigs gained control of the legislature and promptly gerrymandered Johnson out of his congressional seat. "I have no political future," he lamented bitterly—but rather unfairly, for a Democratic legislature had gerrymandered him into his seat in the first place. He quickly rallied, however, and in 1853 through clever maneuvering secured the Democratic nomination for governor. Then, after a vigorous campaign, he defeated a formidable Whig opponent. Two years later he repeated his victory. As governor, Johnson's relations with the state legislature were generally stormy, for at all times at least one chamber was dominated by his political enemies. Even so, he pushed through a law establishing Tennessee's first public school system and successfully sponsored a number of other constructive measures. Moreover, in 1857 when the legislature again became solidly Democratic, it sent him to the United States Senate.[4]

In getting to the top in Tennessee politics, Johnson had overcome men of superior learning, intellect, and status. None could match him in appealing to the "plebians," as he liked to call the small farmers and self-employed tradesmen who comprised the vast majority of Tennessee's voters, especially in the mountainous eastern part of the state. They were, he told them, the true foundation of society, whereas the wealthy aristocrats in their big mansions were merely parasites. He himself, Johnson constantly reminded them, was a "plebian mechanic, and not ashamed nor afraid to own it." Hence they could trust him to uphold the cause of democracy, which he extolled as the only true political religion, with Constitution as its Bible and Jefferson and Jackson as its prophets.

Johnson's enemies accused him of demagoguery. In a sense they were correct. But the most effective demagogue is a sincere one—and there is no reason to doubt Johnson's sincerity. Certainly his followers in eastern Tennessee did not. Long after he was dead, one of them declared that "Johnson was always the same to everybody, . . . he was free from ostenation and . . . the honors heaped upon him did not make him forget to be kind to the humblest citizen." Or, as another admirer put it in 1853, "God Bless him! He has a heart as big as a fodder stack!"[5]

In the rough and tumble election contests of semifrontier

Tennessee, stump speaking—debates between rival candidates or between a candidate and hostile persons in the audience—usually determined the outcome. Johnson was the best stumper in the state —some said in the nation. His appearance was impressive: "He looked," wrote a reporter in 1853, "as rarely ever man looked, turning slowly his deep, dark Webster-like orbs to various parts of the crowd . . . which seemed scarcely to breathe." He had a pleasant, compelling voice which carried far and never grew hoarse. In debates he "cut and slashed right and left . . . running his opponents through and through with a rusty jagged weapon; chopping to mincemeat and grinding to powder his luckless adversary."[6] He turned heckling to his own advantage, answering insults with insults and portraying himself as an underdog battling overwhelming odds.

After 1852, when the Whig party disintegrated nationally, the Democrats tended to dominate Tennessee, and Johnson benefited accordingly. His margin of victory, however, in both of his gubernatorial races was quite narrow and owed more to his own efforts than to his party's backing. Moreover, most of the top Tennessee Democrats were upper-class lawyers and planters who made no secret of the fact they disliked Johnson and would dump him were he not so popular with the masses. Hence, it is understandable that Johnson relied mainly on his own political machine consisting of devoted friends who served him as advisers, leg men, and wire pullers. He was not merely boasting when he declaimed on entering the Senate: "I am no party man, bound by no party platform, and will vote as I please."[7]

In part, Johnson's success was due to his great stamina. A well-muscled 5' 8", he was a tireless campaigner, able to endure long hours of traveling over wretched roads to speak or debate at town after town, day after day. He wore down and wore out less vigorous opponents.

Furthermore, his courage was extraordinary. Often he cowed hostile crowds; more than once he defied murder threats. Nor was his bravery just physical. On issues he deemed fundamental, he ignored political expediency and risked his popularity. Thus, during the 1855 gubernatorial campaign, he resisted the xenophobic flood of Know-Nothingism which seemed about to engulf Tennessee, denouncing it in scathing terms as undemocratic and un-American. He believed that although the people might be deceived for a while, sooner or later they would see the truth—and follow those leaders who had remained faithful to it.

But the most important reason for Johnson's rise to power was his desire for power. It was, testified a discerning fellow-resident of Greeneville, his "consuming passion." He sought it with single-minded dedication. "For society or idle pleasures he had no taste, and in common everyday affairs he took no interest." He preferred solitude and "lived in his own home in almost exclusive retirement." Only during campaigns could he be seen often on the streets. Then he "generally gathered a little crowd around him and talked as if making a speech." He always appeared in public impeccably dressed; he was stiff and formal in manner; and his few close friends were all politicians. His mind worked slowly and followed narrow, hidden channels, but once he reached a conclusion Johnson stuck to it doggedly. Compromise was alien to his nature, opposition increased his determination, and defeat only made him fight harder.[8]

The forces behind Johnson's drive for power were bitterness over the hardships of his boyhood and resentment against the rich, well-born, and highly educated who in his adulthood he felt looked down on self-made men like himself. These so-called gentry, he once declared, were filled with "false ideas of their own superiority, mixed with a superabundance of self-esteem which causes them to feel that the great mass of mankind were intended by their Creator to be 'hewers of wood and drawers of water.' . . ." And on another occasion—in a typical, semiliterate fashion in a letter to a friend—he denounced the wealthy residents of Greeneville as "God forsaken and hell deserving, money loving, hypocritical, back bighting, Sunday praying scoundrels. . . ." There was a core of truth in the nasty remark of one of his enemies: "If Andy Johnson were a snake, he would hide in the grass and bite the heels of rich men's children."[9]

Power for Johnson meant vengeance and vindication. "Some day," he vowed in 1836 after being snubbed socially in Greeneville, "I will show the stuck-up aristocrats who is running the country." His life was "an intense, unceasing, desperate, upward struggle." He had "a deep-seated, burning hatred of all men who stood in his way." Political combat was personal combat, and he engaged in it with savage ferocity. A Whig opponent described him as a man "who cuts when he does cut not with a razor but a case knife."[10]

By 1857 Johnson had cut his way to the Senate. He was also, thanks to shrewd bond and land investments, a well-to-do man who lived in a handsome brick house on Greeneville's Main Street and owned four "household slaves"—two adults and two children. But what a friend termed his "towering ambition" remained unsatisfied.

As early as 1852 he had hoped, on the basis of his advocacy of the homestead law, to win the Democratic vice-presidential nomination, and he was disappointed when he failed. Four years later he obtained the endorsement of the Tennessee Democrats as their favorite-son presidential candidate, in hopes of getting at least second place on the party's national ticket. And in large part presidential ambition prompted his move to the Senate in 1857. "In public life," he commented at the time, "the true policy is to move upward and onward."[11]

In the Senate he continued to champion homestead legislation. Again, most of the opposition came from his Southern Democratic colleagues whereas Northern Republicans provided the strongest support. Finally in June 1860 both houses passed by huge majorities a watered-down version of his bill. President James Buchanan, however, ever-anxious to appease the South, vetoed it, and Southern votes sustained the veto in the Senate. Bitterly disappointed, Johnson declared that presidents should never veto bills passed by a two-thirds majority.[12]

Meanwhile Johnson was still angling for the presidency. In April 1860 he sent his two older sons, Charles and Robert, along with Sam Milligan, his chief political henchman, to Charleston, South Carolina, to represent his interests at the Democratic Convention. Although the Tennessee delegation voted for Johnson on thirty-six consecutive ballots, the convention broke up without nominating anyone. Most of the Southern delegates walked out after failing to pass a platform calling for federal protection of slavery in the territories. Subsequently, Northern Democrats named Stephen A. Douglas and Southern Democrats put forth John C. Breckinridge. Johnson supported the latter, but without hope of success, for he recognized that the Democratic split had made Republican victory certain.

Lincoln's election in November precipitated the secession of the Lower South. In the Senate, during the winter of 1860–61, Johnson took a prominent part in attempting to arrange a new sectional compromise, despite his earlier declaration that he was against such compromises in principle. At the same time he staunchly opposed secession which he branded as treason. He believed in states' rights and defended the right of slavery, but his concept of the Constitution derived from Andrew Jackson and not John C. Calhoun. Johnson argued that slavery could be best protected inside rather than outside the Union and that the preservation of the Union must come above all else. He also denounced the "red-hot disunionists" whose "unhallowed ambition" would plunge the South and the nation into disaster. His pro-Union speeches received great publicity, both because of their power and because he was the only Southern senator to take such a stand. In the North, they helped arouse determination to maintain the Union; in the South, they resulted in his being condemned as a traitor to his section.

Even so, the people of Tennessee backed him at first. Early in February 1861 they rejected by a large majority prosecessionist Governor Isham B. Harris's proposal for a convention to take the state out of the Union. But in April came Fort Sumter and Lincoln's call for volunteers to suppress the rebellion. In Tennessee, as in the rest of the Upper South, the current of public opinion changed course. Governor Harris entered into a "military league" with the Confederacy, and the legislature ordered a referendum on the question of secession.

Johnson hastened home to champion the Union cause. While traveling there by train through Virginia he braved hostile demonstrations and threats of death. On arriving he toured eastern Tennessee, sometimes speaking with a pistol on the podium in front of him. William G. "Parson" Brownlow, Horace Maynard, T. A. R. Nelson, and Oliver Temple—all Whigs and long-standing political foes—joined him in the antisecessionist crusade. On June 8 the predominantly Whig and nonslaveowning mountaineers of eastern Tennessee voted 33,000 to 14,000 against secession. But the middle and western regions favored it 67,000 to 14,000; hence Tennessee formally joined the Confederacy. Ten days later Johnson, who had been warned that if he stayed in the state he surely would be assassinated, fled to Kentucky. He left behind his wife, his two daughters, and his six-year-old son, Andrew, Jr. Charles and Robert took to the mountains to organize resistance to Confederate rule.

Johnson's valiant struggle against secession won him the acclaim of the North: He was called "the greatest man of the age" by the *New York Times*. Moreover, as the only senator from a rebel state to remain in Congress, he became the symbol and spokesman of Southern Unionism. Acting in that role, in July 1861, he joined John J. Crittenden of Kentucky in sponsoring a resolution, which Congress passed almost unanimously, declaring that war was being waged solely to preserve the Union and not to subjugate the South or to destroy its institutions, e.g., slavery. But unlike many Border state Unionists, Johnson eventually supported emancipation—not out of any sympathy for the slaves but strictly as a means of winning the war and breaking the power of the Southern aristocrats. "Damn the negroes," he told a Northern general; "I am fighting those traitorous aristocrats, their masters!"[13]

8

Early in 1862, Ulysses S. Grant drove the Confederates out of the middle and western parts of Tennessee. At Lincoln's behest Johnson went to Nashville as military governor. During the next three years he was virtually the dictator of Tennessee—or at least of the portion controlled by the federal army. At times, as the tide of war swept back and forth across the state, that area was quite small. For two months in the fall of 1862, rebel forces practically surrounded Nashville. Johnson, however, rejected all suggestions of evacuating the city: He would burn it first! Finally a Union counteroffensive drove back the Confederates, who meanwhile had permitted his family to rejoin him.

Throughout his tenure as military governor Johnson struggled to establish a pro-Union civil government in Tennessee. But not until early 1865, with the inauguration of "Parson" Brownlow as governor, did Johnson succeed. Even then he had to resort to the large-scale disfranchisement of Confederate adherents and a rigged constitutional convention through which he rammed an amendment abolishing slavery in the state. He justified these high-handed tactics as being necessary to restore Tennessee to the Union and declared that sometimes ordinary laws had to be disregarded in order to maintain the fundamental law.

In 1864 the Republicans changed their official name to the Union party so as to attract support from prowar Northern Democrats and Border state Unionists. In pursuance of this strategy, Lincoln had them nominate as his running mate Andrew Johnson, whose conduct of affairs in Tennessee had favorably impressed him. Thus it was that late in February 1865 Johnson headed for Washington to be inaugurated as vice-president.

He arrived still weak from a severe bout of typhoid fever. On the night before the inauguration he attended a party in his honor at which he drank a good deal of wine. He awoke on the morning of March 4 with a hangover. When he reached the Capitol, where he was to take the oath, he felt faint. He asked out-going Vice-president Hannibal Hamlin for "some good whisky." Hamlin procured a bottle and Johnson drank two stiff wallops, saying, "I need all the strength for the occasion I can have."[14]

He then went into the Senate chamber to deliver his inaugural address. The heat of that poorly ventilated and densely crowded hall combined with the whiskey to make him drunk or at least tight. The result was a rambling, maudlin, almost incoherent harrangue delivered in a slurred voice and filled with such statements as: "I'm a-going' for to tell you—here today; yes, I'm a-going' for to tell you

9

all, that I'm a plebian! I glory in it; I am a plebian! The people—yes, the people of the United States have made me what I am; and I am a-going' to tell you here today—yes, today, in this place—that the people are everything." Some of the spectators tittered, several of the Republican senators covered their faces with their hands, and Lincoln's head drooped in humiliation. At last Johnson stumbled to a halt, whereupon Hamlin hastily swore him in as vice-president.[15]

Most Democrats deemed Johnson a political apostate, and in reporting the inauguration the New York World, the leading Democratic newspaper, described him as a "drunken clown." Many mortified Republicans agreed. Led by Charles Sumner they clamored for his resignation. Lincoln, however, took a more charitable and also a more realistic view: "I have known Andrew Johnson for many years," he told a worried cabinet member. "He made a bad slip the other day, but you need not be scared; Andy ain't a drunkard."[16] In fact, in May 1864, prior to the Republican Convention, Lincoln had sent an agent to Nashville to check out Johnson on this score and had received a report that although the Tennessean liked his whisky, he did not habitually over-indulge—which was more than could be said about many other public figures of the period.

Johnson, aware that he had disgraced himself, did not preside over the Senate during the short time Congress remained in session following the inaugural. Instead he spent the next two weeks recuperating physically and emotionally at the Silver Springs, Maryland, mansion of Francis Preston Blair, Sr., who had offered him sanctuary. When Johnson returned to Washington late in March, it was with the intention of leaving soon for Tennessee. He wished to rejoin his family and reestablish them in Greeneville, where the Confederates had used his house as a hospital.

However, Grant's capture of Richmond, heralding the end of the war, caused Johnson to postpone his trip home. On Friday, April 14, he conferred with Lincoln at the White House—about what is not known. This was his first meeting with Lincoln since the inauguration.[17] As vice-president—and a disgraced one at that —Johnson had little part or influence in the affairs of the government. Politically, he had hit a dead end.

Then, that night, came the pounding on his hotel door.

Some twelve hours later, shortly after ten o'clock on the morning of April 15, 1865, in the parlor of the Kirkwood House, where a dozen or so cabinet members, congressmen, and others had gathered, Chief Justice Salmon P. Chase administered the oath of office to Andrew Johnson, the seventeenth president of the United States.

10

He became president in the closing days of the most emotional and revolutionary experience in the history of the American people. During the past four years they had been engaged in a titantic civil war. For the North the object of that struggle had been to preserve a nation and, secondarily, to destroy slavery; for the South the purpose had been to create a nation and to preserve slavery. Both sections had poured into the conflict immense amounts of passion, treasure, and blood. When Robert E. Lee surrendered at Appomattox, just six days before Johnson took the oath of office, it was evident that the South had lost: The United States would remain one nation headed by a supreme federal government dominated by the North; the extreme doctrine of states' rights now lay in the historical scrap heap; and slavery was dead, although its corpse would be a long time decomposing.

The North had paid a stiff price for its victory.[18] The federal government had spent directly on the war over $3 billion; the states and local communities, hundreds of millions of dollars more. The national debt stood at $2.8 billion, the tax rate was the highest in the world, and the value of the dollar had declined sharply. Also, during the past four years, the North had mobilized nearly 3,000,000 soldiers and sailors. Of this total, 360,000 were dead (110,000 from battle, the rest from disease) and approximately 275,000 had been wounded but survived. Little wonder that the jubilation in the North over winning the war was mixed with resentment over its cost—a resentment which Lincoln's assassination intensified.

Despite its heavy expenditure of money and men, however, the North emerged from the war stronger than when it had entered. The birthrate had remained high, and the number of immigrants (mainly German, Irish, and English) had averaged one hundred and sixty thousand a year since Fort Sumter—less than in peacetime but still sizable. Furthermore, approximately 15 percent of the Union's dead were foreign enlistees and white and Negro soldiers from the Border states and the South. Hence, in all likelihood, the population of what were still called the free states stood at well over twenty million in 1865 as compared to nineteen million in 1860. Significantly, the War Department calculated that at the end of the war there were more men in the "loyal" states "properly subject" to military duty than when it began.

Between 1861 and 1865 Confederate cruisers had driven the previously flourishing United States merchant marine from the oceans, and New England's textile mills had had to shut down for lack of cotton. But on the whole, Northern industry, agriculture,

11

commerce, and technology had continued to develop, although for the most part at a rate slower than the rapid prewar pace.[19] Thus, for example, three thousand more miles of railroad track had been laid, one hundred thousand additional miles of telegraph line had been strung, and the woolen mills—stimulated by the army's need for uniforms— had doubled their output. Most spectacular of all were the oil fields of northwestern Pennsylvania: There, derricks and entire towns sprouted like mushrooms following a spring rain. Elsewhere, everywhere, new businesses were starting and old ones expanding. To be sure, prices were high, but so was employment. The nation, declared the federal revenue commissioner in August 1865, "is infected with a spirit of enterprise which seems to redouble its energy with every additional burden placed upon it." In the summer of 1865 a former Union army officer in Kansas wrote a friend, expressing the thoughts of thousands of ambitious and enterprising men all over the North: "There is going to be a chance to make some money in the next five or ten years which neither of us may ever have again. I have determined to avail myself of it. I shall devote all my energy and powers to securing my share of it."[20]

Last, but far from least, the war had boosted the pride and confidence of the Northern people. They had battled and conquered the twin evils of secession and slavery. They had not only saved the nation but had also created a better nation, a nation which was *theirs*. They had been tested in the fiery blast of combat and been found tough and true. The glory of the present guaranteed an even more glorious future. Walt Whitman spoke what they felt:

> Race of veterans—race of victors!
> Race of the soil, ready for the conflict—race of the con-
>   quering march!
> (No more credulity's race, abiding temper'd race)
> Race henceforth owing no law but the law itself,
> Race of passion and the storm.

No such exaltation existed in the South. Defeat there had cost far more than victory had in the North. Some two hundred and forty thousand soldiers had died, another two hundred and sixty thousand had been wounded or incapacitated by illness. This loss, moreover, had been suffered by a white population of only 5.5 million, out of which approximately one million men had seen military service. Also, many of the ragged rebel veterans were so worn-down with hunger and privation that they had difficulty making their way home; when they did arrive, they were too weak to perform arduous labor. In fact, thousands of the survivors were literally physical wrecks: In 1866 Mississippi would set aside 20 percent of its meagre budget to purchase artificial limbs for disabled veterans, and most of the other Southern states made equivalent appropriations for the same purpose.

All of the major campaigns of the war—except Lee's well-mannered invasion of Pennsylvania—had taken place in the Border states and in the South. There the armies had fought, marched, confiscated, plundered, ransacked, and burned. When the smoke of battle lifted in the spring of 1865, a scene of horrible destruction appeared. Northern Virginia and the Shenandoah Valley were desolated, large areas of Tennessee, Mississippi, Louisiana, and Arkansas lay in ruins, and a broad path of devastation marked the passage of Sherman's conquerors across Georgia and South Carolina. The central portions of Richmond, Charleston, and Columbia were mere heaps of scorched rubble. In Atlanta only one short block of buildings remained standing in the business district and Jackson, Mississippi, had been almost completely obliterated. Countless smaller towns, villages, plantations, and farms had been reduced to shambles. Hundreds of miles of track had been torn up and the rails that remained were so warped and worn that the few ramshackle trains still operating had to creep along them. Most Southern factories—and before the war there were fewer factories in the entire South than in New England alone—had been wrecked. Once bountiful, productive fields now were overgrown with weeds and brush. Where great battles had occurred, as around Petersburg, Virginia, farmers were unable to plow and plant because the ground was so filled with lead, hunks of iron, unexploded shells, and half-buried skeletons.

The Confederacy (not counting the state governments) spent an estimated $2.3 billion financing the war—an effort which in proportion to resources far surpassed that of the North. Most of this expense took the form of paper money and bonds. With defeat both became worthless, and tens of thousands of Southerners were left literally penniless. Formerly wealthy men and women wore patched and threadbare clothes; people accustomed to dining on hams and chickens considered themselves lucky to have a few ears of corn or some potatoes. In some areas only the distribution of food by the Union army prevented mass starvation. For most Southerners life had become, and for many it would long remain, "mostly a matter of not dying."

Before the war Southern leaders had boasted that "cotton is

king." It was the main money crop of the South, the single most valuable export of the entire United States. But during the war, planters greatly curtailed their cotton acreage in order to grow food for the army and because of the extremely limited market. When the war ended they eagerly sought to resume full-scale production of cotton, for they anticipated big profits and badly needed the income. But a combination of factors—a shortage of labor, lack of horses and mules, destroyed gins and other equipment, inadequate transport, and insufficient capital were the major ones—frustrated their efforts. As a consequence the South marketed only three hundred thousand bales of cotton in 1865 as compared to five million in 1860. Not until the early 1870s would cotton production regain its antebellum level.

Added to the heavy toll of dead and crippled men, to the immense physical destruction, and to the poverty and privation was the psychological and emotional shock of defeat. Southerners began the war supremely confident of victory. During the ensuing years, despite the mounting reverses and odds, most continued to strive and to hope. When Lee surrendered they felt grief, anger, and the awful agony of failure and frustration, all mixed with a sense of relief that at least, and at last, the killing was over. In the end, most Southerners accepted the harsh fact of defeat: They had fought the good battle, and if they had lost, it was because they were lacking in might, not right. What now concerned them, apart from simply surviving, were the consequences of defeat—Northern domination and, above all, Negro liberation.

The single most revolutionary outcome of the war had been the emancipation of 3.5 million Negro slaves in the eleven Confederate states and of another half million or so in the four Border states. The labor, the social, and the racial systems of the Old South were no more. But what would replace them? In the spring of 1865 no one knew, least of all the great mass of illiterate, ignorant, and destitute Negroes. They did know, however, that they were free and that to be free was better than being enslaved. Hence, unlike the Southern whites, they hailed with joy what the war had brought and looked to the uncertain future with hope.

Such, then, was the United States of America at the close of the Civil War and at the beginning of Andrew Johnson's presidency. Obviously the states were united only in the sense that the federal government had imposed its authority on the eleven rebel states through superior power. Otherwise the nation was still profoundly divided: on one side the triumphant, exultant, and prosperous

North; on the other the vanquished, embittered, and devastated South. And between them stood the newly freed Negroes whose fate rested in the hands of the whites of both sections. Much had been decided during and by the war, but many things remained undecided with the advent of peace. During the next four years the "second American Revolution," which had begun in 1861, would continue.

2

★★★★★

THE PRESIDENT PROCLAIMS
HIS POLICY

"The conduct of Mr. Johnson," Secretary of the Treasury Hugh McCulloch wrote later, "favorably impressed those who were present when the oath was administered to him. He was grief-stricken like the rest, and he seemed to be oppressed by the suddeness of the call upon him to become President . . . ; but he was neverthless calm and self-possessed."[1]

After taking the oath Johnson read a short speech in which he stated that "any policy which may be pursued by me in the administration of the Government" must be left to subsequent development. He then asked the cabinet members present—McCulloch, Secretary of War Edwin M. Stanton, Secretary of the Navy Gideon Welles, Attorney General James Speed, Secretary of the Interior James P. Usher, and Postmaster General William Dennison—to remain at their posts. All agreed to do so until Johnson saw fit to dispense with their services. (Usher, however, was merely serving until his already designated successor, James Harlan of Iowa, arrived in Washington.) As the cabinet left, recalled McCulloch, it felt "not entirely relieved of apprehensions" stemming from Johnson's "unfortunate" speech of March 4, but "hopeful that he would prove to be a popular and judicious President."[2]

Few presidents on coming into office—and no nonelected one with the possible exception of Harry S. Truman—ever faced a greater problem than did Andrew Johnson in the spring of 1865. This problem even then was summed up in one word: Reconstruction. The war had settled the question of Southern independence and had emancipated the Negro slaves. But when, by what process, and under what terms would the Confederate states rejoin the Union? And what would be the future legal, political, and social status of the black man in white America?

To these peacetime questions the wartime policies of the federal government provided no clear answer. In 1863 Lincoln had promulgated for Louisiana, Arkansas, and Tennessee (all more or less under federal military occupation) a program whereby 10 percent of the voters, on taking an oath of allegiance to the United States, could form state governments and elect congressmen. The Republican majority in Congress, however, opposed this "Ten Percent Plan" as inadequate and overly lenient. Declaring that Reconstruction was a legislative rather than an executive function, they refused to seat the Southern congressmen elected under the plan. In July 1864, Congress passed the Wade-Davis Bill which disfranchised all high-ranking Confederates, stipulated that 50 percent of the voters in a rebel state must take a loyalty oath before elections could be held, and made the abolition of slavery a condition for readmission to the Union. Lincoln, in turn, pocket-vetoed this measure on the grounds that Reconstruction policy should be kept flexible—that is, in presidential hands. Finally (confusing the situation even more), just before his assassination Lincoln had hinted that with the coming of peace he might take a different approach to Reconstruction, one involving voting rights for those Negroes who had served in the Union army or who could read and write. Yet he continued to defend the Ten Percent Plan and considered it fortunate that Congress was not scheduled to reconvene until December. That way he would have ample time to reconstruct the South as he saw fit.

Thus the war ended without the federal government's having established a Reconstruction policy—or to be more precise, with the Republicans who controlled the government divided over what that policy should be and who should determine it. One faction, the Radicals, tended to believe that high-ranking Confederates should be punished severely for their treason, that the Southern states should not be granted full membership rights in the Union until their future loyalty was assured, and that Negroes should receive equal civil and political rights both as an act of justice and as a means of securing Unionist (Republican) domination of the South. The principal Radical leaders were Charles Sumner of Massachusetts, Benjamin Wade of Ohio, and Zachariah Chandler of Michigan in the Senate; Thaddeus Stevens of Pennsylvania, George W. Julian of Indiana, and George Boutwell of Massachusetts in the House; and outside of Congress, Wendell Phillips, Ben Butler, and Chief Justice Chase. The Radical Republicans enjoyed the backing of many influential preachers, intellectuals, and newspapers—notably Horace Greeley's *New York Tribune* and Joseph Medill's *Chicago Tribune*.

More numerous and powerful, particularly in Congress, were the Moderate Republicans. Their primary desire was to prevent the secessionist leaders from returning to power in the South and the Democrats from regaining control of the federal government. As regards the Negro, they recognized the need for securing his basic personal and civil rights, but as a rule the Moderates either opposed or lacked a strong commitment to giving him the vote—in part because they doubted his competency to exercise it, in part out of fear of adverse repercussions among Northern voters. In the Senate they were led by William Pitt Fessenden of Maine, Lyman Trumbull of Illinois, and John Sherman of Ohio (brother of General William T. Sherman); in the House by John Bingham and James Garfield of Ohio and James G. Blaine of Maine; and beyond Washington by Governors John Andrews of Massachusetts and Oliver P. Morton of Indiana. Representing the Moderates' viewpoint in the press were such publications as the *Boston Journal*, the *Springfield* (Massachusetts) *Republican, Harper's Weekly*, and a newly founded but instantly influential magazine, *The Nation*.

The differences between Radicals and Moderates were essentially ones of emphasis, timing, and temperament. Up to a point these differences were substantial but under the pressure of necessity they could be compromised. Both factions, however, were in fundamental disagreement with Conservative Republicans. The Conservatives saw no justification for going beyond what already had been achieved: preservation of the Union and destruction of slavery. Hence they held that the Southern states should be readmitted as soon as was expedient and that the Negro's future should be left to the future. Although weak in Congress—they numbered no more than six senators and barely a dozen representatives—the Conservatives were strong in the cabinet: McCulloch, Secretary of Navy Welles, and, above all, Seward. In addition they had a powerful voice in the *New York Times*, whose editor, Henry J. Raymond, was also a House member and chairman of the Union (Republican) National Executive Committee.[3]

Ironically, in view of later events, the Radicals welcomed Johnson's accession to the presidency. Had he not repeatedly demanded stern punishment for Southern "traitors"? Had he not in October 1864 promised a crowd of Nashville Negroes that he would be their Moses, leading them from slavery to freedom? Thus it was on April 16, when the Radical-dominated congressional Joint Committee on the Conduct of the War (on which Johnson had served before becoming military governor of Tennessee) called on the new president, its chairman, Senator Wade, cosponsor of the Wade-Davis Bill, declared enthusiastically: "Johnson, we have faith in you. By the gods, there will be no trouble now in running the government!" To which Johnson replied: "I hold that robbery is a crime, rape is a crime, murder is a crime; treason is a crime, and the crime must be punished. Treason must be made infamous, and traitors must be impoverished."[4]

These words could scarcely have been more encouraging to the Radicals. "Johnson is *right*," wrote Senator Chandler to his wife. "He now thinks just as we do and desires to carry out radical measures and punish treason and traitors. . . ." Their main concern was that he would succumb to the wiles of the Blairs. This was an ambitious political clan of former Democrats consisting of Frank Blair, Sr., who had been one of Andrew Jackson's henchmen, and his two sons—Montgomery, who had been postmaster general until dismissed by Lincoln in 1864 in order to appease the Radicals, and Frank, Jr., a former congressman and presently a high-ranking general. The family had been on close terms with Johnson since the elder Blair had taken him under his wing after the inauguration fiasco. Besides favoring a conservative Reconstruction policy, the Blairs were in the process of drifting back into the Democratic party. The Radicals also worried about the potential influence of Seward should he recover from his wounds (something he soon was doing). They believed that the secretary of state had been the gray eminence behind Lincoln and did not want him to continue in that role with Johnson.[5]

Seeking to keep the new president "*right*," top Radicals visited him and wrote him frequently during the remainder of April and throughout May. The most persistent was Sumner. Handsome, erudite, courageous, idealistic, vain, and humorless, he was an ultra-Radical, the self-appointed conscience of the American people, and the champion of causes-yet-to-be-won. Taking advantage of his position as chairman of the Senate Foreign Relations Committee, he conferred with Johnson as early as the evening of April 15, then visited him often thereafter. Each time he urged the moral justice and practical necessity of Negro suffrage. By the end of April he was reporting joyfully to his friends that the president "accepted this idea completely, and indeed went so far as to say 'There is no difference between us.'" And on May 12 he and Wade told a caucus of congressional Radicals that Johnson was "thoroughly radical" and favored Negro suffrage "as much as anyone here."[6]

However, the Radicals were far from being the only ones to have their hopes raised by the new president. There were also the Northern Democrats. For them the Civil War had been a disaster. Prior to 1861 they had, in alliance with the Southern Democrats, held sway over the national government. Then the issue of slavery and the secession of the South had enabled the Republicans to take over. Following Fort Sumter most Northern Democrats had rallied behind the Union cause, but a large portion of them—the so-called Copperheads—had sympathized with the Confederacy. Furthermore, as a whole, the Northern Democrats had opposed emancipation and during the 1864 presidential campaign had declared the war a failure. As a consequence they had become discredited in the eyes of most Northerners and had lost both voters and elections to the Republicans. By 1865 they held barely one-fourth of the seats in Congress and only one Northern governorship.

The obvious remedy for this lamentable state of affairs was, they felt, the speedy return of their Dixie political brethren to the polls and to Congress. Hence they advocated the immediate and unconditional restoration of the Southern states to the Union, arguing that constitutionally the states had never been separate. At the same time the Northern Democrats opposed—in the name of "white supremacy"—civil and political rights for the Negroes and accused the "Radicals" (as they labeled all Republicans) of favoring "nigger equality." By so doing they hoped, now that the war was over and the slavery issue settled, to increase their strength in the North. Despite recent setbacks, they still largely controlled the Ohio Valley, the Border states, and the cities; they had the financial backing of many wealthy Eastern businessmen, especially in New York; and they possessed the propaganda support of numerous newspapers. Moreover, the Republican victory margin in many areas of the North had been very narrow in 1864.

Lincoln's death opened up for Northern Democrats the very exciting prospect of a fellow Democrat in the White House. For, as they quickly noted, Johnson never had joined the Republican party as such; on the contrary he continued to describe himself as a "Jacksonian Democrat." Should he renew his old political ties, make available presidential patronage, and—above all—restore the South to the Union, then, they hoped, it would not be long before the Democratic party was back in power.

Accordingly scores of Democratic politicians and organizations hastened to pledge their support to Johnson, and the Democratic press, hitherto hostile, began praising him. In particular Samuel L. M. Barlow, co-owner of the *New York World* and a top Democratic leader, promised Johnson (via Montgomery Blair) "the united support of the whole democracy, North and South," provided the president broke away from the Republicans. There is no record of Johnson's replying directly to these overtures. Some of his public statements, however, could only have increased Democratic optimism. For example on April 21 he told an Indiana delegation that the Southern states had not become (as the Radicals maintained) mere territories; instead "their life-breath has only been suspended," and constitutionally, he said, they still were states. By the end of April, Barlow was predicting confidently that "Johnson's policy will be such as to give us a speedy peace with all of its blessings"—in other words, the return of the South to the Union and of the Democrats to power.[7]

In the South itself initial reaction to Johnson's becoming president was mixed. To some battered and bitter Confederates he was a "vulgar renegade" who "stunk like carrion." Aware of his oft-repeated denunication of "traitors," such persons feared the worse from him: "We sit and wait until the drunken tailor who rules the United States of America issues a proclamation," wrote a South Carolina lady in her diary. Other Southerners, however, reassured by the same statements that were so pleasing to Northern Democrats, predicted that he would adopt a lenient Reconstruction policy. After all, a *New Orleans Times* correspondent pointed out, "He was born in North Carolina and raised in Tennessee. . . . He does not pass his entire time in singing psalms through his nose . . . he has never peddled a clock or palmed off a wooden nutmeg. . . ." Hence, "the wonderful effects of New England culture are not manifested in any growth of horns upon his forehead."[8]

Johnson began formal consideration of a Reconstruction policy on April 16 at his first regular cabinet meeting. Secretary of War Stanton outlined two plans which he had drawn up at Lincoln's request. One pertained to Virginia and simply called for recognizing as its government the Unionist regime which had been set up there early in the war. The other applied specifically to North Carolina but would set the pattern for all the other Southern states except Louisiana, Arkansas, and Tennessee, which had been provided for already by Lincoln's Ten Percent Plan. Some discussion ensued but no attempt was made to reach a decision. For the time being, there were more pressing matters to be dealt with: the apprehension of Booth and his fellow conspirators, arrangements for Lincoln's funeral, and military operations against the Confederate forces still in the field.[9] Also Johnson needed more appropriate quarters than the Kirkwood House while waiting for Mrs. Lincoln to vacate the White House. (The wait promised to be long; half-crazed with grief, she raved that Johnson was responsible for her husband's murder.) At McCulloch's suggestion Johnson established an office at the Treasury Department, and he accepted an invitation from Representative Samuel Hooper to move into his Massachusetts Avenue mansion.

It was at Hooper's house on the evening of April 21 that Johnson received two unexpected visitors: Stanton and Lieutenant General Ulysses S. Grant, commander of the army. They excitedly told him that dispatches had just arrived from Major General William T. Sherman, commanding the federal forces in North Carolina. The messages were so alarming that Stanton, on his own initiative, had called a cabinet meeting.

Less than an hour later, at 8 P.M., Johnson met with the cabinet at the Treasury Department. They noted with interest that Preston King accompanied him as a personal adviser. A former senator from New York, King was a Conservative Republican of Democratic background who was on close terms with the Blairs but who also had links to Seward. Johnson and King had become friendly while serving together in the Senate early in the war, and following Johnson's return to Washington their association had been resumed under the auspices of the Blairs.

Grant opened the meeting by reading the communications from Sherman. These dispatches reported that on April 18 Sherman had signed a "memorandum" with General Joseph E. Johnston, commander of the last major Confederate army. Under its terms, all rebel forces throughout the South were to surrender. In addition, however, it promised federal recognition of the existing Confederate state governments as soon as their officials swore allegiance to the United States; declared that in those states where there were Union and Confederate governments, the Supreme Court would decide which was legitimate; provided for the reestablishment of federal courts in the South; called for a general amnesty; guaranteed property and voting rights for all peaceful Southerners; and authorized the Confederate troops to store their arms in state arsenals.

In effect this memorandum placed political control of the South in Confederate hands, contrasting sharply with the simple military surrender Grant had obtained from Lee at Appomattox. Clearly Sherman had exceeded his authority.

Johnson did what had to be done. He instructed Stanton to inform Sherman that the government disapproved of the agreement and that he was to notify the Confederates that hostilities would be resumed in forty-eight hours. Grant hastened to North Carolina and delivered this message personally. As a result, on April 26 General Johnston surrendered on the same basis as Lee.

Sherman was not surprised by the rejection of his treaty. Although he believed that it afforded the best means for rapid restoration of peace and national unity, he admitted that he had done "a little bending to policy." But he was incensed when he learned that Stanton had published a statement implying that he had been driven by discreditable, even treasonable, motives. Henceforth he refused to have any except official dealings with Stanton. When Sherman's army marched in review through Washington on May 24, he publicly snubbed the secretary of war.[10]

Stanton was the most important man in Johnson's administration during its early weeks—in some ways more so than the president himself. Fifty years old, goggle-eyed, and grotesquely bearded, he was a hard-working, hard-driving administrator, an excitable man and something of a bully. Before the war he had been a leading Ohio lawyer and Democrat who had served as President Buchanan's attorney general. Then late in 1861 he took over as secretary of war and proceeded to play a key role in organizing Northern might for victory. He also became personally very close to Lincoln and enjoyed more influence with him than anyone else in the cabinet except Seward. Politically, Stanton moved—as did many other War Democrats—into the Republican party. Conservative Republicans and Democrats considered him a Radical, but in fact he was so only in the company of Radicals. With Moderates he was a Moderate, and with Conservatives he tended to be a Conservative.

Following Lincoln's murder, Stanton devoted himself to tracking down the assassins and capturing Jefferson Davis and other Confederate officials whom he believed had instigated the deed. Agents acting under Stanton's direction quickly rounded up most of Booth's co-conspirators plus a number of suspects. On April 26 a cavalry detachment trapped Booth and his henchman, David Herold, in a Virginia barn. The soldiers took Herold alive, but one of them, acting contrary to orders, shot and mortally wounded Booth. Stanton had Booth's body secretly buried beneath a floor in the Washington Arsenal. Evidence gathered by the army's Bureau of Military Justice apparently confirmed that high-ranking Confederates had been behind the assassination plot. Hence on May 2, Johnson, who already had leaped to the same conclusion, issued a proclamation offering a $100,000 award for the apprehension of Jefferson Davis. Eight days later, the federal cavalry captured him in Georgia, and on May 22 Stanton had him imprisoned in chains at Fortress Monroe—an act so brutal that public outcry in the North soon led to the removal of the shackles.

Meanwhile Stanton sought swift punishment for Booth's collaborators. To that end he asked Johnson to authorize their trial by a military commission. Johnson readily agreed—a decision which drew criticism from numerous newspapers and lawyers protesting that the civil courts were open and that there was no need for haste. On May 9 the trial, which was conducted in secret until clamor from newspapers opened it to the press, began. Eight defendants appeared before the commission: Herold, Atzerodt (who had failed to kill Johnson), Lewis Payne (who nearly had murdered Seward), Michael O'Laughlin, Samuel Arnold, Edward Spangler, Dr. Samuel Mudd, and Mary Surratt. (She was the owner of the Washington boardinghouse where Booth had hatched his plot and the mother of John Surratt, a member of Booth's circle who had escaped.) Judge Advocate General Joseph Holt, assisted by Representative John Bingham, served as prosecutor.

While overseeing the arrest and trial of the Booth conspirators, Stanton also took the lead in formulating a Reconstruction program. On April 16 he presented to the cabinet recommendations for Virginia and North Carolina. Subsequently he made a number of revisions in these proposals, the most important of which was to add to the pattern-setting North Carolina plan a clause granting suffrage to all "loyal citizens." He incorporated this change, which had the potential effect of conferring voting rights on Negroes, at the insistence of Sumner and House Speaker Schuyler Colfax.[11]

By early May all of the Confederate armies had surrendered or were in the process of doing so; it was now both possible and pressing to focus on postwar policy. At a May 8 cabinet meeting Johnson ordered Stanton's Virginia plan, somewhat modified, put into effect. The next day the cabinet discussed his North Carolina proposal. Welles, a rigid and highly contentious Connecticut Yankee, pounced on the "loyal citizens" phrase. What did it mean, exactly? Negro as well as white suffrage, Stanton replied. Welles, McCulloch, and Usher objected: This was contrary to the Ten Percent Plan and "subversive" of states' rights. On the other hand, Dennison and Speed backed Stanton. Seward, still convalescing, was not present. President Johnson himself merely stated that he would postpone a decision on the matter pending further study. He followed the same course with respect to an amnesty proclamation introduced by Attorney General Speed.[12]

During the next two weeks Johnson revised the drafts of the North Carolina and Amnesty proclamations. He often consulted Stanton and Grant. He also interviewed several leading North Carolina Unionists. Meanwhile Seward, although barely able to talk, resumed regular attendance at cabinet sessions; and Harlan succeeded Usher as secretary of the interior. Both Seward and Harlan opposed Negro suffrage and Stanton himself let the matter drop.[13]

Finally, on May 29, Johnson issued the proclamations, both of which had been approved unanimously by the cabinet. The amnesty statement pardoned all participants in the rebellion, restored their property (except slaves and that which had been or might be legally confiscated), and required them to take a loyalty oath. It excluded, however, fourteen categories of people from the general pardon. Mainly these were upper-echelon Confederate civilian and military officials and all persons possessing over $20,000 in taxable property. Such individuals would have to apply to the president for a restoration of their rights to vote and to hold office.

The North Carolina Proclamation provided for the appointment by the president of a provisional governor who would summon a convention to draw up a new constitution establishing a "republican form of government," whereupon the state would resume its proper relationship to the Union. But instead of all "loyal citizens," only those men who had been eligible to vote in 1861 and who had taken the loyalty oath could elect delegates to the convention. In other words, Negroes would be barred from the polls, although either the convention or a subsequent state legislature could grant them the franchise if it so desired.[14]

The proclamations delighted Democrats, pleased Conservative Republicans, and relieved Southerners (although many of them criticized the disfranchisement of Confederate leaders). The early restoration of the Southern states seemed assured, and as a Democratic newspaper observed, "Mr. Johnson had set his foot down against permitting the negroes having anything to do with putting the State governments into operation."[15]

On the other hand, the proclamations worried most Moderate Republicans. The policy these statements embodied was acceptable as far as it went, but were there sufficient safeguards against unrepentant rebels taking control of the new Southern governments and electing congressmen who would combine with the Northern Democrats to dominate the nation again? And what about the Negro—was his fate to be left entirely in the hands of his former masters? Obviously, much depended on how Johnson's program worked in practice. So, for the time being, the Moderates chose to regard it as an "experiment" which, if need be, could be supplemented or corrected by Congress.

As for the Radicals, they were shocked and surprised by Johnson's failure to give at least some Negroes the vote. Had he deceived them on this score? They thought so and, to a degree, they were right. It was Johnson's habit, Gideon Welles noted, to listen while others talked, "but unless he squarely and emphatically disapproved, [he] is disinclined to controvert." Quite possibly Sumner, Chase, and other Radicals who had advocated Negro suffrage to Johnson mistook his silence for agreement. It should be noted, however, that in fact Johnson did "squarely and emphatically" disapprove of their ideas on this subject and yet made no effort to "controvert."[16]

Despite their disappointment and resentment over the May 29 proclamations, the Radicals still hoped that they could persuade Johnson to support Negro suffrage: "With the President on our side," declared Sumner, "it will be carried by simple *avoirdupois*." At the same time most of them soft-pedaled their public criticisms of his policy for fear of driving him into the waiting arms of the Democrats. "He is our President," wrote Sumner to Chase on June 25, "and we must keep him ours unless he makes it impossible to go with him."[17]

Many contemporaries attributed the Reconstruction policy outlined in the proclamations to the influence of the Blairs and/or Seward, an explanation some historians have echoed. No doubt these men did influence Johnson. But so did a number of others. Chief among them were Preston King, the president's closest confidant at the time; Senator James Doolittle, a Conservative Republican from Wisconsin who was one of his most devoted friends; Welles, whose arguments against Negro suffrage made a strong impact; Grant, whom Johnson frequently consulted; Stanton and

Speed, who, after all, provided the basis for the proclamations; and even Chase, who while touring the South in April and May sent the president several letters filled with suggestions on Reconstruction policy, some of which Johnson adopted. To try to isolate the influence of the Blairs and of Seward from the rest is impossible, and it is absurd to argue that they controlled Johnson. He was not that pliable. In fact, he was just the reverse.[18]

Another frequent explanation of Johnson's Reconstruction policy is that he was merely carrying out Lincoln's plans.[19] This is true in the sense that Johnson shared his predecessor's view of the constitutional status of the rebel states and in the sense that he also gave top priority to the reconcilation of North and South. But the disfranchisement clauses of the Amnesty Proclamation had more in common with the Wade-Davis Bill than the Ten Percent Plan, and the North Carolina Proclamation showed none of the concern Lincoln had expressed before his death about giving at least some Negroes the right to vote.

The truth of the matter is that Johnson followed Lincoln's precedents and the advice of others only to the extent that they harmonized with his own ideas about Reconstruction; these ideas, in turn, were determined mainly by his personal and political objectives.

First of all, Johnson wished to restore the Southern states as functioning members of the Union as quickly as possible. To him this was a moral imperative, the goal for which the Civil War had been fought (as stated in the Crittenden-Johnson resolutions of 1861), and the justification and culmination of all the suffering and struggle that he and other defenders of the Union had undergone during the past four years. He simply could not conceive of any honest, intelligent person thinking otherwise. Consequently, like Lincoln (and like the Conservative Republicans and Democrats) he reasoned that constitutionally the Southern states had never been out of the Union and, hence, that there was no need for "reconstruction" at all—only for "restoration." By the same token, he believed that only the minimum necessary conditions should be placed on the states' return to the national fold, with Negro suffrage definitely not being among them. In his opinion Negro suffrage was a minor issue, the raising of which would encumber and delay restoration. Moreover, in accordance with traditional constitutional doctrine and practice, he maintained that only the states had the right to decide who should vote.

Secondly, Johnson hoped to transfer political power in the South from the aristocracy of landed wealth to the democracy of the "plebians and mechanics." That was the motive, along with punishment, behind the disfranchisement clauses of the Amnesty Proclamation. Negro suffrage, especially if unlimited, would merely thwart this purpose. Although now legally free, blacks remained bound economically to the big planters, who therefore would be able to control them politically. Or, as Johnson put it to a Tennessee friend, the Negro "would vote with his late masters, whom he does not hate, rather than with the non-slaveholding whites, whom he does hate."[20]

Johnson's third goal was to be elected president in 1868. Like every vice-president who has succeeded to the presidency through death or resignation, he wished to hold it in his own right. The only question was how best to go about accomplishing this—something neither John Tyler nor Millard Fillmore before him had managed to do. Should he return to the Democrats (as the Blairs were urging him to do), he would be condemned as another Tyler who had betrayed the party which had made it possible for him to become president. Besides, Johnson needed much more support in the politically dominant North than the enfeebled Democrats alone could give him.

On the other hand, as a Southerner and a Democrat he did not feel comfortable in the Northern-based Republican party with its prewar abolitionists and postwar Radicals. Only by abandoning lifelong attitudes and principles, could he hope to satisfy the Radicals. Moreover, he shared a belief—widespread in 1865—that now that the Union had been saved and slavery destroyed, the disparate elements comprising the Republican party would fall apart, creating a political vacuum.

Johnson saw this as his opportunity. He would form a new political coalition consisting of moderates and conservatives from North and South and from both parties, but excluding all extremists (unrepentant secessionists and fanatical Radicals). He would do so by using the power and prestige of the presidency to promote what he was confident most Americans favored—sectional reconciliation—and to oppose what he was sure only a few of them wanted—Negro equality. In the process of thus reshuffling the political deck, of course, he would deal himself the winning hand: four more years in the White House.[21]

Some modern historians argue that another, indeed the main, motive behind Johnson's Reconstruction program was a racist desire on his part to maintain white supremacy. They are not entirely wrong. Like the vast majority of whites of his time, in the North as well as the South, Johnson regarded blacks as inherently inferior. The Negro leader Frederick Douglass detected in him a "bitter contempt and aversion" for blacks, and Johnson's private secretary recorded that "the President has at times exhibited a morbid distress and feeling against the negroes."[22] Nevertheless, ideology and political considerations played a bigger role in molding Johnson's Reconstruction policy than did racial prejudice. As he saw it, any attempt to impose Negro suffrage on the South would not only be unconstitutional but would also alienate Southerners and even most people in the North—where, after all, only five New England states with minuscule black populations gave Negroes an unqualified right to vote. On the other hand, by leaving the question of Negro suffrage to the Southern states to decide, he believed that he was satisfying all elements in the nation except the Negroes (who, of course, did not count politically) and the Radicals, who certainly had no place in his own political calculations.

Finally, some historians contend that Johnson made a great mistake—possibly his greatest—by putting a Reconstruction program into effect without consulting Congress. They correctly point out that Congress—meaning specifically the Republican majority—had sent him signals by the Wade-Davis Bill, by refusing to seat the congressman elected under Lincoln's Ten Percent Plan, and in numerous verbal declarations that it intended to have a voice—indeed, a decisive voice—in the formulation of Reconstruction. And, of course, these analysts can and do point to the ultimate rejection by Congress of Johnson's program in favor of one of its own. Hence they conclude that Johnson (who was, after all, a nonelected president without his predecessor's prestige) should have waited until Congress met in December or else called it into special session before proposing a Reconstruction policy.[23]

There is much validity to this viewpoint; it ignores two crucial factors, however. The first is Johnson's prior executive experience, his personality, and his political philosophy. As governor of Tennessee during the 1850s he had battled a hostile legislature; as military governor of that state he had ruled without a legislature. By nature he was a seeker and a user of power who relied not on collaboration but on determination to achieve his objectives. And he possessed a Jacksonian concept of the president as the tribune of all the people, whereas each congressman represented merely a fragment of the people.

The second factor is the status of the presidency at the end of the Civil War. For four years Lincoln had exercised powers of unprecedented degree and scope. In some respects he had been a constitutional—at times, even an unconstitutional—dictator. Repeatedly he had made and executed fundamental policy decisions while Congress was absent from Washington, thereby leaving it little choice except to ratify the *faits accomplis* when it returned. Lincoln had rarely failed to get his way with Congress, and never on any important matter had it imposed its will on him. As a consequence, Northerners had become accustomed to a dominant president—and so too had Congress, despite warnings from such Republican leaders as Fessenden that what had been permitted the president in war would not be allowed in peace. Thus in the spring of 1865, nearly everyone expected and even desired Johnson to do what Lincoln obviously had planned to do—formulate and implement a Reconstruction program while Congress was not in session. Only a few unhappy Radicals urged a special session of Congress, and even they did so half-heartedly. The vast majority of Republican spokesmen both in and out of Congress were more than willing to let the president, at least for the time being, handle the onerous and perilous chores of Reconstruction. Indeed, had Johnson called a special session, most Republican congressmen would have been embarrassed and annoyed; and had he waited until December to propose a Reconstruction program, he would have created an impression of timidity and weakness.

As it was, the public reaction to the May 29 proclamations indicated that Johnson had done what was expected of him and had done it well. At the same time, it encouraged Johnson's hope of creating a new and dominant party of the center, headed by himself. As we have seen, only the extreme Radicals complained about the proclamations, and even they hesitated to express overt opposition. On the other hand, as has been noted, Northern Democrats, Conservative Republicans, and Southerners acclaimed the proclamations, and Moderate Republicans considered them to be at least a good beginning. In addition, General Grant, the most popular man in the North, endorsed the president and his policy at a June 7 meeting in New York; and James Gordon Bennett's independent *New York Herald*, with the nation's largest circulation, heralded Johnson as "the right man in the right place" and called for his election as president in 1868. All in all, as the spring of 1865 turned into summer, Johnson seemed, in the words of the historians John and LaWanda Cox, "the master of his own and the nation's political future."[24]

3

★★★★★

PRESIDENTIAL RECONSTRUCTION
IN ACTION

At the time of the Amnesty and North Carolina proclamations
Johnson still resided in Congressman Hooper's house and still conducted public business at the Treasury Department. McCulloch,
who occupied an adjoining office, kept a careful eye on the Tennes-
seean, particularly for signs of drinking. Much to his relief, he
found Johnson a model of industrious sobriety. "He was there every
morning before nine o'clock and he barely left before five. There
was no liquor in his room. It was open to everybody. His luncheon,
when he had one, was like mine—a cup of tea and a cracker." His
only serious fault seemed to be a penchant for delivering "intemperate" speeches to visiting delegations, something McCulloch attributed to "the habit of denunciatory declamation which he had
formed in his bitter contests in Tennessee."[1]

On June 9 Johnson finally was able to move into the White
House. Preston King also took up quarters there; and on June 19
Johnson's oldest daughter, Mrs. Martha Patterson, and her two children joined him. Most of the president's time was taken up with
seeing swarms of office-seekers, pardon-seekers, and favor-seekers,
as well as the merely curious. To them all he listened courteously,
although occasionally displaying impatience with the more flagrant
time-wasters. Late in his presidency Johnson remarked that there
was a "difference between those who were office seekers and those
who came to pay their respects. You can distinguish between them
as quickly as you can distinguish from the pure waters of a river, the

muddy torrent that flows into it from the deep ravine of clayey soil."[2]

Through June and early July, he did not once set foot outside the White House grounds. He became pale and haggard, and late in June severe kidney pains forced him to take to his bed for ten days. Concerned that "the President would break down" unless he got some recreation, Welles and Speed urged Johnson to take a cruise on the Potomac. He did so on July 9, and although he suffered from a bad headache, Welles believed the excursion benefited him. At the beginning of August, however, Johnson again was so ill that he was unable to meet with the cabinet for several days. Responding to his plea for help in the matter, Seward drew up an order designed to reduce the flow of visitors.

It was during Johnson's first illness that the trial of the Booth conspirators concluded. On June 30 the military commission sentenced Payne, Herold, Atzerodt, and Mrs. Surratt to death, Mudd and O'Laughlin to life at hard labor, and Spangler to six years. Five of the nine members of the commission, however, signed a petition requesting that Johnson commute Mrs. Surratt's sentence to life imprisonment because of her age and sex. On July 5—the first day since June 26 that Johnson was well enough to conduct business— Judge Advocate General Holt brought the court's proceedings to the White House for the president's review. Dedicated to bringing his close friend Lincoln's murderers to justice and convinced that Mrs. Surratt deserved execution, Holt did not mention the clemency petition to Johnson and arranged the trial documents so that the president would be unlikely to see it. Johnson thereupon approved Mrs. Surratt's sentence along with the rest and at the same time gave orders that he did not wish to see anyone who came on "errands of mercy." Consequently, on the following morning when Anna Surratt appeared at the White House to plead for her mother's life, Preston King and Senator James H. Lane of Kansas denied her admittance to the president. On July 7 Mrs. Surratt died beside Payne, Herold, and Atzerodt at the end of a rope.

Subsequently, after learning of Holt's deception, Johnson declared that had he known of the clemency petition he would have spared Mrs. Surratt's life. All of his biographers and most historians concur. The major exceptions are Stanton's biographers, Benjamin Thomas and Harold Hyman, who point out that Holt, Stanton, and various other cabinet members had discussed clemency for Mrs. Surratt with Johnson and that on each occasion he had rejected it. They also note that Johnson took no heed of letters he received prior to the execution discrediting some of the testimony used to convict Mrs. Surratt. Therefore, they conclude that "it seems unlikely that Johnson would have been moved by the petition whether or not he saw it."[3]

Possibly, possibly not. In their conversations with Johnson, Holt, Stanton, and the rest opposed clemency for Mrs. Surratt, arguing that she was clearly guilty. As for the letters denouncing the testimony against her, they had come from dubious sources. In all liklihood Johnson simply acted on the advice of those presumably in a position to know the facts, unaware that one important fact—the clemency petition—had, in effect, been withheld from him.

On August 6 the remainder of Johnson's family joined him at the White House: Mrs. Johnson, Robert, Andrew, Jr., and the Johnsons' second daughter, Mrs. Mary Stover, with her three children. Missing was the president's son, Charles, who had been killed in 1863 when he was thrown from a horse. Earlier, in June, Johnson's older brother, William, had also shown up in Washington—as usual impoverished. Johnson gave him $1,000 and appointed him to a minor government post in Texas, where he had lived since 1857; in October William died as a result of a hunting accident.

Robert Johnson, who had been compelled to resign a colonel's commission because of drunkenness, joined his father's personal staff. For a while he performed his light duties competently enough. But early in 1866 he not only began hitting the bottle again, he also went so far as to bring prostitutes into the White House. Reports of his debauchery circulated around Washington, with some of them confusing the son for the father. Finally, at the president's behest, Welles and Seward arranged an ostensible diplomatic mission for Robert, who early in May 1866 set forth aboard a naval vessel on a cruise that took him to Africa, South America, China, and Japan, thus keeping him out of Washington for the better part of a year. He then resumed his rather nominal duties on the White House staff, apparently without causing his father any further serious embarrassment. Andrew Johnson, it should be noted, personally paid all the expenses of his son's trip.[4]

Andrew Johnson, Jr., who was eleven and afflicted with tuberculosis, enrolled in a Catholic school in Georgetown. Mrs. Johnson, now an invalid slowly dying of consumption, retired to a second floor bedroom from which she seldom emerged. As a consequence Martha Patterson, whose husband recently had been elected to the Senate from Tennessee, assumed the duties of First Lady. Well educated and sensible, she performed them capably, with the result that social life at the White House during Johnson's tenure possessed a simple, if somewhat somber, dignity.

The presence of his family caused Johnson to relax more. He began taking carriage drives in the country and occasionally picnicked with his grandchildren along Rock Creek. Nevertheless he maintained an arduous schedule, made all the more so by chronic attacks of gravel which were accompanied by "physical pain amounting to torture"—a condition which one of his secretaries believed accounted for his grim expression and generally humorless attitude. Rising shortly before dawn, Johnson read, wrote, or studied for several hours and then interviewed callers from ten until eleven, when he ate lunch. At noon he usually met the cabinet or received distinguished visitors, following which there would be more interviews. At four he ate supper with his family and friends; then at five he retired to his study, carrying a coffee pot and accompanied by a cat. There he held private conferences and labored on official business until midnight, emerging briefly at eight for tea with his family.

Eventually a staff of six secretaries assisted him. They kept a record of all official transactions, filed incoming correspondence, and preserved copies of his letters, nearly all of which he dictated or had written according to his instructions. (Since breaking his right arm in an 1857 train accident, Johnson rarely wrote anything in his own hand; in any case, he probably was self-conscious about his erratic grammar and spelling.) Not since John Quincy Adams had a president conducted the affairs of office in so systematic a fashion. By modern standards, however, Johnson devoted an excessive amount of time to petty bureaucratic and patronage matters. Also, despite Seward's order curtailing access to the White House, the president continued to see large numbers of time-wasting applicants and supplicants daily. During that era, the public expected presidents to be readily available, and Johnson considered himself obligated, in the words of one of his secretaries, "to be bored frequently by Tom, Dick, and Harry."[5]

According to McCulloch, Johnson followed Lincoln's practice of leaving the "management of affairs of the different departments of the Government" to their "respective heads." Only rarely did a cabinet member present, at a cabinet meeting, "a departmental subject for consideration or advice." Instead, matters of general domestic or foreign policy would be discussed, with Johnson usually listening more than he talked. Normally the cabinet met on Tuesdays and Fridays, but during the early weeks of his presidency and at other periods when crucial decisions had to be made, it would gather almost every day, Sundays included.[6]

In Seward, Stanton, McCulloch, and Welles Johnson inherited from Lincoln four highly able ministers—indeed, Stanton and Welles were among the most competent administrators ever to occupy their respective posts. For reasons that will be described later, the other cabinet members appointed by Lincoln did not remain with Johnson long enough to establish a definite performance record. Johnson replaced them with men who, if not distinguished, were at least capable. All in all, during Johnson's presidency the civil service was not inferior in honesty and efficiency to what it had been under his predecessor, and it was far superior in those respects to what it would be under his successor. Most of the corruption that did exist involved, as was customary in those days, revenue officers of the Treasury Department and Indian agents of the Interior Department—positions which carried with them unusually great temptations and opportunities to engage in graft. Likewise some of the personnel of the Freedmen's Bureau, an agency of the War Department charged with providing for the welfare of the newly liberated Negroes of the South, were guilty of malfeasance and misfeasance. The head of the bureau, however, the "Christian General," Oliver Otis Howard, whom Johnson had appointed on the recommendation of Grant and Sherman, possessed undenied integrity, and on the whole the record of the bureau was good.

Johnson took over a government which had expanded greatly in size and scope during the war. Most of this increase had occurred in the Treasury Department, which administered the host of new and wide-ranging revenue laws that had gone into effect after Fort Sumter. The Treasury staff numbered 6,333 in 1865 as compared to 3,403 in 1861. And, as it extended its operations into the conquered South and the ever-advancing West, the department continued to add personnel, reaching 7,851 in 1867 and 8,168 in 1869. Next in the rate of wartime increase was the War Department, which grew from 820 civilian employees in 1861 (301 of whom were in Washington) to 2,517 by 1865 (with 1,427 in Washington). Moreover, it continued to grow after Appomattox, largely because of the creation of the Freedmen's Bureau, attaining a total of 3,272 civilian employees by 1867 (with 1,273 in Washington). By the end of Johnson's administration, however, the bureau had been phased out, with the result that in 1869 the War Department employed only 1,514 people (710 of them in Washington).

All the while the postal service remained by far the largest department. Despite the secession of the eleven Confederate states, the number of postal employees grew from 30,817 in 1861 to 33,646 in 1865—probably reflecting the extraordinary flow of mail occasioned by the absence of so many soldiers from their homes. After the spring of 1865, the restoration of service to the South compensated for the reduced volume of mail that came with the demobilization of the army; in 1869 the department still had over 33,000 employees. Likewise the ending of the war brought no decrease in the Interior Department staff; on the contrary, it grew from 1,342 officials and employees in 1865 to 1,875 in 1869, with the bulk of them working in the Bureau of Indian Affairs. As for the Navy and State departments, they experienced only a modest increase during the war. At the former, the civilian staff grew from 91 in 1861 to 131 in 1865; at the latter the growth was from 398 to 427 officers and clerks. By 1869, however, the navy's civilian personnel numbered a mere 111, whereas the State Department had expanded to nearly 500 persons in 1867 and then declined to 466 by 1869. (The drop came mainly because of the Senate's politically motivated refusal to confirm new appointees.) In sum, the number of federal civilian employees, which had been 36,672 in 1861, was about 50,000 by the time Johnson left the White House. It was a significant manifestation of the greater role that the Civil War and the needs of a rapidly developing nation gave to Washington.[7]

Apart from Reconstruction, the most pressing problem Johnson faced after taking office was the demobilization of the army. The people of the North wanted "the boys back home" and so did the boys. Johnson entrusted this task to Stanton and Grant. Under their direction 641,000 troops were discharged by August 7, 1865, and by the end of the year the great Union host which had numbered 1,000,000 at the time of Appomattox had been reduced to 150,000 men, of whom nearly one-half were Negroes. In October 1866 the last volunteers were mustered out, by which time Congress had established the regular army's strength at 54,000. Only a handful of the top generals—Grant, Sherman, Meade, Thomas, Sheridan, Halleck—retained their wartime ranks. The rest dropped a grade or more, becoming colonels, majors, or even captains; some left the service for careers in politics or business.

Welles and Assistant Secretary of the Navy Gustavus Fox carried out a similar dismantling of the fleet. At war's end it contained over 600 ships and was equal, if not superior, in power to Britain's. But by the fall of 1865 it had only 115 vessels in service. All of the others had been sold or drydocked. Unlike the army, which still had occupation duties to perform in the South and Indians to fight in the West, the navy no longer had any major missions to perform.

Spurring this rapid reduction of the land and sea forces was the condition of the nation's exchequer. The federal debt in the spring of 1865 totaled nearly $3 billion—an enormous sum by the standards of the day. Most of it was in the form of short term bonds paying high interest. Also, during the war, the government had issued over $600 million in paper currency, two-thirds of which consisted of "greenbacks" unsupported by gold or silver specie. Because of this influx of "legal tender," gold and silver had practically ceased to circulate, and monetary inflation ran rampant. At the same time, taxes, especially the tariff, had climbed to unprecedented heights.

Throughout his career Johnson had championed governmental frugality. He also had a Jacksonian distrust of banks and paper money, as well as a Southern distaste for protective tariffs. Beyond these prejudices, though, he was, like most politicians, an economic illiterate. Consequently, for the time being at least, he was quite willing to let McCulloch—who had been head of the Indiana State Bank and then comptroller general before becoming secretary of the treasury in March 1865—manage the nation's fiscal affairs.

McCulloch, whose appearance suggested his native New England's granite, believed that top priority should be given to reducing the amount of paper money and to restoring the nation to a specie basis. Accordingly in his report to Congress on December 5, 1865, he called for currency contraction—that is, taking greenbacks out of circulation. At first Congress agreed. Then it had second thoughts, inspired by the fear that too quick a contraction might produce a politically embarrassing panic. Hence in April 1866, Congress empowered the secretary of the treasury to withdraw from circulation only $10 million of the $428 million in greenbacks during the next six months and no more than $4 million per month thereafter—limitations which McCulloch considered calamitous. Likewise, Congress in 1866 rejected a plan put forth by the special commissioner of revenue, David Wells, to lower the tariff and otherwise reform the tax structure. As always, many favored such action in principle but few agreed as to specifics.[8]

Johnson possessed at least some prior experience with economic matters. When it came to diplomatic affairs he had none. Yet during the spring of 1865 there existed the distinct possibility of a foreign war which would have blasted all hopes of reducing the armed forces and restoring the nation to fiscal virtue. In 1864 Napoleon III of France, after sending an army into Mexico on the pretence of collecting unpaid claims, installed Austrian Archduke Maximilian on the throne of the Montezumas. This, of course, constitued a brazen violation of the Monroe Doctrine. But as long as the United States was preoccupied with subduing the Confederacy, there was little it could do except to express concern over French activities and continue to recognize the government of President Benito Juarez as the legitimate authority in Mexico.

With the end of the Civil War, the need for American restraint also ended—or at least so thought General Grant. On the day after Appomatox he announced gleefully to his staff, "Now for Mexico!" Soon he was urging Johnson to let him drive the French out, and late in May Grant ordered fifty-two thousand troops to the Rio Grande. In addition he instructed Major General John M. Schofield to go to northern Mexico and recruit Union and Confederate veterans to bolster the Juarez forces, which were to be supplied with American arms.

Grant's aggressive plans had both popular and congressional backing, along with the president's tacit acquiescence. During the 1864 campaign, Johnson had asserted that "an expedition into Mexico would be a sort of recreation to the brave soldiers who are now fighting the battles of the Union. . . ."[9] Secretary of State Seward, however, took a different view of the matter.

Sixty-four years old and with a "head like a wise macaw," Seward had been playing a star role on the national political stage for twenty years as governor of New York, United States senator, and one of the main leaders of first the Whig and then the Republican parties. In 1860 he had expected, with good reason, to win the Republican presidential nomination and was sorely disappointed when he lost out to Lincoln. Appointed secretary of state by Lincoln in recognition of his party standing and personal talent, Seward consoled himself with the notion that he would be president in fact if not in name. He quickly learned otherwise, yet he did become Lincoln's most influential associate. At the same time, he conducted diplomatic affairs with a firmness and a finesse that did much to prevent the disaster of British intervention on the side of the Confederacy.

As the Civil War drew to a close, Seward possessed a prestige surpassed among political leaders only by Lincoln's. Moreover, Lincoln had indicated his intention of passing the presidency on to Seward; the main obstacle was the enmity of the Radicals. Hence, during the winter of 1864–65, Seward and his astute political lieutenant, Thurlow Weed of New York, began maneuvering to recast the Republican party along conservative lines. Lincoln's death did not cause them to abandon that project. Seward still entertained presidential aspirations, and even if they proved impossible to realize, he could at least be Andrew Johnson's Warwick—or so he hoped.[10]

In the Blairs, however, Seward had dangerous rivals where Johnson was concerned. Not only were they urging the president to return with them to the Democratic fold, they were advocating the use of force to expel the French from Mexico. Should Johnson follow their advice, Seward's political plans would be wrecked and the United States involved in what he regarded as needless war. Therefore, as soon as he recovered sufficiently from Payne's attack, he moved to counter their influence.

First, late in May, he reached an understanding with Johnson that there was to be no change in foreign policy—which meant that he would continue to direct it. Next he sidetracked Grant's scheme to send Schofield to Mexico by appointing him as special agent to France with instructions "to get your legs under Napoleon's mahogany and tell him that he must get out of Mexico." On the grounds that the time for the mission was not yet ripe, however, Seward did not authorize Schofield to leave until mid November. Meanwhile, through regular diplomatic channels, Seward began prodding the French government to withdraw its troops from Mexico; their presence, he warned, created "a future if not immediate antagonism" between France and the United States.[11]

Seward's refusal to engage in sabre-rattling drew fire from the Democrats and numerous Radicals; these otherwise disparate elements were united by their mutual dislike of the secretary of state. In addition the general public clamor against the French intervention became so loud that in October Johnson showed signs of taking matters into his own hands with a view to a more aggressive approach. Alarmed, Seward placated the president and preserved his own control over foreign policy by serving notice on the French early in November that peace would be impossible unless they soon began to withdraw from Mexico. Faced with this virtual ultimatum and growing disenchanted with the ever-mounting cost (in money and in men) of his Mexican adventure, Napoleon III decided in January 1866 to bring his army home. In April 1866 the French minister to Washington informed Seward that France would conduct a three-stage withdrawal of its forces from Mexico beginning in November and ending a year later. That same month a threat by

Seward to suspend diplomatic relations caused the Austrian government to drop plans for raising a volunteer army to aid Maxmilian.[12]

Historians unite in praising the skillful fashion in which Seward dealt with the French intervention. On the other hand, the only credit they give Johnson is for not interfering with his secretary of state. This is fair enough. Yet it could be argued that by impelling Seward to increase pressure on the French during the fall of 1865, Johnson indirectly hastened Napoleon's decision to evacuate Mexico. Furthermore, a bellicose policy towards France might have paid Johnson rich political dividends. It would have been highly popular and in all probability successful, given American power and French military incompetence. Also, it most likely would have assured the acceptance of Johnson's Reconstruction program by a nation and a Congress preoccupied with the possibility of war. Indeed, fear that a conflict with France would divert Republican attention from "guarding the poor freedmen" and would lead to the immediate readmission of the Southern states caused Sumner to part company with most of his fellow Radicals and support Seward's Mexican diplomacy.

There never was much chance, however, that Johnson would seek to promote his Reconstruction policy by overruling Seward's foreign policy. First of all, Johnson was confident that his Reconstruction plan would prevail in any case. Secondly, the president respected and needed Seward's diplomatic expertise. Thirdly, Johnson was grateful to Seward for having (along with Weed) played a key role in securing the vice-presidential nomination for him and also for not joining in the criticism of his inaugural conduct. Finally, Seward's support was vital to Johnson's plans of forming a new party—plans which Seward (at least to a degree) shared and, perhaps, helped inspire. To have caused Seward to resign by repudiating his diplomacy would have deprived the president of his main source of Republican backing and left him almost totally dependent on the Democrats.[13]

To make the president thus dependent was precisely the object of the New York Democratic leader, Samuel Barlow. On July 19, obsessed with a desire to break the Seward-Weed domination of New York politics, Barlow wrote a letter to Montgomery Blair (who showed it to Johnson) threatening to withdraw Democratic support of the administration unless Seward was removed. Five days later, however, after hearing from a prominent former Confederate general that the Southern people were "universally pleased with the Johnson course" on Reconstruction, Barlow sent word to Blair that the "whole [Democratic] party is today a Johnson party; that the South just as rapidly as his reconstruction plans are carried out, will be a Johnson party."[14]

During the next several weeks Johnson met privately with a number of top Democrats. The result was an understanding that in return for their backing he would adhere to his policy of speedy restoration of the South. He also gave some of them the impression that he would dismiss Seward and Stanton as soon as was expedient. Johnson refused, however, to commit himself openly to the Democrats, and when asked in a public interview about reports that he was "going over" to them, the president replied that on the contrary they were moving to his position.[15]

Johnson's independent attitude annoyed Barlow, who was aware of what he termed Johnson's "insane" plan to "build up a personal party," but he was confident that sooner or later the president would quarrel with the Republicans, whereupon he would have no choice except to join the Democrats—and on their terms. For, predicted Barlow to a fellow Democrat, once the Southern states were back in the Union, "*we*, not the Pres[ident], will . . . have an absolute majority in both branches of Congress, and he will then be under the control of our organization, or powerless outside of it."[16]

While Johnson established this rather dubious de facto alliance with the Democrats, he took steps to develop his strength among Conservative Republicans. He appointed Preston King as collector of the Port of New York, a position of immense power in New York politics because of the large amount of patronage it controlled. In addition, he named other Conservatives, and also some Democrats, to federal posts as they became vacant; established close ties with James Gordon Bennett of the *New York Herald*; set up the *National Intelligencer* as his "organ" in Washington; controlled the Republican state conventions in Connecticut and Wisconsin via Senators Dixon and Doolittle of those states; and employed his long-time political crony, Lewis D. Campbell, to represent his interests in Ohio. Nor did Johnson neglect the South in constructing a power base. He sent several agents through the former Confederate states, where they extolled his Reconstruction policy and made political contacts.[17]

However useful, politicking of this kind could not be decisive. Johnson's hope of succeeding himself in 1868 depended largely on the success of his Reconstruction program. That, in turn, involved two interrelated factors. First, the South's response to that program; and second, the North's reaction to the South's response. Of the two, obviously the second was more important: Having won the war the North could dictate the peace.

What most people in the North—particularly Republicans—wanted from the South in peace was an acceptance of the results of the war. Specifically, that meant a convincing demonstration by Southerners that they repented their sin of rebellion, that they now gave true allegiance to the Union, and that they intended to deal fairly with their former slaves. Once satisfied on these points, all but the most vindictive Northerners and Republicans were agreeable to the return of the Southern prodigal to the national family.[18]

In principle these peace terms seemed reasonable, but in fact they were unrealistic. Most Southerners regretted not their rebellion but their defeat; they acknowledged the power of the Union but could not love it; and the abolition of slavery did not end their belief in black inferiority or their determination to preserve white supremacy. Therefore, they were prepared to concede to the North only what they must—that and no more. Encouraging them in this attitude was Johnson's Reconstruction policy and the manner in which he implemented it.

Johnson followed the North Carolina Proclamation with identical declarations in June and early July for Mississippi, South Carolina, Florida, Georgia, Alabama, and Texas. Next, during the late summer and the fall, all seven of these states held constitutional conventions. Acting through the provisional governors he had appointed, Johnson directed each state to nullify its secession ordinance, ratify the Thirteenth Amendment, and—after North Carolina proved recalcitrant on this score—repudiate its Confederate debt. All except South Carolina carried out the nullification, Mississippi refused the ratification, and neither of those states repudiated its debt.[19]

At this point Johnson's policy changed from one of requiring the Southern states to satisfy minimal conditions for reentering the Union to one of advising them to do certain things calculated to appease Northern public opinion and thus improve their chances of readmission. His first important move along this line occurred on August 15 when he telegraphed Provisional Governor William L. Sharkey of Mississippi, the first state to hold a convention:

> If you could extend the elective franchise to all persons of color who can read the Constitution of the United States in English and write their names, and all persons of color who own real estate valued at not less than two hundred and fifty dollars, and pay taxes thereon, you would com-

pletely disarm the adversary [by which Johnson meant the Radicals] and set an example the other states will follow.[20]

Moreover, added Johnson, "This you can do with perfect safety, and you will thus place the Southern States, in reference to free persons of color, upon the same basis with the Free States." As a consequence, he continued, "The radicals, who are wild upon negro franchise, will be completely foiled in their attempts to keep the Southern States from renewing their relations to the Union. . . ."[21] Early in September Johnson told a New Orleans journalist in a published interview that Louisiana should give literate Negroes the vote and "stop this Northern clamor."[22]

Neither Mississippi nor Louisiana nor any other Southern state, however, followed the president's advice. In fact none of them so much as gave it serious consideration. The very idea of blacks casting ballots raised the hackles of most Southern whites. "I'll emigrate," vowed the Johnson-appointed provisional governor of Alabama, "if Negroes get the vote." Moreover, many middle and lower class Southerners feared that limited black suffrage, as proposed by Johnson, would merely open the way for all adult male Negroes to vote, which in turn would enable the big planters to increase their political power. (Johnson himself, of course, opposed mass Negro voting for this same reason, and it is significant that most of the few Southerners who at this time did favor enfranchising Negroes were members of the gentry—men such as Wade Hampton of South Carolina and James Lusk Alcorn of Mississippi.) Nor were Southerners in general impressed by Johnson's argument that by allowing a small number of Negroes to vote, Southerners would facilitate their own reentry into the Union. As one of their spokesmen put it, "The absurd project of conferring the right of suffrage upon an ignorant and semi-barbarous population of suddenly emancipated slaves we can never consent to, nor do I believe it would be insisted on by the Northern people when they give it a sober second thought." In any event the majority of Southerners preferred to remain outside the Union rather than enter it at the price of Negro suffrage.[23]

Beyond what has been described, Johnson made no recorded attempt to induce the South to enfranchise at least some blacks. Quite likely, and with good reason, he concluded that it would be futile to do so—and also unnecessary. After all, how could the Northerners insist that the South grant Negroes the vote when so few states of their own region permitted it?

What Johnson did do, however, was to try to convince North-ern proponents of Negro suffrage that although he himself favored the limited enfranchisement of blacks, he had to be guided by what was constitutional and practical. Early in October he gave an inter-view to George Luther Stearns, publisher of the Radical *Boston Advertiser*. Suffrage, he told Stearns, was "not a natural right, but a political right." For Johnson as president to dictate to states who should vote would, he said, create a "central despotism." "Our only safety lies in allowing each state to control the right of voting. . . ." Were he simply a citizen of Tennessee, Johnson continued, "I should try to introduce negro suffrage gradually; first to those who had served in the army; those who could read and write; and perhaps [with] a property qualification for others, say $200 or $250." But, he concluded, "It would not do to let the negro have universal suffrage now; it would breed a war of races."[24]

The Stearns interview, which was widely published, elicited a favorable response in the North. Even the Radicals expressed re-spect for, if not agreement with, the president's views.[25] Thus Johnson was confirmed in his belief that the failure of the South to grant Negro suffrage would not be a major obstacle to its restoration to the Union.

The same, however, could not be said about the way in which Negroes were being treated in the South. Scarcely a day went by without the newspapers—especially Republican ones—carrying ac-counts of whites oppressing, terrorizing, and even murdering blacks. Northern concern, indeed outrage, mounted.

Johnson noted this. He also recognized that as a practical mat-ter the legal status of free Negroes needed defining. Therefore, in November he urged the provisional governors of Mississippi, South Carolina, and North Carolina (the states which had progressed the farthest in the Reconstruction process) to have their legislatures pass laws "for the protection of freedmen in person and property," laws which "will be acceptable to the country"—meaning the North.[26]

This time Johnson's advice was acted on, but not precisely in the way he had intended or hoped.

At war's end the South's greatest need and wish was to get its farms and plantations producing again. However, the majority of Negroes, understandably enough, conceived of freedom as meaning at least a temporary release from labor, particularly labor under their former masters. Ofttimes too, they believed reports that the federal government would soon—say by Christmas 1865—give them land of their own. As a consequence thousands of them refused to work, or if they did, to work as hard as they had as slaves. Still thousands more left the plantations to wander about the countryside or crowd into towns where they lived in squalor and subsisted off of private charity and government relief. Wherever these migrants went, disease, debauchery, and crime accompanied them.

Planters, unable to obtain or retain laborers, faced ruin. Southerners in general saw this as proof of their prewar contention that the Negro would not work unless he was a slave and that he would become demoralized if given his freedom. Also Southerners were angered by what they regarded as insolent behavior on the part of blacks who acted as if they were the equals of whites and were alarmed by rumors that the Negroes were plotting a mass "rising" to seize the land. Hence, almost unanimously, white Southerners resolved to regain control over black labor and reassert white supremacy.

Thus it was that in November the Southern states, with Mississippi and South Carolina leading the way, began enacting the Black Codes. Under the Mississippi code, Negroes under eighteen years of age who were orphans or whose parents could not support them were to be apprenticed to a white person, preferably their former owner. Also Negroes who were vagrants, or who committed a long list of offenses ranging from theft to preaching without a license, could be hired out to whites should they fail to pay a stipulated fine. A Negro who left a white employer without permission could be arrested and—unless he paid a fine—required to work without wages for the employer. No Negro could practice a skilled trade without a license, possess firearms or other weapons, or rent land outside an incorporated town. The South Carolina code contained the equivalent of most of these provisions, as well as a section stating that "stubborn or refractory servants" were liable to a fifty dollar fine which, if unpaid, would be worked off by six months of unremunerated labor. Both codes, in sum, had the effect of placing blacks in a position of subordination approaching peonage.

To be sure, these and other Black Codes did give Negroes the right to sue and be sued, to acquire and sell property, and to marry on the same legal basis as whites. Also, they required that all labor contracts between whites and blacks be in writing and that they be explained to the latter before witnesses; and they allowed Negroes to testify in courts when they were a party to a case. Moreover, to a large extent the codes were modeled—deliberately, in fact—after Northern laws applying to apprentices, vagrants, and free Negroes; and those provisions designed to compel Negroes to work for whites

47

were no harsher than some of the orders which previously had been issued for the same purpose by United States Army officers and the Freedmen's Bureau, the agency which Congress had set up in the South in 1865 to aid the ex-slaves. Finally, the codes were framed and passed by moderate Southerners and were not nearly as drastic as the measures advocated by extreme white supremacists.[27]

Nevertheless, they were, in the words of a South Carolinian who opposed his state's code, "scarcely compatible with a state of freedom" for the Negro. And to many Northerners they seemed nothing less than a brazen attempt to restore slavery. "We tell the white men of Mississippi," roared the Radical *Chicago Tribune*, "that the men of the North will convert the State of Mississippi into a frog pond before they will allow such a law to disgrace one foot of soil in which the bones of our soldiers sleep and over which the flag of freedom waves."[28]

Just as disturbing to the North—perhaps even more so—were the results of state and congressional elections held throughout the South during the late summer and fall. With few exceptions the successful candidates were men who had supported the Confederacy. Many of them, in fact, had held high positions in the Confederate government and army—notably Alexander H. Stephens, former vice-president of the Confederacy, whom the Georgia legislature named to the United States Senate. Only in Tennessee, thanks to the disfranchisement of nearly everybody who had supported the Confederacy in any way and to the use of out-and-out fraud by Governor Brownlow, did the Unionists prevail.

Johnson neither desired nor expected this Confederate resurgence. It contradicted his cherished belief (shared by Seward) that the mass of the Southern people had remained loyal at heart to the Union; it frustrated his hope of breaking the power of the old ruling class in the South; and it jeopardized the early restoration of the Southern states because of its adverse effect on Northern opinion. Indeed, this last consideration had prompted Johnson and Seward to urge Southerners to send to the House and Senate men who never had voluntarily served the Confederacy and, hence, could take the so-called iron-clad oath which, since 1863, Congress had required of all of its members. It would be better, Seward had advised a Virginia friend, "to send an idiot or a child to Congress who can take it [the oath] than to send a wise man who cannot." And when Johnson had learned of the impending election of Stephens to the Senate, the president had tried to forestall it by indirectly letting the Georgia politicians know his feelings: "There seems, in many of the elections something like defiance, which is all out of place at this time."[29]

Some Southerners themselves advocated electing Unionists as a matter of expediency. But this "Uriah Heep" strategy, as its opponents termed it, succumbed to a number of arguments: First, that sending Unionists to Congress would be sheer and obvious hypocrisy; second, that it would be rewarding with power men who otherwise lacked the ability to win it; third, that the South at this time of crisis needed its best men in positions of leadership; fourth, that it would be better not to be represented in Washington at all than by men who did not speak for the majority of the Southern people and who probably would sell out to the Radicals; and finally, that sooner or later the North would have to accept the South back into the Union regardless—that it could not be kept out forever. The South did attempt to placate the North to the extent of electing to Congress men who, for the most part, had not been original secessionists, but more than that it refused to concede.[30]

Johnson, of course, could have forced or at least strongly pressured the Southerners to elect Unionists simply by refusing to recognize the election of Confederate adherents. But in fact he did nothing of the kind. On the contrary, he actually abetted the return of the Confederates to power by the course he pursued with respect to pardoning men disfranchised by his Amnesty Proclamation.

At first he granted pardons very sparingly. Then he began handing them out at the rate of a hundred a day, and by late fall they could be had practically for the asking, not only from him but from the provisional governors and a White House clerk to whom he delegated much of the task. In fact, numerous Southern politicians received pardons merely in order to make them eligible to occupy the offices to which they had been elected in defiance of the Amnesty Proclamation. Among them was the new governor of Mississippi, ex-Confederate General Benjamin G. Humphreys, who was pardoned ten days after being inaugurated! Many Southerners also flagrantly perjured themselves when they took the "iron-clad oath" in order to qualify to vote and hold office.

Johnson's wholesale distribution of pardons contrasted strongly and strangely with his earlier denunciations of "traitors." It also undermined his plan to transfer political power in the South to the middle classes. How, then, can it be explained?

Perhaps in part the president simply succumbed to the strain of listening to so many pardon-seekers; they made up the bulk of the daily White House throng and the rapid increase in the number of successful applicants following his illness in June and July. It is also conceivable that he was influenced to a degree by flattery from his petitioners or else derived satisfaction from pardoning high-born aristocrats after they or their wives had humbled themselves before him, the ex-tailor. And quite likely too, he believed that he was fostering the reconciliation of the South to the Union by, in effect, forgiving Southerners who showed repentance for the sin of treason by soliciting a pardon. In his interview with Stearns, Johnson stated that he "did not expect to keep out all [Southerners] who were excluded from the amnesty, or even a large number of them"; rather he "intended they should sue for pardon, and so realize the enormity of the crime they had committed."[31]

But probably the primary motive behind his pardon policy was political—the advancement of his presidential ambitions. By late summer it was clear that the Confederate leadership retained the allegiance of the Southern masses, his faith in their essential loyalty notwithstanding. At the same time, it became evident that in most parts of the South the Unionists were few in number and low in ability. For example, McCulloch could not find enough qualified Unionists to serve as Treasury agents and so asked and received Johnson's permission to appoint men who were ineligible to take the required "iron-clad oath." Thus Johnson must have realized that whether he liked it or not, he would have to work through and with the followers of Jefferson Davis and Robert E. Lee if he were to bring the South back into the Union and keep himself in the White House. That, in turn, meant pardoning top Confederates and allowing them to take the offices to which they had been elected. By so doing he would facilitate the restoration of normal government and, he hoped, promote the rebirth of Southern loyalty to the Union. In any case, to do otherwise would merely produce the opposite effect, as well as alienate the Northern Democrats. In short, Johnson did what practical necessity and political expediency seemed to dictate.[32]

A lenient pardon policy was not the only way in which Johnson endeavored to gain favor in the South. On September 12 he directed that land confiscated from Confederates during the war be returned to its former owners. As a consequence several thousand Negroes who had been settled on plantations taken over by the Union army were dispossessed. On November 1 he ordered that a cotton tax which had been enacted by Congress at the behest of Thad Stevens not be collected on the grounds that the Southern people "are oppressed greatly now and they are little able to bear it in this transition state."[33] Furthermore, he removed Negro occupation troops or, where that was impossible, ordered their number reduced as much as possible. Southern whites bitterly resented the presence of black soldiers—an attitude with which Johnson sympathized after receiving a report (apparently erroneous) that Negro soldiers stationed in Greeneville had converted his own house into a brothel.[34]

Johnson also encouraged the revival of civil government and courts in the South while at the same time restricting the role of the occupation forces and of military tribunals. Apart from Unionists and Negroes, Southerners welcomed this development. Jurisdictional clashes, however, began to occur between the army and local authorities, with some of the latter going so far as to bring legal action against United States officers and soldiers for acts performed during the war.

Finally, he permitted the organization of Southern militia. At the end of the war, much of the South bordered on anarchy, with robbery, murder, and violence of all kinds rampant. This was especially true in Mississippi, where on August 17 Provisional Governor Sharkey issued a proclamation calling for the formation of militia companies, to be made up of former Confederate soldiers, for the purpose of restoring order and guarding against Negroes "who are bold in their threats." Alarmed at the prospect of rebel veterans once more in arms, Major General Henry W. Slocum, commanding the Department of Mississippi, countermanded the proclamation, only to be overruled and rebuked by Johnson. Soon several other states followed Mississippi's example.[35]

Little wonder then that the vast majority of Southerners became convinced that Johnson was sincere when he stated in an interview on September 11, "I am of the Southern people, and I love them and will do all in my power to restore them." Throughout the South, newspapers hailed him as a "savior" and "a statesman of God's creation." More significantly, numerous Southern editors and politicians endorsed the idea of a "great conservative party" combining Northerners and Southerners and headed by Johnson, "our choice for our next President."[36]

But while Johnson was winning the plaudits of former Confederates, Northerners had been watching the South closely, looking for the desired signs of repentance and acceptance. Instead they saw notorious rebels resuming power, conventions refusing to repudiate secession and slavery, and Confederate veterans rearming. They also read in their magazines and newspapers that the Southerners were arrogant and defiant, that they took the oath of allegiance with sneers on their faces, that they scorned the federal occupation troops, and that they even plowed up Union graves. Last but not least there were the Black Codes and the constant reports of Negroes being maltreated and killed. Was it for this that three hundred and fifty thousand Northern soldiers had died?

As he told a Tennessee friend, Johnson himself was "not at all pleased with the conduct of the South's politicians, newspapers, conventions, and legislatures." In particular he resented the fact that although his pardon policy had gone "to the utmost verge of generosity in order to encourage the rebel leaders to repent and act as national men," they had failed to follow his advice regarding the treatment of Negroes and the election of congressmen. He manifested his annoyance by permitting Major General Oliver Otis Howard, head of the Freedmen's Bureau, to suspend that part of the Mississippi Black Code which prohibited Negroes from renting rural land and by letting stand an order by Major General Dan Sickles, commanding in South Carolina, which rejected that state's code and placed Negroes under military jurisdiction. Also, he retained the provisional governors although every Southern state except Texas had, by the end of 1865, chosen regular governors.[37]

Yet despite disappointments in the South and grumblings in the North, Johnson remained confident, as November gave way to December, that his Reconstruction policy was a success when measured by the all-important criterion of popular support. Testimony to this effect came daily from speakers, editorials, visitors, letter-writers, and his own advisers. Thus, just to cite two examples, early in December the historian George Bancroft of Boston assured him that "public opinion is all with you,"[38] and Republican Senator Lot Morrill of Maine declared that Johnson was "probably the most popular President in our history."[39] More concretely, during the fall elections in the North both Republicans and Democrats vied with each other in proclaiming themselves to be the true champions of his policy—obviously both parties agreed that backing the president was good politics.

Victory in the elections went to the Republicans, who carried every state. This too could be interpreted as a popular endorsement of Johnson's policy, which *The Nation* stated has "the miraculous property of appearing to satisfy all parts and parties of the country." On the other hand, it was evident that the Democrats still suffered from the contamination of Copperheadism and that in order to be successful, a new party would have to be Republican-based, as Seward contended. However, a setback to achieving that goal—as well as a personal loss to Johnson—occurred shortly after the elections when Preston King committed suicide, apparently as a conseqence of the strain of trying to reconcile the irreconcilable patronage demands of Republicans and Democrats in New York.

Another significant aspect of the elections was that in no state did the Republicans come out in favor of imposing Negro suffrage on the South, although in a number of states they advocated voting rights for blacks in principle. Furthermore, Connecticut, Wisconsin, and Minnesota defeated Negro suffrage proposals by large majorities. Could it be that the Radicals were merely voices crying in the political wilderness?

The Radicals themselves began to fear this. During the summer and fall, Sumner, Stevens, Wendell Phillips, Wade, and other Radical leaders endeavored to mobilize opposition to the president's Reconstruction program, which Sumner, in typical style, described as being "openly against Almighty God." The results of their efforts, however, were discouraging. Sumner was unable even to get the Republicans of his own state to back him, and Stevens had no better luck in Pennsylvania. Likewise their efforts to influence the president directly or through his cabinet proved unavailing. Johnson did not even bother to reply to letters from Stevens urging him to defer to Congress on Reconstruction, and the cabinet members either supported the president or refused to challenge his course, causing Sumner to complain that they were acting like "courtiers" to a king. Also most Republican journals, including some sympathetic to Negro rights, condemned the Radicals' criticism of Johnson as uncalled for and disruptive of party unity.

By November Sumner was admitting that "some of our friends are in great despair," and Wade had concluded that "the colored people of the South will be compelled to hew out their own way to liberty by the power of their own right arm. . . ." The only hope, as Sumner and Stevens saw it, was that Congress would override the president on Reconstruction. But would it? "I fear we are ruined, for I have little faith in Congress," wrote Stevens to Sumner; and Sumner echoed these words in a letter to a British friend: "It is doubtful how Congress will stand."[40]

On the evening of Saturday, December 2, two days before the first session of the Thirty-ninth Congress convened, Sumner visited the White House. His ostensible purpose was the same as it had been when he called on Johnson the day after Lincoln's assassination—to persuade him that the Southern Negroes should be given the vote. But now he knew that this could not be done, hence his real object was to force the president to break openly with the Radicals so that he, rather than they, would be blamed for disrupting the Republican party.

Johnson received the Massachusetts senator coldly. Here was the adversary—the Harvard aristocrat who wrote essays on Latin declensions, the very incarnation of New England fanaticism, and also the man who had taken the lead in condemning his conduct at the inauguration. The Tennessee tailor expected a clash—expected it and welcomed it.

For two hours the two men parried words. Then Sumner burst forth: The president "had thrown away the victories of the Union army." How so? Johnson asked.

> "The poor freedmen in Georgia and Alabama are frequently insulted by rebels."
> "Mr. Sumner, do murders ever occur in Massachusetts?"
> "Unhappily yes, Mr. President, sometimes."
> "Would you consent that Massachusetts should be excluded from the Union on this account?"
> "No, Mr. President, surely not."[41]

The two men sat in the same room but lived in different worlds. Johnson equated Massachusetts with South Carolina. Sumner thought that Negroes were simply whites with dark skins. Further argument was pointless. As he started to leave, Sumner picked up his hat from the floor where he had placed it and was disgusted to find that Johnson had used it for a spittoon.[42]

4

★★★★★

JOHNSON QUARRELS WITH THE REPUBLICANS

The same Saturday evening that Sumner wrangled with John-son, the Republican members of Congress held a caucus. At it they unanimously agreed to support a resolution, presented by Stevens, calling for the creation of a joint House-Senate committee to in-vestigate conditions in the South and recommend appropriate legis-lation. When Congress conveyed two days later it adopted the resolution by a strict party vote. At the same time, both houses refused to seat any of the congressmen elected from the eleven former Confederate states.

This last action could not have surprised Johnson. The North-ern press had been predicting it for over a month, and he himself had advised Southerners not to send delegations to Washington until the question of seating them had been settled. He had, how-ever, expected the House to admit Horace Maynard of Tennessee, an undoubted Unionist, and thus open the way for other Southern congressmen.[1] Nevertheless, Johnson remained confident that sooner or later Congress would seat most of the Southerners who had been elected to it. Otherwise it would be repudiating the very purpose for which the war had been fought—the restoration of the Union. Should Congress do that, then the Republicans responsible would suffer political destruction. For Johnson also was confident that the majority of Northerners would turn against anyone who tried to perpetuate sectional division and animosity—particularly if they did so in the name of Negro rights. After all, Northerners were whites. Outside of a few New England states, they denied the Negro the vote and systematically discriminated against him with regard to public transport, theaters, restaurants, churches, schools, and housing. Obviously, Johnson concluded, the North was as committed to white supremacy as the South, and men like Sumner and Stevens were hypocrites or fools. In either case, Johnson believed that he had the proper strategy for defeating them and their fellow Radicals—a strategy which he put into effect with his annual message to Congress, presented on December 5.

In the message he rehearsed in eloquent language supplied by his ghostwriter, Bancroft, the historian, what by now had become his familiar themes: that the Southern states constitutionally had never been out of the Union because only individuals, not states, could commit treason; that the continuance of military rule in, or the imposition of Negro suffrage on, the South would be contrary to the Constitution and to democracy; and that the sole legitimate purpose of Reconstruction was the restoration and reconciliation of the Southern people to the Union. Johnson then went on to declare that his policy—by reestablishing civil government in the South, pardoning repentant rebels, and requiring the Southerners to repeal their secession ordinances, repudiate their Confederate debts, and, above all, ratify the Thirteenth Amendment—had accomplished the essentials of that purpose. All that remained to complete the work of restoration "was the admission of loyal Senators and Representatives from the States whose people had rebelled against the lawful authority of the General Government." This the president trusted Congress would quickly do. To delay would accomplish nothing, he said, for the "efflux of time" would change nothing: "Ten years hence, if these States remain as they are, the right of representation will be not stronger, the right of exclusion will be no weaker."[2] On the other hand, great benefits would be realized by admitting them now:

> This would consumate the work of restoration and exert a most salutary influence in the re-establishment of peace, harmony, and fraternal feeling. It would tend greatly to renew the confidence of the American people in the vigor and stability of their institutions . . . and show to the world the inherent recuperative power of a Government founded upon the will of the people. . . . The admission of loyal members from the States now excluded from Congress, by allaying doubt and apprehension, would turn capital, now awaiting an opportunity for investment, into the channels

of trade and industry. It would alleviate the present troubled condition of those States . . . and lead to an increased production of those staples which have added so greatly to the wealth of the nation. . . . New fields of enterprise would be opened to our progressive people, and soon the devastations of war would be repaired, and all traces of our domestic differences effaced from the minds of our countrymen.[3]

The message did two things and did them well. First, in terms calculated to appeal to nearly everyone except Radicals, it justified Johnson's Reconstruction policy; and second, it placed the Republicans on the spot by saying to them in effect: You may either keep the South out of Congress and hence keep America divided, or you may seat most of the Southern congressmen and thus bring peace, unity, and prosperity to the nation. Johnson had no doubt that the Republicans would find themselves forced to choose the first alternative. In turn, Johnson felt this would mean the successful culmination of his Reconstruction policy and practically guarantee his election in 1868.

Reaction to the message could only have increased Johnson's optimism. Letters praising both its style and content poured in from all quarters. Governor Oliver P. Morton of Indiana, a Moderate Republican, wrote: "I can't be mistaken, the great body of the people of the North will endorse your doctrine and policy, and this the members of Congress will find out before they are ninety days older." Bancroft, who naturally was elated by the message's reception, predicted, "In less than twenty days the extreme Radical opposition will be over. *All* of all parties approve the ground you have taken." A fellow Tennessee Unionist informed Johnson that "the South looks upon you as a pillar of cloud by day and of fire by night." The press likewise made pleasant reading. The *New York World* dubbed the message a vindication of Democratic doctrine, the Conservative Republican *New York Times* said it was "full of wisdom," the Moderate Republican *Harper's Weekly* called it a "model," and even the Radical *New York Tribune* stated that it was doubtful "whether any former message has contained so much that will be generally and justly approved."[4]

Had Johnson at this juncture suddenly died, then, as David Donald has remarked, "he would have gone down in our history books as one of our most politically astute Presidents."[5] But he did not die—and instead of being remembered as a skilled politician, his name became and remained a synonym for political blunderer.

Why did this happen?

To a .large extent the rest of this book is an attempt to answer that question. But as for congressional acceptance of Johnson's Reconstruction program by means of seating the Southern delegations, there are two basic reasons why he failed when he was so confident of success: First, he overestimated the backing that he and his policy had in the North; and second, he underestimated the determination and ability of the Republican party to preserve itself and its power.

As noted earlier, throughout the summer and fall of 1865 most Northerners and Republicans expressed approval of Johnson and his conduct of Reconstruction, and as we have just seen they continued to do so following his message to Congress. This approval, however, did not stem from a wholehearted acceptance of his Reconstruction policy and its outcomes. Rather it reflected a belief—or more accurately, a desire to believe—that this policy was simply an experiment intended to ascertain how the South would respond to leniency. If it did so by "accepting the results of the war," fine. But if it did not, then a different approach would be in order.

By December most Northerners and Republicans had concluded—and here the enactment of the Black Codes was decisive —that the experiment had failed, or at least needed a number of corrections and additions. At the same time they hoped, in fact expressed confidence, that Johnson himself took the same view of the situation. The possibility that he did not or would not was almost unthinkable, for that would mean that he deemed satisfactory and final a Reconstruction policy which had resulted in the restoration of rebels to power in the South, the near-restoration of slavery for the Negro, and the possible reestablishment of Democratic control of the nation.

The last prospect, understandably, was of particular concern to Republicans. To be sure they presently had an overwhelming majority in Congress—39 to 11 in the Senate, 140 to 43 in the House. But if the Southerners were seated, then the Democratic minority would be increased to as much as 33 in the Senate and 101 in the House. Moreover, once the Thirteenth Amendment formally went into effect (which it did on December 18, 1865) the three-fifth's clause of the Constitution no longer would be operative and the South would be entitled to at least a dozen more representatives, thus further narrowing the Republican margin in the House. With the aid of a few Conservative Republicans, the Democrats could immediately dominate the Senate and at least make things difficult for the Republicans in the House. By picking up a few more seats in the 1866 elections—a likely enough prospect—the Democrats would, as they were frankly and gleefully predicting, be back in power.[6]

Thus the question of admitting the Southern congressmen was, for the Republican party, one of survival. But there was more to it than that. Should the Democrats—in Republican eyes, a coalition of Copperheads and Rebels—regain control of Congress, Republicans feared repeal of their party's wartime economic legislation (such as the protective tariff), cancellation of the federal war debt, and even the assumption of the Confederate debt. In any event one thing would be sure not to happen: There would be no government intervention on behalf of the Negro, who thus would be left to the obviously not-so-tender mercies of his erstwhile owners.

At this point let us discuss motives. Historians have long and lengthily debated whether the Reconstruction-era Republicans (sometimes referred to as "Radicals") were driven by a "selfish" lust to retain power for themselves or inspired by an "idealistic" desire to help the Negro. Pro-Southern and pro-Johnson historians have maintained the former, while modern neo-Radical historians argue the latter. As often is the case in such matters, both are right and both are wrong. Being politicians the Republicans naturally wanted to stay in office. But being human they just as naturally were capable of altruism, humanitarianism, and idealism—provided such noble sentiments did not interfere overmuch with staying in office. And given the mood of the North following the Civil War, in most places advocating Negro rights was a political asset rather than liability.[7]

Johnson was right in assuming that the mass of Northerners opposed, or had no desire for, Negro equality. What he failed to realize was that a great and growing number of them favored rights for the Negro, at least in the South. They did so not so much out of sympathy for the Negro per se (although that too existed, especially since it cost little or nothing); instead, the sentiment derived basically from what most Northerners perceived as the state of affairs in the South. A typical expression of this attitude is to be found in the statement made by an Ohioan who had journeyed down the Mississippi to Louisiana, as reported early in 1866 by a correspondent of *The Nation* who met the traveler in Baton Rouge:

> You must understand . . . that in 1860 I was a strong Douglas man. I didn't like Lincoln, and the abolitionists I hated; but of course I was Union. As the war went on I

59

began to believe in Lincoln, and, by the time the Emancipation Proclamation was issued, I had been educated up to it and endorsed it. . . . Well, since the war ended I've been a conservative; I've considered Stevens and Sumner dangerous men, who didn't understand the South, wanted to humble it and so on, and were standing in the way of peace. I believed what we used to hear, that the North didn't understand the South. I believe it yet, but in a very different sense. This journey has been the greatest that I ever experienced. I came out with the kindest feelings for these people down here; I wanted to see it made easy; we had whipped them, and I wanted it to rest there. I thought the South wanted it to end there. But I was tremendously mistaken. They hate us and despise us and all belonging to us. They call us cut-throats, liars, thieves, vandals, cowards, and the very scum of the earth. They actually believe it. . . . And they say they are the gentlemen; we are amalgamationists, mudsills, vandals, and so forth. And I've heard and seen more brag, and lying, and profanity, and cruelty, down here, than I ever saw or heard before in all my life. The only people I find that a Northern man can make a friend of, the only ones that like the Government and believe in it, are the Negroes. I'm convinced they can vote just as intelligently as the poor whites. A Southerner would knock me down if I said that to him; but it's true. I tell you I'm going home to be a radical. Fight the devil with fire. I've learned to hate Southerners as I find them, and they can hate me if they want to. I'm a Sumner man after I get back. . . .[8]

The majority of the Ohioan's fellow Northerners were not Sumner men and never would be in the sense of sharing his dedication to Negro equality. But like the Ohioan, they were angry at the South for what they deemed to be its lack of repentance and its excessive arrogance. Accordingly, they were disposed to compel the Southerners to behave properly, particularly with regards to the former slaves whose freedom had been won by Northern blood. This, in turn, meant that for the time being, and up to a certain point, Northerners would support and even demand measures designed to establish and maintain Negro rights. Most Republicans being Northerners, felt the same way. Johnson, a Southerner, had no such feelings and could not understand them in others.

Of course Johnson was aware that dissatisfaction with his Reconstruction policy and its outcomes existed in the North. But he did not think that it was great, and he believed that it was confined largely to the Radical minority. Hence, as he saw it, the need was to combat the efforts of that minority to convert itself into a majority. In his message to Congress he had sought—effectively, so it seemed —to accomplish that purpose. His next move was to throw the prestige of Grant against the Radicals.

Back in June the president had appointed Carl Schurz to tour the South and report to him on conditions and attitudes there. Schurz was a former Union general, a leader of the German-American community, and a Radical Republican. In sending him on this mission (the idea for which had originated with Schurz), Johnson probably hoped to win the Republican over or at least appease him. Schurz, however, who traveled through the South from July through October, angered Johnson by interfering in the matter of arming the Mississippi militia and by publishing articles in the *Boston Advertiser* highly critical of the way in which Reconstruction was proceeding. When Schurz returned to Washington, Johnson told him that he need not submit a report. Nevertheless, Schurz sent him one stressing the need for federal protection of the Negro.[9]

Shortly after Congress convened, Sumner, who knew the contents of the report and who, in fact, had helped finance Schurz's trip, introduced a resolution which the Senate passed calling for the president to make the report available. On December 18 Johnson complied. But he also sent to the Senate a message of his own in which he challenged Schurz's findings. Affairs in the South, the president stated, were more promising than one had a right to expect; the Southern people had evidenced a laudable desire to renew their allegiance; and although there were occasional disorders, "Systems [i.e., the Black Codes] are gradually developing themselves under which the freedmen receives the protection to which he is justly entitled."[10] In support of these contentions Johnson asked the Senate to consider the report of General Grant, a copy of which he transmitted.

In October, following Schurz's return, Johnson had requested Grant to make a similar tour, confident of a different outcome. He was not disappointed. Traveling through the South during November and early December, Grant was, on the whole, favorably impressed by what he saw and heard. Therefore, in his report he said as much and concluded that "the mass of thinking men of the South accept the present situation of affairs in good faith." He made no reference to the plight of the Negro.[11]

Sumner, incensed by Johnson's reference to the Black Codes as a "protection" for the Negro, denounced the president's message as "white washing" and compared it to Franklin Pierce's condonement of proslavery outrages in Kansas in 1856. But neither Sumner nor anyone else publicly criticized Grant's report—the general was too popular for that. Thus Johnson could believe, probably with considerable justification, that he had canceled out Schurz with Grant: Who were people more likely to credit—a third-rate German political general or the "hero of Appomatox"? Moreover, by association, Grant appeared to be supporting the administration and its Reconstruction policy.

So, through December Johnson held the Radicals at bay. In fact many Moderate Republicans criticized Sumner for his savage attacks on the president. Senator Edwin D. Morgan of New York even wondered if Sumner was "demented," and *The Nation* dismissed his Reconstruction proposals as utterly impractical. Furthermore, although the Republican caucus appointed Stevens to the Joint Committee on Reconstruction which he had originated, it filled the committee mainly with Moderates—including the chairman, Senator Fessenden. Sumner, who disliked Fessenden and was detested by him, did not even become a member, much to his chagrin. In the House, Stevens's bill reducing the Southern states to territorial status got nowhere.

Meanwhile public opinion in the North remained, on the whole, favorable to Johnson. There the prevailing premise continued to be that he would cooperate with Congress in supplementing his Reconstruction program with measures to protect the Negro. When Johnson received a number of Negroes at the White House New Year's Day reception—the first president ever to do so—it seemed to some Northerners and Republicans an auspicious sign.

On the other hand, the Democrats and the Southerners also looked for a sign from Johnson. They wanted him to declare open war on the Radicals, whom they blamed for the rejection of the Southern congressmen and for the continuation of military occupation in the South. Consequently, throughout December and January their spokesmen called on the president to "strike" at the Radicals either by removing Stanton or by vetoing one of the "unconstitutional acts of the present Congress." Such action on his part was needed, stated one Democratic newspaper, before the Democrats could put their "entire faith in him." Southern leaders expressed similar sentiments.

Added to this pressure were the promptings of the Blairs, Welles, Campbell, and other confidants. Only by moving decisively against the Radical "conspiracy," they told Johnson, could he—in

Welles's words—"maintain and carry into effect his administrative policy" and create a new political coalition committed to him. Bennett's *New York Herald* likewise urged him to hurl down the gauntlet to the Radicals and so open the way for the formation of an "Andrew Johnson Party."[12]

By late January, if not before, Johnson himself had concluded that a showdown with the Radicals was necessary to the success of his policy and ambitions. The only question in his mind was when and over what. He rejected dismissing Stanton because that would offend Stanton's personal friend Seward as well as the large numbers of Northerners who regarded the secretary of war as one of the architects of Union victory. Instead Johnson decided to challenge the Radicals on what he deemed—correctly—to be their most vulnerable ground: Negro suffrage. Furthermore, an opportunity to do this seemed conveniently at hand, for on January 25 the House passed a bill, sponsored by Stevens, which granted the vote to Negroes in the District of Columbia. Here was an issue, the president was confident, on which he could surely win, especially since the citizens of the District had defeated Negro suffrage in a recent referendum by a vote of 7,369 to 36.[13]

Johnson began his campaign against Stevens's bill in a published interview with Senator Dixon on January 28. This measure, he told Dixon, was "ill-timed, uncalled for, and calculated to do great harm." Indeed, "it would engender enmity, contention, and strife between the two races" and result in the "certain extermination of the negro population." Moreover, the president disapproved of the numerous proposals that were being made in Congress to amend the Constitution and enable Negroes to vote. But if such were to be done, Johnson said, he would favor an amendment stating that "Representatives shall be apportioned among the several states . . . according to the number of qualified voters in each State." Thus, it still would be left to the states to decide whether or not they wanted Negro suffrage.[14]

Stevens responded by calling the interview a "proclamation" which "centuries ago, had it been made to Parliament by a British king, it would have cost him his head." Promptly, most Republicans joined with Democrats in denouncing Stevens for his extreme language. At the same time Johnson's declared willingness to support an amendment tying representation to the number of qualified voters put Sumner in an awkward position: Because a large number of nonvoting emigrants resided in Massachusetts, such an amendment would reduce his state's House membership. Hence Sumner

63

was bound to oppose it—as in fact he did—and so leave himself open to the charge of hypocrisy on the question of Negro suffrage. Indeed, all New England congressmen took the same attitude towards such an amendment for the same reason, thereby dooming any chance it had for adoption. Johnson knew this when he proposed the amendment—which, no doubt, is exactly why he did so.[15]

Another opportunity for Johnson to express himself on Negro suffrage came on February 7 when a delegation of Negroes, headed by Frederick Douglass, visited him at the White House. Only the ballot, stated Douglass, could make the Negro truly free. Therefore he asked Johnson to support voting rights for the Negro, saying, "You have the power to save or destroy us, to bless or blast us—I mean our whole race." Johnson answered by repeating his standard argument that imposing black suffrage on the South against the will of the whites would lead to a race war. The two then engaged in what at times was a heated argument over the past, present, and future status of the Negro, with Douglass stressing the ideal of justice and Johnson what he considered to be the practical considerations. Finally as his delegation started to leave, Douglass declared, "The President sends us to the people, and we go to the people." To which Johnson answered, "Yes, sir; I have great faith in the people. I believe they will do what is right." Then, after the Negroes were gone, he turned to one of his secretaries and (according to a *New York World* reporter) "uttered the following terse Saxon: 'Those d———d sons of b———s thought they had me in a trap! I know that d———d Douglass; he's just like any nigger, and he would sooner cut a white man's throat than not.' "[16]

Historians, understandably enough, have used this quotation to illustrate Johnson's racial prejudice, but possibly the most significant word is *trap*. For the day before Johnson's encounter with Douglass, the House had passed a measure earlier approved by the Senate, namely the Freedmen's Bureau Bill; meanwhile the Senate had buried Stevens's District of Columbia Bill. Thus, instead of being able to veto that bill as anticipated, Johnson found himself confronted with a fundamentally different piece of legislation.

The Freedmen's Bureau Bill had nothing to do with Negro suffrage; rather, it was designed to promote Negro welfare. It extended indefinitely the life of the Freedmen's Bureau (which had been slated to expire in March 1867), increased the number of its agents, set aside three million acres of public land in the South for allotment to Negroes and loyal whites, confirmed for three years South Carolina Negroes in the possession of farms granted them in the Sea Islands, authorized the establishment of asylums and schools for freedmen and white loyalists, and empowered the bureau to protect the civil rights of Negroes by means of military tribunals.

Furthermore, it was not a Radical scheme. It originated from the Senate Judiciary Committee, chaired by Moderate Republican Lyman Trumbull of Illinois, and had passed both House and Senate with the unanimous support of Republicans and against the solid opposition of Democrats. Clearly it was a Republican party measure. Should he veto it, Johnson would not be challenging merely the Radicals. He would be going against the will of the party which had placed him in power and of which he was titular head.

The Republican congressional leadership not only hoped but expected him to sign the bill. In fact, while it was in the process of passage, both Trumbull and Fessenden had visited Johnson to ask him if there was anything in the bill to which he objected; if so, they said, they were prepared to change it. Both had come away from the White House confident of the president's approval or at least his acquiescence. They also felt relieved. Along with the majority of Republicans—even many Radicals—the two wished to avoid a quarrel with Johnson. Such an occurrence, they feared, would be calamitous for the party and the nation. In particular it would lead to Johnson's siding with the Democrats and using his great patronage powers against Republicans. Indeed, Republicans had grown increasingly uneasy over Johnson's Democratic associations and the claims by Democrats that they, not the Republicans, were the president's true adherents.

Either Trumbull and Fessenden were new victims of Johnson's taciturnity, or else he deliberately deceived them. Probably it was a combination of both. In any case, at no time did he consider signing the Freedmen's Bureau Bill. Johnson would have preferred to veto the District of Columbia Bill but this one would do; given his political situation and ambition, he saw no practical alternative. Southerners hated the Freedmen's Bureau; to them it was the main instrument perpetuating Northern domination and blocking white supremacy. Should Johnson allow it to exist, all he had gained in the South might be lost. In addition, if he let the bill become law, the Democrats, with their demand that he back his words with deeds, would turn against him. All hopes of forming a new party would be ruined.

To be sure, the majority of Republicans would resent a veto. But in the end, Johnson calculated, most of them would accept it, and with it, his leadership. Public opinion would force them to.

Faced with a choice between a president who sought to reunite the nation and politicians who were keeping it divided, the people of the North, he concluded, would back the former.

Last but not least Johnson believed that the Radicals were engaged in a revolutionary conspiracy via the Joint Committee on Reconstruction (which he erroneously thought Stevens dominated) to create an all-powerful central government through constitutional amendments calling for federal enforcement of Negro civil and political rights. On February 13 in a conversation with Welles he

> alluded with some feeling to the extraordinary intrigue which he understands was going on in Congress, having nothing short of subversion or change in the structure of the government in view. The unmistakable design of Thad Stevens and his associates was to take the government into their own hands, the President said, and to get rid of him by declaring Tennessee out of the Union [actually, the Joint Committee was then giving favorable consideration to admitting Tennessee]. A sort of French Directory was to be established by these spirits in Congress, the Constitution was to be remodeled by them, etc.[17]

By blocking enactment of the Freemen's Bureau Bill, Johnson hoped to demonstrate that the Radical plot to alter the Constitution was as impractical as their vision of Negro equality. They then would be isolated and rendered impotent. Also, a veto would provide him with an occasion for rallying public opinion behind the immediate seating of the Southern congressmen—and once that was accomplished, there no longer would be the slightest chance of pro-Negro amendments magnifying federal power.[18]

So, during the days that followed the passage of the Freedmen's Bureau Bill, Johnson's main concern was framing a veto message that would have maximum popular appeal. To that end he consulted Seward, Welles, Doolittle, and several other advisers, all of whom furnished him with either drafts of a veto message or data pertinent thereto. He then selected the materials he wished to use and had one of his secretaries, or possibly some confidant, write the message in final form. For the most part he followed the suggestions of Seward and Welles, but he rejected the basic approach proposed by Seward, which was to disapprove of the bill on technical grounds while holding out to Congress the possibility of compromise. That would not have satisfied the Democrats and Southerners, nor would it have had the impact on public opinion the president desired.

On the morning of February 19 Johnson presented the veto message to the cabinet. His purpose was to announce his decision, not to solicit advice. Seward and Welles, of course, expressed approval, as did McCulloch and Dennison; on the other hand, Welles recorded in his diary that Stanton was "disappointed," Speed was "disturbed," and Harlan was "apprehensive." That afternoon Johnson's staff delivered copies of the message to Congress and to the press.[19]

The Freedmen's Bureau Bill, Johnson declared, was unnecessary since the act establishing it remained in effect; second, it was unconstitutional because it extended military power in peacetime and invaded areas reserved to the civil authority and the judiciary; and third, it was unjust in that it would "take away land from its former owners." Furthermore, he asserted that the bureau itself was excessively expensive, its procedures unfair, and it conferred privileges on blacks that were denied to whites. At best it could only be justified as a temporary expedient to assist the Negro in the transition from slavery to freedom. At worse it would, if allowed to operate indefinitely, impair this transition by discouraging the freedom from developing habits of self-reliance.[20]

Having thus blasted the bill, Johnson then fired a salvo at Congress itself: "At the time . . . of the consideration and the passage of this bill, there was no Senator or Representative in Congress from the eleven States which are to be mainly affected by its provisions." Although Johnson did not question the right of Congress to judge the qualifications of its own members, he said that "that authority can not be construed as including the right to shut out in time of peace any State from the representation to which it is entitled by the Constitution." Therefore, as president, "chosen by the people of all the States," he considered it his duty to present the "just claims" of the unrepresented states to the Congress, each member of which was chosen merely by a "single district or State." Such being the case, Johnson continued, "It is hardly necessary for me to inform Congress that in my own judgment most of those States, so far, at least, as depends on their own action, have already been fully restored, and are to be deemed as entitled to enjoy their constitutional rights as members of the Union."[21]

Southerners and Democrats hailed the veto message—they could not have asked for more. By the same token most Northerners and Republicans reacted to it with dismay. Despite published reports to the contrary they had expected Johnson to sign the Freedmen's Bureau Bill or at least offer to accept a modified version of it.

Nearly the entire Republican press condemned the veto and also Johnson's claim as president to a superior authority over Congress. Only the Radicals, however, attacked Johnson personally. Most Republicans, reluctant to face unpleasant facts, took the line that the difference between the president and Congress was merely one of means rather than ends, and they continued to insist that Johnson had adhered to their party and had not gone over to the Democrats.

The day after the veto, Trumbull called for repassage of the bill, declaring that in advocating the extension of the Freedman's Bureau he thought he had been "acting in harmony with the views of the President." Trumbull's motion, however, failed by a vote of 30 to 18 to secure the needed two-thirds majority. Ten Conservative and Moderate Republicans—Cowan, Dixon, Doolittle, Lane of Kansas, Morgan of New York, William Stewart of Nevada, and Peter Van Winkle and Waitman T. Willey of West Virginia—joined the ten Democratic senators to sustain the veto. To a large degree, Morgan, Stewart, and Willey were motivated by a desire to avoid a total break between the president and their party; Lane's primary concern was to maintain his friendly personal relations with Johnson and thus retain control over federal patronage in Kansas, the key to his political power.

Johnson was exultant. Ignoring the very thin and shaky margin by which his veto had been upheld, he believed that he had successfully defied the Radicals and their revolutionary schemes. He may also have misunderstood or underestimated the adverse reaction to the veto in the North: Nearly all the letters he received and the press clippings assembled by his staff expressed approval. In any case, he had faced storms of opposition many times before, above all in Tennessee in 1861, but always had fought through to victory and vindication. He would do so again. Were not the Radicals merely the Northern counterparts of the Southern secessionists?[22]

It was in this mood that he spoke on the evening of February 22, Washington's Birthday, to a crowd of supporters who had marched to the White House, with torches burning and bands playing, to demonstrate their approval of the veto. Johnson began by proclaiming his devotion to the Union and recalling how he had suffered in the struggle to preserve it against traitors in the South. Now, however, he said, those traitors had been defeated and had repented. Hence his policy was one of forgiveness, based on the example set by Jesus, who "went forth with grace and attested by His blood and His wounds that He would die and let the nation live." But unfortunately, Johnson continued, new rebels had appeared, this time in the North. They were men who plotted to concentrate all power in the hands of a few at "the federal head, and thereby bring about a consolidation of the Republic, which is equally objectionable with its dissolution." The instrument of their evil ambition he said, was "an irresponsible central directory"—the Joint Committee on Reconstruction—which had assumed "nearly all the powers of the government" and which was preventing the restoration of the Union. These men, the president announced, were just as treasonable as "the Davises and Toombs, the Slidells and a long list of such."[23]

> "Give us the names!" called a voice from the crowd.
> "A gentleman calls for their names," answered Johnson. "Well, I suppose I should name to you those whom I look upon as being opposed to the fundamental principles of the Government and as now laboring to destroy them. *I say Thaddeus Stevens, of Pennsylvania—I say Charles Sumner, of Massachusetts—I say Wendell Phillips, of Massachusetts.*"[24]

The crowd cheered at the mention of each name. Johnson then went on to accuse his enemies of wanting to remove him from office—even of inciting his assassination. "Are they not satisfied with the blood which has been shed? Does not the murder of Lincoln appease the vengeance and wrath of the opponents of this government? However," Johnson continued, "if my blood is to be shed because I vindicate the Union and the preservation of this government in its original purity and character, let it be shed; let an altar to the Union be erected, and then, if it is necessary, take me and lay me upon it. . . ."[25]

Yet, despite everything the Radical revolutionaries might do, he was confident of the outcome: "They say that man Johnson is a lucky man, that no man can defeat me. I will tell you what constitutes luck. Doing right and being for the people. The people . . . are frequently underrated or underestimated; but somehow or other the great mass of the people will find out who is for them and who is against them." Although he had been placed in many a trying position during his career, "so far, thank God, I have not deserted the people, nor do I believe they will desert me."[26]

Earlier in the day, concerned about Johnson's propensity to get excited when talking to an audience, McCulloch and Doolittle had urged him not to speak extemporaneously when his supporters marched to the White House that evening. Johnson had promised merely to thank them, but their cheers and an inner need to lash out at his enemies caused him to change his mind. The president's comments to the crowd justified McCulloch's and Doolittle's worst fears. The vast majority of Northerners felt outraged and shamed as they read, or read about, Johnson's speech. In their eyes he had disgraced himself and the presidency. Many of them suspected—or concluded—that he had been drunk again. In particular, they resented his denunciation of Stevens and Sumner; whatever else they might be, the two were not traitors to the Union. Indeed, Johnson's attack on them enhanced the prestige of both the Radical leaders, with Sumner probably being saved from defeat in his bid for reelection to the Senate. Even Johnson's friends expressed regret over his performance: It "lost to our cause 200,000 votes," moaned Doolittle. All in all, Johnson had committed an act of great personal and political folly.[27]

Yet not all had been lost. He soon had a chance to redeem himself and the situation—in fact, to gain the upper hand over the Radicals. Along with the Freedmen's Bureau Bill, Trumbull's Senate Judiciary Committee had prepared and reported a civil rights bill. Designed to protect Negroes against oppression in general and against the Black Codes in particular, the bill declared them citizens of the United States; it bestowed on all persons born in the United States (except Indians) an equal right to make and enforce contracts, to sue and be witnesses in the courts, to own land and other property, and to enjoy equal protection under the law; it stipulated punishments for anyone violating these rights; and it conferred broad enforcement powers on the president and the federal judiciary. The Senate had passed the bill on February 2 by a vote of 33 to 12, and on March 13 the House followed suit, 111 to 38. Like the Freedmen's Bureau Bill, this was a Moderate measure. Furthermore, Trumbull and other leading Moderates once again visited Johnson to solicit his views on the bill. He expressed no objections, and they went away assuming that it was acceptable to him. This was a great relief to them, for they still hoped to achieve harmony between the executive and legislative branches—and within the Republican party—on Reconstruction policy.[28]

But their hope proved as unfounded as their assumption false. On March 27 Johnson delivered another stern, unbending veto. The bill, he declared, was an unconstitutional invasion of states' rights, "another step, or rather stride, towards centralization, and the concentration of all legislative powers in the national government." Furthermore, he continued, since Negroes were not qualified for citizenship, it discriminated against "large numbers of intelligent, worthy, and patriotic foreigners." And, in an appeal to racial prejudice, he asserted that the measure would "operate in favor of the colored and against the white race."[29]

Had Johnson signed the Civil Rights Bill he would have become—as Governor Cox of Ohio told him when urging him to do so—"master of the situation." Johnson would have satisfied the North's desire to protect Negroes in the South and thus would have regained much of the support and respect he had lost by his Freedmen's Bureau veto and by the Washington's Birthday harrangue. He also would have kept the Moderate Republicans, who did not insist on Negro suffrage, divided from the Radicals, who did. All of this would have added up to enough popular and congressional backing to enable Johnson to block the Radicals and to open the way for the early restoration of at least some of the Southern states.

But as it was, the veto, and the manner in which it was expressed, angered most Northerners and broke the last link between Johnson and most Moderate Republicans. Johnson, the latter concluded, had indeed gone over to the Copperhead Democrats and the Southern rebels; in alliance with them, he was seeking to destroy the Republican party and undo the results of the war. Therefore the Moderates felt that they had no choice except to join the Radicals in all-out opposition to the president. Only in that way could they preserve Northern victory, Republican power, and Negro freedom.[30]

On April 6 the Senate, by a vote of 33 to 15, repassed the Civil Rights Bill. Three days later the House did the same, 122 to 41, thereby making it law. In the Senate the three Republicans—Morgan, Stewart, and Willey—who had sustained the Freedmen's Bureau veto in hope of preventing a party split now voted with the majority. In the House just one Northern Republican—Raymond—remained loyal to Johnson. It was the first time in history that Congress had overturned a presidential veto.[31]

Contemporaries and historians agree that Johnson's rejection of the Civil Rights Bill was one of the great blunders of his presidency—perhaps the greatest. He turned friends into enemies, united Moderates and Radicals, and made the issue between him and Congress not the Negroes' political rights, on which he probably could have won, but their civil rights, on which he was doomed to lose. Moreover, he ruined any realistic chance he had of retaining the presidency (although he continued to aspire to that goal) and set in motion forces which rendered him nearly impotent as presi-

71

dent. Finally and most fundamentally, he made it impossible for Reconstruction to be conducted rationally and thus made it inevitable that the process would be full of passion and conflict.

Why did Johnson commit this terrible blunder? It was not for lack of sound counsel. Just one member of the cabinet—Welles—wholeheartedly endorsed the president's decision to veto the Civil Rights Bill. The rest either advised him to sign it or—like Seward—attempted to persuade him to reject it only partially, while offering to compromise with Congress. In addition, a number of Moderates still friendly to Johnson despite the Freedmen's Bureau veto —notably Senators Morgan, Sherman, and Grimes, and Governor Cox of Ohio and ex-Governor Morton of Indiana—urged him to approve it, warning that otherwise they too would be forced into opposition. Indeed, even such staunch Johnsonites as Bennett, Raymond, and Dixon expressed approval of the bill, with the latter two voting for it when it passed initially.

No doubt the standard explanations of why Johnson disregarded all this advice are, to a high degree, correct: his racial prejudice, his dedication to states' rights, and his desire to retain the support of the Democrats and the South. Yet there was more to it than this. Johnson sincerely believed that his Reconstruction program was all that was necessary and practical. The Republicans, he told a reporter, knew nothing about the "real state of the South" and were equally ignorant of the true nature of the Negro. Moreover, the president's personal ambition was tied to the success of that program. The refusal of the Republican majority in Congress to accept it filled him with bitter resentment. He took it as a personal challenge, both to Johnson the president and to Johnson the man. His reaction was to fight, and to fight relentlessly, regardless of the odds. "Sir," he declared to his private secretary one evening during the height of the furor over the civil rights veto, "I am right. I know I am right, and I am damned if I do not adhere to it."[32]

Johnson's pugnacious response to the frustration of his plans and ambitions also helps account for his stubborn refusal to compromise on the bill. Seward had proposed a veto message in which Johnson would have objected only to the enforcement provisions of the bill and then invited Congress to revise them so as to make them constitutional. Following the veto, Fessenden and Morgan had sought an accommodation with the president, and Doolittle prepared another civil rights bill which he hoped would be satisfactory to Johnson. Johnson, however, rejected the overtures of the first two senators (thereby causing Morgan to cast what was, in effect, the decisive vote to override the veto); and he did not even consider Doolittle's bill. In each instance Johnson threw away an opportunity to retain enough Republican support to uphold his veto. By the same token, had he delivered a conditional veto and then compromised, he probably would have lost little or no Democratic and Southern backing. Although the Democrats and Southerners denounced the Civil Rights Bill as "dangerous and atrocious," their more perceptive leaders privately expected the president to sign it out of political expediency, and after the veto they were alarmed to see the Republicans uniting against him. More importantly, the Democrats and the South would have found it difficult to oppose Johnson. Whom else could they support?[33]

But Johnson lacked the finesse and the flexibility to follow the course marked by Seward and urged by his other advisers. It was not in his nature. He preferred all-out enemies to lukewarm friends. And those who were not for him, he regarded as being against him. This is what two very moderate Republican representatives, Godlove Orth of Indiana and Shelby Cullom of Illinois, discovered when they called on him in hopes of achieving a reconciliation between the president and their party. "He received us politely enough," recorded Cullom, "and without mincing any words he gave us to understand that we were on a fool's errand and that he would not yield. We went away, and naturally enough joined the extreme radicals in the House, always voting with them afterwards."[34]

Johnson further demonstrated his determination to battle the "Radicals" (by which he, like the Democrats, now meant the great majority of Republicans) by issuing on April 2 a proclamation which declared the rebellion at an end and the Southern states back in the Union. This was done four days before the Senate overrode the civil rights veto. Then, a few days later, he ordered that military trials of civilians be halted in the South, citing as his reason the recently announced preliminary verdict of the Supreme Court in the *Ex Parte Milligan* case. The intent of both the president's proclamation and his order was to undermine military rule in the South. Their only real effect, however, was to further antagonize the North and the Republicans and to irritate Stanton and Grant.

Meanwhile, all through the winter and into the spring the Joint Committee on Reconstruction had been hearing testimony on conditions in the South, collecting relevant data, and considering possible legislation. Finally, on April 30—the same day, coincidentally, that a white mob began a three-day rampage of pillage, arson, rape, and murder against blacks in Memphis, Tennessee—the committee reported a constitutional amendment designed to make permanent and undeniable the protections granted Negroes by the Civil Rights Act. More than two months of congressional debate followed, during which many changes were made and unmade in the amendment. When adopted by the Senate on June 8, 33 to 11, and by the House on June 11, 120 to 32, the amendment contained five main clauses. First, all persons born or naturalized in the United States would become citizens thereof and of the state in which they resided. No state was to make or enforce any law abridging the privileges or immunities of United States citizens, nor "deprive any person of life, liberty, or property, without due process of law; nor deny to any person . . . the equal protection of the laws." Second, all persons residing in a state, excluding untaxed Indians, were to be counted for the purpose of representation in the House, but a state denying or "in any way" abridging the right of male, adult citizens to vote was to have its representation reduced proportionately. Third, no person was to hold any federal or state office who, through engaging in rebellion against the United States, was guilty of violating an oath to uphold the Constitution. Congress, by a two-thirds vote of both houses, could "remove such disability." Fourth, the validity of the United States public debt was not to be questioned, and all rebel debts were illegal and void. And finally, "The Congress shall have the power to enforce, by appropriate legislation, the provisions of this article."[35]

Like the Freedman's Bureau Bill and the Civil Rights Act, the Fourteenth Amendment was a moderate measure in its origin and intent. Representative Bingham of Ohio, leader of the House Moderates, was the primary author of the crucial first clause; and Senate Moderates were responsible for the third clause, which replaced a more drastic House-passed version disfranchising all rebels until 1870. Even the second clause, which Stevens had authored, was more a move to reduce Southern representation than to secure Negro suffrage. In fact, Sumner, Stevens, and other Radicals were unhappy with the amendment because it did not grant Negroes the vote, and they supported it only because it was the most that could be obtained for the time being.[36]

In effect the amendment constituted the peace terms of the North, of Congress, and of the Republican party. Implicitly if not explicitly the Republicans declared to the Southern states that if they ratified it—thereby indicating acceptance of the *sine qua non* of equal civil and personal rights for the Negro—they would be readmitted to the Union. On the other hand, should they reject it, then they could expect something much more drastic. But most Republicans, in particular the dominant Moderates, hoped it would not come to that.[37]

As president, of course, Johnson had no legal role in the amending process. But should he endorse the Fourteenth Amendment, it might improve the chances of ratification in the South and certainly it would be a step towards reconciliation with Congress. Hence numerous Conservatives and some Moderates joined the *New York Times* in expressing hope, even confidence, that Johnson would at least acquiesce in the amendment. These elements again deluded themselves, however, with wishful thinking. On June 22, in an unprecedented act, Johnson sent Congress a special message regarding the amendment. The fact that Secretary of State Seward, Johnson stated, had performed the "purely ministerial" function of transmitting the amendment to the states for ratification was not to be construed as meaning that he, the president, approved of the amendment. On the contrary, he questioned the constitutional authority of Congress to amend the constitution at all while it unconstitutionally denied eleven states representation. In other words, Johnson argued that Congress had no right to adopt an amendment without the participation of congressmen whose very presence would make its adoption impossible![38]

So the war between president and Congress continued. Early in July the latter passed another Freedmen's Bureau Bill, basically the same as the first. On July 16 Johnson vetoed it, repeating his earlier objections. That same day both houses overrode the veto. In the Senate, where the vote was 33 to 12, the only Republicans to join the Democrats in sustaining the veto were Doolittle, Norton, and Van Winkle. Thus, Johnson's only semblance of a victory over the Republicans was transformed into a defeat. Indeed, worse than defeat—humiliation.

Next, on July 20, Congress replied to Johnson's attack on the Fourteenth Amendment in the most effective manner conceivable: It seated the congressmen (among them Johnson's son-in-law, Senator Patterson) from Tennessee. Just four days before, under the almost dictatorial sway of Governor Brownlow, Tennessee had ratified the Fourteenth Amendment "amid some of the most violent and irregular scenes in the history of parliamentary government in America" and against the will of the state's largely disfranchised citizens. "Give my compliments to the dead dog in the White House," sneered Brownlow in a telegram to Washington announcing the event. By thus admitting Tennessee, the Republicans not only had embarrassed Johnson but confirmed their implied promise that if the South accepted the Fourteenth Amendment it would be accepted back into the Union.[39]

On July 28 the first session of the Thirty-ninth Congress ended. When it began seven months before, the nearly universal hope had been that it would complete the process of restoring unity and peace to the nation. Instead it had witnessed a bitter quarrel between the president and its Republican majority over whether or not the federal government should provide and protect civil rights for Negroes. Now the Republicans headed for their homes to seek the endorsement of the Northern people in the fall elections. Johnson, on the other hand, looked to the North to repudiate the Republicans. If that happened, all would be well for him and his Reconstruction policy. But if it did not . . .

5

★★★★★

JOHNSON LOSES HIS QUARREL

Back in March when he was vainly attempting to persuade the president to sign the Civil Rights Bill, Morton of Indiana warned Johnson that failure to do so would produce an irreparable rupture between the president and the Republicans. But Johnson, "laboring under great emotion" and with "beads of perspiration" on his brow, stated that he intended to build a new party which would assure the triumph of his policy. To this Morton replied that "all roads out of the Republican Party lead into the Democratic." Soon afterwards Morton, hitherto a Johnson supporter, opened a successful campaign in Indiana for the United States Senate, running as a Radical.[1]

As for Johnson, following the overturning of his civil rights veto, members of his inner circle began laying the organizational groundwork for his proposed new party. First, Alexander W. Randall, the assistant postmaster general and a political associate of Seward's, formed the National Union Club, which consisted mainly of proadministration Republican officeholders. Then Montgomery Blair took the lead in setting up a predominantly Democratic National Union Johnson Club; it soon merged, however, with Randall's group. On the evening of June 11, the day Congress passed the Fourteenth Amendment, Johnson met with several of his confidants at the White House and agreed to the calling of "a convention of the friends of the country" to combat the Radicals. "We must rescue the power from their hands," Johnson declared. "I am willing to put in all the capital I have. I will give $20,000 in cash and all the influence I have as President. . . ." Four days later, in a conference with Welles and Doolittle, he affirmed this decision to call a convention.[2]

Hence, on June 25—three days after Johnson's message to Congress criticizing the adoption of the Fourteenth Amendment—the Executive Committee of the National Union Club issued in Washington a "Call for a National Union Convention" to meet on August 14 in Philadelphia. Its purpose, stated the "Call" (which had been written by Doolittle) was to uphold the "undoubted right" of each state to "prescribe the qualifications of its own electors" and to "control its own domestic concerns," while at the same time it would oppose the "unjust and revolutionary" exclusion from Congress of "loyal Senators and Representatives" and the "usurpation and centralization of power in Congress." It was to consist of at least four delegates from each congressional district, two from every territory and the District of Columbia, and four delegates-at-large from all thirty-six states.[3]

The summoning of the National Union Convention formally launched Johnson's campaign to defeat the Republicans in the 1866 elections. It also was another step towards the realization of his goal of creating a new political party. He did not plan, however, for the convention as such to organize the party. Instead he envisioned its basic function to be the formation of a working coalition of Conservative Republicans and Northern Democrats who would back candidates favorable to his Reconstruction policy. His hope—indeed his assumption—was that these candidates would either win control of Congress and the Northern states or else substantially reduce Republican strength therein. At a minimum, this would enable him to frustrate further "revolutionary" congressional legislation with the veto. At a maximum, the way would be opened for the seating of the Southern congressmen and the transformation of the Conservative Republican–Democratic coalition into a full-fledged party.

Implementing this strategy, however, promised to be difficult. Although Republican Conservatives and Northern Democrats united in opposing the "Radicals," they had precious little else in common except mutual distrust. Thus Seward, Weed, and Raymond, the principal Conservative leaders, were determined to keep the National Union movement, or (if it became such) party, under Republican (i.e., their own) control. On the other hand, the Democrats had no intention of merely being privates in an army, commanded by Seward and for which they obviously would provide most of the troops. Hence their initial reaction to the convention was one of skepticism and criticism. Not until the Executive Committee of the National Union Club promised them one-half of the delegates and a fair share in presidential patronage did Democrats give their adherence. Likewise Southern leaders were at first hesitant about participating in the convention because of its Republican auspices, but eventually most of them rallied behind it, seeing in it a chance to return to the mainstream of national politics and help defeat the Radicals' nefarious schemes.[4]

To complicate matters more, Johnson's own entourage disagreed as to the best way to advance the National Union movement. Seward and his cohorts believed that it was both imperative and possible to attract the support of Moderate Republicans. Hence Doolittle's call for the convention (written under Seward's direction) emphasized readmitting the Southern states and only by implication criticized the Fourteenth Amendment, which Moderates generally supported. In contrast, the Blairs, Welles, and McCulloch urged Johnson to break formally from the Republican party and to rely on Democratic backing, which they argued could be obtained in full strength only by all-out opposition to the Fourteenth Amendment. Privately Johnson concurred with them about the Republican party, but as a matter of practical politics he went along with Seward's approach. This had the advantage of enabling him and his followers to claim that they, not the "Radicals" (by which they meant all antiadministration Republicans), were the true disciples of Lincoln and the Union party of 1864.

The Republicans, of course, promptly and scathingly denounced the National Union movement. It proved, they charged, that Johnson had sold out to the Copperheads and rebels, thereby betraying the party which had made it possible for him to become president. On July 12 the Republican congressional caucus adopted a resolution declaring that the forthcoming Philadelphia convention was nothing but a plot to break up the party and, in effect, excommunicated any Republican who took part in it. Only Raymond, to whom Johnson and Seward had entrusted the task of organizing the convention in his capacity as chairman of the Union (Republican) party National Committee, voted against the resolution. Stevens thereupon gave him a vicious verbal whiplashing.

Seward also came under fire from the Republicans for championing Johnson in opposition to the party which he, Seward, had done so much to create. Why he followed this course, which led to his political ruin, puzzled many contemporaries as it has historians. The explanation seems to be fivefold. First, Seward had always considered the division between the North and South a tragedy which was both unnatural and unnecessary. Consequently, on the eve of the Civil War, he had been willing to go to almost any length to appease the South in order to preserve the Union. Now, after the war, he was prepared to support practically anything that would quickly restore the South to the Union. Second, despite his anti-slavery background, his attitude towards the Negro was identical to Johnson's. In an off-the-record interview with the editors of *The Nation* in March 1866, Seward bluntly stated that he had no more concern for Negroes in the South than he had for Hottentots—"they were," he said, "God's poor and always would be, and must take their level." Moreover, as he told a French correspondent who had criticized him for being callous to the plight of the Negro, he believed that the highest priority should be given to reconciling the whites of the South and that if this meant sacrificing the blacks, so be it. Third, Seward had far-reaching diplomatic ambitions which could be achieved only if he remained secretary of state—something he could not do if he broke with Johnson. In addition, his foreign policy aspirations provided an extra reason for wanting to reestablish national unity as quickly as possible. Fourth, by remaining in the cabinet Seward felt he could exercise a moderating influence on Johnson, who otherwise would be left to extremists, like the Blairs, and doctrinaires, like Welles. Finally, Seward suffered from a chronic over-optimism which, despite his skill as a political manipulator, often made him unrealistic when it came to major issues. Thus he actually believed that under his direction Johnson could overcome his enemies in the 1866 elections and bring about the formation of a new party which would gain power in 1868.[5]

For reasons previously described, Johnson valued and needed Seward, although contrary to what many then and later thought, he was not dominated by him. (Had Johnson been, he would not have made so many blunders, or the blunders he did make might not have been so bad.) Also Johnson could rely on the support of McCulloch and Welles. But he had good cause to doubt the loyalty of the rest of the cabinet. Therefore in mid July he had Doolittle, acting as spokesman for the National Union Club, write to each member of the cabinet requesting a public endorsement of the upcoming Philadelphia convention. Seward, McCulloch, and Welles promptly complied. Dennison, Harlan, and Speed, on the other hand, resigned, with the latter speaking for all three when he declared that he could not support any organization that opposed the Fourteenth Amendment and said that he did not consider the Philadelphia convention as representing the "great Union Party of the country." Johnson replaced Dennison as postmaster general with Randall, a logical enough choice. To succeed Harlan as secretary of the interior, Johnson named Orville H. Browning, a former senator from Illinois; Speed gave way as attorney general to Henry Stanbery, an Ohioan whom Johnson had earlier nominated unsuccessfully to the Supreme Court. All were Conservative Republicans but none possessed significant political influence, which is perhaps one reason why the Senate routinely approved their appointments.[6]

As for the seventh cabinet member, Stanton, on July 16 he wrote a reply to Doolittle. In it he stated his support of the Fourteenth Amendment and his opposition to the Philadelphia convention, which he said had as its object "the organization of a party consisting mainly of those who carried on the war (Rebellion) against the government . . . and those in the Northern States who sympathized with them." But after writing the letter to Doolittle, Stanton did not send it. To have done so would have been tantamount to resignation. And that he had no intention of doing, despite his wife's urgings and his precarious health.

By normal standards Stanton was wrong to remain in the cabinet of a president whose basic policies he rejected. The situation during the summer of 1866, however, was not normal. Johnson was openly trying to destroy what nominally was his own party; he was publicly challenging the authority of Congress; and he was instigating or countenancing measures designed to make it impossible for the army to maintain control over the South and to protect the freedmen. Therefore it was easy for Stanton to convince himself that he had a patriotic duty to continue as secretary of war—a post second only to the president's in actual power—in order to combat Johnson's schemes. Besides, at this particular time Stanton faced several potentially disastrous lawsuits arising from certain of his official acts. Thus added to the politician-bureaucrat's normal desire to cling to power was the practical necessity of preserving the legal protection provided by his cabinet status.

Johnson was well aware of Stanton's attitude. Those pro-Johnson historians who claim that Stanton deceived him on this score are, in effect, saying that their hero was a fool. Accordingly, he had good cause and every right to remove Stanton. Yet, in spite of the repeated urgings of the Blairs, Welles, and other confidants, Johnson held back. He feared that such a step might produce a dangerously adverse reaction in the North, where the Republicans would be sure to proclaim it as further proof that the president had sold out to the

Copperheads and rebels. Also, he lacked a clear-cut reason for dismissal: Stanton had carefully refrained from directly or publicly opposing Johnson's Reconstruction policy as such, although he had expressed disagreement with certain aspects of it. Therefore Johnson decided to ignore Stanton's failure to respond to Doolittle's inquiry and, for the time being, put up with his presence in the cabinet.[7]

Soon, however, Johnson had ample reason to regret this decision. On July 14 Major General George H. Thomas, commanding occupation troops in Tennessee, wired Grant that Governor Brownlow had requested military assistance in compelling the attendance of Democratic members of the legislature in order to muster the quorum to ratify the Fourteenth Amendment. "Shall I furnish it?" asked Thomas. Grant passed the message on to Stanton. But the secretary of war did not answer, and not until July 17—the day after the Tennessee legislature ratified the amendment—did he show the message to Johnson. Obviously and quite deliberately Stanton had sought to prevent Johnson from ordering Thomas not to intervene. As it turned out, in the absence of positive instructions to do so, Thomas refused to comply with Brownlow's request, with the result that Brownlow used sergeants-at-arms to round up enough legislators to obtain the desired quorum. Nevertheless, Stanton's conduct bordered on malfeasance.[8]

But the Tennessee affair was a mere trifle compared to what happened two weeks later in Louisiana. There Governor J. Madison Wells, a Unionist who had been elected under Lincoln's Ten Percent Plan and who had subsequently gravitated into the Radical camp, decided to reconvene the Unionist Constitutional Convention which had met last in 1864; his object was to retain power by enfranchising black "loyalists" and disfranchising white "rebels." The lieutenant governor, the attorney general, and the New Orleans mayor—all Democrats and ex-Confederates—moved to forestall the Unionist convention by having a state judge issue an injunction against its meeting. The mayor then informed Major General Absalom Baird, commanding the Department of Louisiana during the temporary absence of Major General Philip Sheridan, that he intended to disperse the convention should it defy the injunction, as it gave every sign of doing. Baird responded by questioning the mayor's authority to take such action and by declaring that he would use military force if need be to protect the convention from violence. The lieutenant governor thereupon telegraphed Johnson asking him if he intended to permit the army to interfere with the enforcement of the judge's injunction. On the evening of July 28 Johnson wired back: "The military will be expected to sustain, and not to obstruct or interfere with, the proceedings of the courts." The lieutenant governor, however, failed to transmit this or any other communication to Baird, who that night sent a telegram to Stanton:

A convention has been called, with the sanction of the Governor . . . to meet here on Monday. The Lieutenant-Governor and city authorities think it unlawful, and propose to break it up by arresting the delegates. I have given no orders on the subject, but have warned the parties that I could not countenance or permit such action without instructions to that effect from the President. Please instruct me at once by telegraph.[9]

Stanton did not answer Baird. And he did not show the general's request for instructions to Johnson. His purpose, as it had been with Thomas in Tennessee, was to promote the Republican cause by tacitly encouraging a general to do something which he knew the president would prohibit if aware of the situation. This time the ploy succeeded. Baird assumed that he had Stanton's sanction for protecting the convention and therefore announced that he would do so. This, in turn, caused the organizers of the convention, who had begun to waver, to go ahead with their plans.

Early on the afternoon of July 30, the convention—about thirty white delegates and between three and four hundred Negro supporters—began assembling at the Mechanic's Institute in New Orleans. A white mob made up in large part of former Confederate soldiers attacked with clubs, knives, and revolvers. The New Orleans police, instead of combating the assailants, joined them in the slaughter. When it ended, at least 38 participants in the convention—34 of them Negroes—had been murdered and 146—of whom 119 were blacks—had been wounded. Not until after the massacre ended did Baird's soldiers arrive on the scene. Either because of a misunderstanding or because he had been deceived by the mayor, Baird had thought that the convention was not scheduled to meet until 6 P.M. Hence his troops were still in their barracks, three miles away, when the mob struck.[10]

Primary and direct blame for the New Orleans riot, as it was rather euphemistically called, falls on the Louisiana Democratic leaders and the New Orleans mayor, mob, and police. But Johnson, Stanton, and Baird also share indirect responsibility. Johnson was wrong to back the Louisiana Democrats in their campaign to suppress the convention. Although of dubious legality, the delegates had a right to assemble—which is about all they could have done since not enough attended to constitute a quorum.

Stanton's inexcusable act was to withhold from Johnson Baird's request for instructions. Had Johnson seen it, he would have ordered Baird not to protect the convention. In that case the group would not have attempted to meet and there would have been no massacre. As for Baird, Johnson did not, as he should have, send him a copy of his July 28 telegram to the lieutenant governor expressing his desire that the army "sustain . . . the proceedings of the courts." On the morning of July 30, however, the lieutenant governor showed the general Johnson's message, whereupon Baird promised to provide troops to keep order. Baird's failure lay in not keeping himself accurately informed about the plans of the convention and the mood and intentions of the new Orleans mob.

Historically, the main importance of the New Orleans riot was its impact on the North. The majority of the people there were horrified and outraged as they read of helpless blacks being butchered by Southern whites. Here, as in Memphis two months before, was the bloody fruit of the president's lenient Reconstruction policy. Here, too, was further proof that the South remained unrepentant and unregenerate. Many Northerners who hitherto had doubted the need for the Fourteenth Amendment no longer did so. Those who already supported it now became convinced that it was an absolute necessity. No other single event did more to rally the North behind the Republicans and against Johnson. And, as if he were determined to make a bad situation even worse, Johnson failed to utter a single word of sympathy for the New Orleans victims or to condemn their murderers. *The Nation* spoke for most Northerners when it declared on August 9, "The coolness with which he [Johnson] refrained from expressing one word of honest indignation at the slaughter, in an American city, of unarmed men by a mob of their political opponents for political reasons . . . is, perhaps, the most alarming incident in this sad affair."[11]

Not until nearly two weeks after the New Orleans riot did Johnson learn of Baird's telegram asking for instructions and of Stanton's withholding of it.[12] At this point the president should have dismissed Stanton. But, probably fearful of intensifying the storm of criticism that was raging, he took no such action. Also, the Philadelphia convention was about to meet and firing Stanton would have distracted public attention from it. Thus Johnson decided to put up with Stanton awhile longer, no doubt hoping that success in the forthcoming elections would make it easy as well as safe to dump him later.

On August 14 the National Union Convention met in Philadelphia in a ramshackle wooden "wigwam" which had been hastily constructed for the purpose. Cheers went up as General Darius N. Couch of Massachusetts and Governor James L. Orr of South Carolina, arms linked, entered at the head of a procession of delegates from all thirty-six states. A self-appointed executive committee consisting of Randall, Doolittle, Browning, and Montgomery Blair carefully controlled proceedings with an eye to preserving harmony and forestalling excesses. Among the rank-and-file delegates, however, Republicans were conspicuously scarce. Democrats and Southerners predominated and only a desperate behind-the-scenes effort by the executive committee prevented two notorious Copperheads, Clement L. Vallandigham of Ohio and Fernando Wood of New York, from taking the seats to which they had been elected. Also most of the Southern delegates were former Confederates, among them ex-Confederate Vice-president Stephens (he, however, did not attend any of the sessions, giving illness as his excuse).

After listening to a great many speeches hailing the return of sectional peace and friendship, denouncing the "Radicals," and praising Johnson, the convention closed on August 16 by adopting unanimously a set of resolutions drafted by Raymond which repeated these sentiments and urged voters not to elect anyone to Congress who did not support the president and the immediate readmission of all the Southern states. Originally Raymond had also proposed resolutions calling for acceptance of the Freedmen's Bureau, the Civil Rights Act, and the Fourteenth Amendment (except the disfranchisement clause), but he had withdrawn them in the face of Southern protests. Immediately following adjournment, the executive committee issued a proclamation inviting all "friends of peace, Union, liberty and law in every county" (by whom it meant members of the "Johnson Clubs" which had been or were being organized throughout the North and especially in the Border states) to hold mass meetings to ratify the convention's resolutions and rally the people behind the National Union movement.[13]

Republican newspapers derided the "arm-in-arm convention." Making much of the presence of Vallandigham, Wood, and Stephens, they charged that the meeting was nothing but a gathering of Copperheads and rebels, the purpose of which was to trick Republicans into voting for Democrats. And in fact, many Moderate and Conservative Republicans who otherwise were sympathetic to

85

the president felt uneasy about the predominance of Democratic and Southern delegates; this was not their idea of a "national union" movement. All in all, the convention gained no additional support for Johnson and probably lost him some of his previous backing.[14]

In the eyes of its organizers, however, the convention was a huge success. At least they acted as if it were. On August 18 Raymond published an editorial in the *New York Times* in which he asserted that an "organized National Union Movement" now existed which "will sweep everything before it." That same day a group of delegates from the convention visited the White House where Johnson received them with Welles standing on his left side and Grant on his right. The latter, who recently had been promoted to full general by Johnson, was present most reluctantly at the expressed invitation of the president, who thus sought to make it appear that the hero of Appomattox supported his administration. The spokesman for the delegation, Democratic Senator Reverdy Johnson of Maryland, declared, "If you could have seen the men of Massachusetts and South Carolina coming into the Convention . . . hand in hand, amid the rapturous applause of the whole body, you would have felt, as every person present felt, that the time had arrived when all sectional or other perilous dissension had ceased. . . ." To this the president replied that when he had read of "South Carolina and Massachusetts, arm in arm, marching into that vast assemblage," which he described "as more important than any Convention that has met—at least since 1787," at that moment "my own feelings overc[a]me me." Then, after comparing himself to a "learned and wise physician" who had sought to "pour oil into the wounds of the nation," he continued:

> We have witnessed in one department of the Government every endeavor to prevent the restoration of peace, harmony, and Union. We have seen hanging upon the verge of the Government, as it were, a body called, or which assumes to be, the Congress of the United States, while in fact it is a Congress of only a part of the States.[15]

The fatuity of Johnson's statements was exceeded only by their provocativeness. In effect he was questioning the legality of Congress. By so doing, he lent credence to rumors that he intended to proclaim as the true Congress an assemblage of proadministration and Democratic members, to which would be added the congressmen elected by the Southern states. Consequently, still more erstwhile or potential Northern supporters turned away from him.

Along with launching the National Union movement, Johnson employed a number of other devices in his campaign against the Republicans. One was the publication, during the summer, of a series of "official reports" on the Freedmen's Bureau. These documents, which had been prepared at Johnson's behest by two pro-administration generals, made false or exaggerated charges of corruption against the bureau. Also, Johnson sought to attract Irish and labor votes. In the former case, he waited until the last possible moment before issuing a proclamation ordering federal officers to prevent incursions across the Canadian border by the Fenians, an organization of Irish-Americans which was attempting to further the good cause of Irish independence by the hare-brained method of conquering Canada! Then, following the tragic-comic failure of the Fenian invasion early in June, Johnson ordered the release of all arrested Fenians and had the State Department intervene on behalf of Fenians imprisoned in Canada. Nevertheless, the Fenians believed that they had been betrayed by the Johnson administration —and not without reason, for in a private interview Johnson and Seward had told one of their leaders that should a Fenian republic be established in Canada, the United States government would recognize it. As a result in New York many Irishmen temporarily abandoned their traditional Democratic allegiance, thereby helping the Republicans carry that state in November. As for labor, shortly after the Philadelphia convention Johnson received a delegation from the newly founded National Labor Union (which favored speedy readmission of the South) and assured it of his sympathy for the working class. He refrained however, from repeating what earlier he had told the British minister in Washington—that he believed that the big city poor should be disfranchised. When Johnson praised "plebians," he had in mind artisans, not proletarians.[16]

In the opinion of some historians writing during the 1930s, Johnson should also have challenged the Republicans on such "economic issues" as the protective tariff, fiscal policy, and business monopoly. Indeed, one of these historians, Howard K. Beale, went so far as to contend that Johnson's failure to do this enabled the Republicans to win in 1866.[17] But as Eric McKitrick and a number of other more recent scholars have pointed out, the all-dominant issue in 1866 was Reconstruction, and had Johnson by some miracle escaped from his own obsession with it and started talking about the tariff and other issues, he merely would have bored or bewildered most voters. Besides, many of Johnson's adherents favored the protective tariff as well as the government's fiscal policy (which after all had been largely established by his own secretary of the treasury). For the president to have attacked protection or opposed monetary contraction or adopted an anticapitalistic stance probably would have produced McCulloch's resignation, certainly would have alienated many of the wealthy businessmen who continued to support him out of a desire for a return to economic normality, and in general would have cost rather than gained him votes. Hence he was well advised to confine his references to economic matters to broad generalizations and declarations that restoration of the Southern states would promote prosperity.[18]

In the estimation of both his friends and enemies, the most powerful weapon Johnson possessed was patronage. The former hoped, and the latter feared, that with it he could undermine the Republican party while building up the National Union movement. As noted, late in 1865 he began to use it for these purposes, although in a restrained fashion. Then, following the Philadelphia convention, he went all out, removing over twelve hundred postmasters alone and replacing them with proadministration men: "Only those sustaining the President should eat his bread and butter," asserted Randall. The results, however, were not what Johnson desired or expected. Most of the replacements he named were Democrats; he could find few Republicans who were willing to accept an appointment from him, and those who did were generally men of little standing—"flunkies," Fessenden called them. Moreover, instead of cowing the remaining Republican officeholders into supporting him, Johnson merely antagonized them, as he did rank-and-file Republicans who resented seeing good Union men being superseded by Copperheads. Indeed, some Republican officeholders went so far as to resign for fear that people would interpret their staying in office as support for the administration![19]

On the other hand, the patronage that Johnson bestowed on the Democrats failed to secure from them the sort of support that the National Union movement needed and on which he, Seward, Raymond, Doolittle, and its other organizers had counted. To most Democratic leaders the National Union movement was merely, in Barlow's cynical words, an opportunity "to turn Cuckoo and lay our eggs in the Republican nest."[20] They had no intention of giving up their separate political identity and they did not. When state and local National Union conventions met to select candidates, Democrats usually dominated them and usually they nominated fellow Democrats. Thus, in vital New York, the National Union convention passed over General John A. Dix, keynote speaker at the Philadelphia convention and the choice of Seward and Weed, to nominate for governor a Tammany Hall politico who had backed McClellan in 1864. In short, the National Union movement, instead of being a coalition of Conservative Republicans and Democrats, headed by the former, turned into a front for the latter.[21] The consequences were two, both bad for Johnson. First, many Conservative Republicans quit the movement in disgust. As an example, William Gray, a prominent Bostonian, wrote to McCulloch that he could not support the movement because "practically [all] the leaders in this movement in Massachusetts were the old political leaders of the remains of the Democratic Party, with which I have never had, nor expect to have any affiliation." Second, in most Northern states and congressional districts the voters found themselves presented with a choice: to vote for a Republican who, although he might have some extreme notions on Negro rights, had supported or even fought for the cause of Union and Emancipation, or else for a Democrat who had opposed the war and the freeing of the slaves while sympathizing with the South. Candidates of the latter type, noted Welles, "can gain no recruits. There is a kinder feeling towards beaten Rebels than towards Copperheads."[22]

Johnson himself was irritated by the Democrats lack of "cooperation." Subsequently he blamed them for the failure of the National Union Movement and charged, correctly enough, that the object of their leaders had been "to use him as they would an orange." Throughout his career Johnson never had relied on party organization. The key to his success had always been his ability to appeal directly to the people. It had worked in Tennessee, why should it not work as well on the national scene? Therefore, late in August, he decided to embark on a speaking tour of the North. The occasion and excuse for doing so was provided by an invitation to deliver an address at the dedication of a monument to Stephen A. Douglas in Chicago (which was somewhat ironic in view of the fact that Johnson had despised "the little giant" while he was alive).[23]

Welles and other friends tried to dissuade him from making the tour. They considered it undignified for a president to "go on the stump," and they feared the consequences of Johnson's tendency to become excited when speaking. But he paid them no heed—the "President . . . manifestly thought I did not know his power as a speaker," commented Welles. On the other hand, Seward both approved of the trip and served as its manager. On August 28 Johnson left Washington on a special train. Only Seward and Welles among the cabinet accompanied him. The others excused themselves for various reasons, with Stanton's being the illness of his wife. Presumably Johnson found his absence tolerable. Also on the train were Grant and Admiral David G. Farragut, plus assorted lesser war heroes. Johnson hoped that the public would interpret Grant's presence as support for his policies—which is why he also had arranged for the general to be on hand when he met the delegation from the Philadelphia convention. Grant, who realized and resented the President's efforts to exploit him politically, consented to join the tour only after Johnson put him in a position where to refuse would have been rude and almost insubordinate.[24]

Johnson's itinerary was north to upstate New York, west to Chicago, south to St. Louis, and then back to Washington via the Ohio Valley. Hence the tour soon became known, and Johnson himself referred to it, as the "swing around the circle." It was also the first presidential whistle-stop campaign in American history, for in addition to major cities the train halted at numerous small towns.

In the beginning all went well. Large and friendly crowds received the president in Baltimore and Philadelphia; in New York City leaders of the business and social community regaled him with a banquet at Delmonico's. His speeches were reasoned expositions of his policies, and his language and manner dignified—although he did engage in a carriage race through Central Park with Grant (who issued and won the challenge). Evidently he was following Doolittle's advice to "say nothing which has not been more carefully prepared. . . . *Our enemies, your enemies,* have never been able to get any advantage from anything you *ever wrote.* But what you have said extemporaneously, in answer to some question or interruption, has given them a handle to use against you."[25]

But then the tour reached Cleveland. There, Johnson's political and historical champions later claimed, the "Radicals" planted hecklers in the crowd in order to provoke the president. This is conceivable. But it should also be noted that Cleveland was a center of prewar abolitionism and postwar Radicalism, thus sentiment in the city was predominantly hostile to Johnson.

In any event a large throng collected outside Johnson's hotel, clamoring for him to come out. Finally Johnson, who had not planned to speak, appeared on a balcony. He thanked the crowd for its welcome and made a few other innocuous statements. At this point he should have returned to his room. But once again he succumbed to oratorical self-intoxication and to his craving for vindication. Those who denounced him today, he declared, would have assailed Lincoln the same way, for he was merely trying to carry out his predecessor's intentions. His enemies called him a betrayer, but, Johnson asked, "Who is he that can come and place his fingers upon one pledge I ever violated, or one principle I ever proved false to?"

A voice from the crowd cried, "New Orleans!" Another, "Why don't you hang Jeff Davis?" And a third yelled mockingly, "Hang Thad Stevens and Wendell Phillips!"

"Hang Jeff Davis?" replied Johnson. "Give us an opportunity!" "However," he continued, "I am not the Chief Justice! I am not the Attorney General! I am no jury! But I'll tell you what I did do. I called upon your Congress that is trying to break up the Government. . . ."

But before he could finish, there were hisses and someone shouted "A lie, a lie!" The crowd became disorderly, almost riotous. Yet at the same time there were cheers and yells of "Give it to 'em, Andy!" "Bully for you, Andy!" and the like. Again, Johnson should have retired from the balcony, but it simply was not in his nature to back down before a mob. In fact, successfully defying hostile audiences was his specialty, a way in which he often had gained sympathy, admiration, and support.

Hence, despite frequent interruptions, he continued to speak and to reply to taunts. When someone called out "Traitor!" he looked in that person's direction and said, "I wish I could see that man. I would bet you now that if the light fell on your face, cowardice and treachery would be seen! Show yourself. If you ever shoot a man . . . you will do it in the dark."

"Is this dignified?" cried an exasperated sounding voice.

"I care not for dignity," Johnson shouted back.[26]

Even in today's Age of Vulgarity Johnson's performance at Cleveland probably would be "counterproductive. By the standards of his own day, it was shocking. Moreover, worse was to come. On September 8 in St. Louis, where he again made an unscheduled speech, he accused the Radicals of being responsible for the New Orleans riot and asserted that "every drop of blood that was shed is upon their skirts." And when a heckler yelled at him "Judas!" he shouted back,

"Judas! There was a Judas once, one of the twelve apostles. Oh yes, the twelve apostles had a Christ."

"And a Moses, too!" a member of the crowd hollered, referring to Johnson's promise to be "Moses" who would lead the Negro from slavery to freedom. There was great laughter.

"The twelve apostles," continued Johnson, "had a Christ and

he never could have had a Judas unless he had had twelve apostles. If I have played the Judas, who has been my Christ that I have played the Judas with? Was it Thad Stevens? Was it Wendell Phillips? Was it Charles Sumner?"

At this point the cry came: "Why not hang Thad Stevens and Wendell Phillips?"

"Yes," said Johnson, "why not hang them?"[27]

The Republicans pounced with glee on Johnson's outbursts at Cleveland and St. Louis, plus similar ones elsewhere. The president, asserted Greeley's *New York Tribune*, has "turned a solemn journey to the tomb of a celebrated American into the stumping tour of an irritated demagogue." *The Nation* characterized Johnson's utterances as "vulgar, egotistical and occasionally profane." Even Raymond deplored in the *New York Times* Johnson's declaration that he did not care for dignity. In addition many Republican papers charged or hinted that Johnson and even Seward were habitually drunk, that the entire tour was "nothing more or less than a big drunk"—or in the words of James Russell Lowell of the *North American Review* "an indecent orgy."[28]

In truth, the only person on the special train who engaged in alcoholic overindulgence (other than the reporters, of course) was Grant. He went on a spree in Cleveland and had to be taken on a sobering-up cruise across Lake Erie to Detroit, where he rejoined the president's entourage. Nevertheless, to millions of Northerners, Johnson now became and forever remained "the drunken tailor." At the same time his speeches, to quote the *New York Post*, one of the most objective newspapers of the period, had "driven people's blood to their heads and aroused a storm of indignation throughout the country."[29]

Almost as damaging to Johnson as his intemperate language was his constant repetition of the same ideas and phrases. He began practically every speech by stating that it was not his purpose to make a speech. Invariably he denied that he was motivated by personal ambition, pointing out that he had "filled all the offices in the gift of the people" from alderman up to that of president. Again and again he compared his pardoning of Southern rebels to Jesus's forgiveness of sinners and asserted that he too was prepared to suffer crucifixion if it would save the country. Rarely did Johnson omit declaring in one form or another that "as I go around the circle, having fought traitors at the South, I am prepared to fight traitors at the North"—meaning the Radicals. And he concluded almost every speech by saying that he was leaving the Constitution, or the Union, or the flag—or all three—in the hands of his audience.

In Tennessee, where newspapers were very limited in their coverage and circulation, using a basic speech when on the stump had served Johnson well. Therefore it is understandable that he did the same thing on the "swing around the circle," especially if one remembers that unlike a modern president Johnson did not have a large staff of literary prostitutes to feed him fresh material to mouth. But now, as president, he was accompanied by a horde of reporters who filed long and often biased accounts of his tour, all of the major newspapers printed his speeches verbatim, and the small town sheets either did the same or provided detailed summaries. As a result most people already knew what he was going to say—and got bored when they heard him say it. Indeed, it became a common occurrence for listeners to interrupt Johnson with calls for Grant and Farragut; and several times the crowds were so unruly that conductors ordered the special train out of the station before the president had finished his address.

Johnson's Republican opponents, of course, were quick to ridicule his repetitiveness. Here the lead was taken by David Ross Locke, editor of the *Toledo* (Ohio) *Blade*, who under the penname of "Petroleum V. Nasby" was one of the most popular humorists of the day. In a series of widely reprinted articles "Nasby" (who was portrayed as a semiliterate Copperhead) described "Swinging Round the Cirkle" with Johnson in the following satirical fashion:

> UTICA. . . . He [Johnson] introdoost here the remark that he didn't come to make a speech; that he wuz goin to shed a tear over the tomb uv Douglas; that, in swingin round the cirkle, he hed fought traitors on all sides uv it, but that he felt safe. He shood leave the Constooshn in their hands, and ef a martyr wuz wanted, he wuz ready to die with neetness and dispatch.
>
> ROME. . . . He menshuned to the audience that he had swung around the Southern side of the cirkle, and wuz now swingin around the Northern side uv it, and that he wuz fightin traitors on all sides. He left the Constitooshun in their hands, and bid em good bye. . . .
>
> LOCKPORT. . . . Ez for himself his ambishn wuz more than satisfied. He hed bin Alderman, Member uv the Legislacher, Congressman, Senator, Military Governor, Vice President, and President. He had swung around the entire cirkle uv offices, and all he wanted now wuz to heal the wounds uv the nashen. He felt safe in leavin the Constooshn in their hands. . . .

93

DETROIT. . . . This bein a Democratic city, the President wuz hisself agin. . . . He gathered together in one quiver all the sparklin arrows he had used from Washington to this point, and shot em one by one. He swung around the cirkle; he didn't come to make a speech; he hed bin Alderman of his native town; he mite hev been Dicktater, but woodent. . . .

YPSILANTI. . . . He asked em, ef he was Judis Iskariot who wuz the Saviour? Thad Stevens? If so, then after swingin round the cirkle, and findin traitors at both ends of the line, I leave the 36 States with 36 stars onto em in your hands, and—

The train wuz off amid loud shouts uv "Grant! Grant!" to which the President responded by wavin his hat.

KALAMAZOO. . . . Grant! The President responded, saying that in swingin around the cirkle, he hed bin called Joodis Iskariot for sacrificin uv hisself for the people! Who wuz the Saviour? Wuz Thad Stevens? No! Then cleerly into yoor hands I leave the Constitution uv 36 stars with 36 States onto em. . . .[30]

Equally devastating, perhaps even more so, were the anti-Johnson drawings of Thomas Nast. These appeared during the 1866 campaign in the mass circulation *Harper's Weekly* and are classics of political cartooning. One of them pictured Johnson as Iago trying to persuade the Negro (Othello) that he was his friend. Another depicted the president as a snake charmer blowing on a flute labeled "Constitution" while a huge Copperhead snake coils around a struggling Negro. And the most elaborate one showed Johnson as King Andrew, sitting on a throne watching the beheading of a group of well-known Radicals.

From St. Louis onward the tour was a dismal fiasco. At Indianapolis a riot prevented Johnson from speaking. At New Market and Steubenville, Ohio, hostile mobs shouted him down, and the same thing happened in Pittsburgh. At Cincinnati Grant quit the special train for good, unwilling any longer, he confided to a friend, "to accompany a man who was deliberately digging his own grave."[31] Earlier Matias Romero, minister of the Juarez government in Washington, had likewise departed when he realized that Seward had brought him along solely for the political purpose of using his presence as proof of the success of the administration's Mexican policy.[32] Only in Louisville and Cincinnati did Johnson receive friendly receptions. In the former, his statement that "there are those who seem to forget that there are any but negroes in America" was greeted with cries of "Put down the nigger, Andy!"[33] In Louisville Seward fell ill with cholera and had to be left behind at Harrisburg. When on September 15 Johnson arrived back in Washington, he had only one reason for feeling happy: The "swing around the circle" was over.

One historian has claimed that the "swing around the circle" was "mildly successful."[34] Even if one were to accept that assessment—and no one else who has studied the subject does—nonetheless, what Johnson needed was not a mild success but a great one. He needed to reverse the tide of Northern public opinion, to turn it against the Republicans and in favor of what he called "my policy." He believed he could accomplish this if only the people had a chance to hear him. "I wish," he had stated in Columbus, Ohio, "that I had a clarion voice to extend to the remotest cabin. . . ." But, either in person or through their newspapers, the voters of the North did hear him—and they rejected him. It was Johnson, not the "Radicals," who appeared to be the revolutionary: he challenged the legality of Congress, favored the readmission of unrepentant rebels into the government, and drew his support from Copperheads. It was he too who talked constantly of the Constitution yet would deny Negroes basic rights under that Constitution; and it was he who attacked the friends of the Negro as traitors while in effect exonerating the butchers of New Orleans. And if he was not a drunkard, then he talked and acted like one, disgracing the presidency. In short, Johnson set out on the "swing around the circle" to persuade the Northern people and ended up frightening and disgusting them.

Elections were held in Vermont on September 4 and in Maine on September 10. In each state, Republicans carried every congressional seat as well as the governorship and the legislature. It was the handwriting on the wall: "I mourn over Andy," wrote Fessenden to McCulloch the day after the Maine election. Soon afterwards both the *New York Times* and the *New York Herald* repudiated Johnson. In the latter's case, declining circulation resulting from its championing of the increasingly unpopular president was the prime motivation—that and Bennett's belated realization that he was backing a loser. The same considerations influenced the *Times*. In addition, however, Raymond resented the way in which the Democrats had taken over the National Union movement in New York, and he was disillusioned by Johnson's conduct during the "swing around the circle." Raymond, concluding rightly enough that he had ruined himself politically by supporting Johnson, abandoned his candidacy for reelection to the House.[35]

On October 10 the Republicans won a landslide victory in Pennsylvania. Faced not merely with defeat but with disaster, Johnson now attempted to play his last remaining political card—dismissal of Stanton. For months the Blairs, Barlow, Welles, Randall, and others had been telling the president that this would arouse otherwise dormant Democratic and Conservative support. And, of course, he had legitimate reasons for getting rid of his marplot secretary of war.

To replace Stanton, Johnson proposed to appoint Sherman, whom he summoned from St. Louis to Washington, where he arrived on October 25. Sherman was second only to Grant in popularity (in the North), an advocate of lenient Reconstruction, and had gained Johnson's gratitude by writing him a letter commending his policies. Should Sherman become secretary of war, however, he would be in the awkward position of giving orders to his close friend and superior in rank, General Grant. Therefore with Seward's cooperation, Johnson sought to get Grant out of the way by having him undertake a mission to Mexico with Lewis Campbell, whom Johnson had recently rewarded for his utterly useless political machinations in Ohio by an appointment as special minister to the Juarez regime.[36]

But Grant had other ideas. Although he remained outwardly friendly to Johnson, in private he disliked the president and opposed his Reconstruction policy. Furthermore Grant had been angered by Johnson's attempts to strip the army of legal authority in the South and by his permitting it to be subjected to harrassment in Southern courts. Last, but far from least, the general suspected Johnson of plotting a coup d'état! On October 12 Grant wrote Sheridan, "I regret to say that since the unfortunate differences between the President and Congress the former becomes more violent with the opposition he meets until now but few people who were loyal to the Government during the Rebellion seem to have any influence with him . . . indeed I much fear that we are fast approaching the point where he will want to declare the body [Congress] unconstitutional and revolutionary."[37]

Of course there was no basis in fact for Grant's suspicions—Johnson was neither that rash nor that foolish. These were, however, fantastic times filled with fantastic events. Hence it is understandable that people would believe that fantastic things were possible. Among them was Johnson himself. While Grant was fearing that the president might attempt to overthrow Congress, Johnson was worried, as a result of reports from various proadministration generals, that the Grand Army of the Republic, the recently formed Union veterans' organization, would march on Washington! Indeed, it is possible that another reason Johnson wanted to make Sherman secretary of war and send Grant to Mexico was so that the regular army would be commanded by a man who could be relied upon to defend the capital against the Grand Army. Johnson could have no such confidence in Grant; undoubtedly he realized that Grant was not in sympathy with his Reconstruction policy; and, like everyone else, Johnson knew that Grant would be the probable Republican presidential candidate in 1868.

In any case, when Johnson asked him to go to Mexico, Grant refused; and when Johnson practically ordered him to go, the general answered that the president had no authority to require him to perform a diplomatic mission as distinguished from a military assignment. In addition, after consulting Grant, Sherman informed Johnson that he would not accept the post of secretary of war if it was offered to him, but that he was willing to accompany Campbell to Mexico in Grant's place. Johnson thereupon dropped his scheme, with the result that Stanton remained in the War Department, Grant stayed in the United States, and Sherman ended up traveling to Mexico. (He and Campbell, however, failed even to locate Juarez's "government," which was in hiding pending withdrawal of the French army.)[38]

During the remainder of October and early November, voters around the country continued to go to the polls. When the last ballots were tallied the Republicans had retained control of every state in the North and increased their already huge majority in Congress. To the degree that is practically possible in the American political system, the North had repudiated Johnson and endorsed the Republicans. Henceforth the course of Reconstruction would be determined in accordance with the feelings of the North and the interests of the Republicans, with no more reference to the president than Congress considered necessary and expedient. At the same time Johnson's hope of forming a new party and of succeeding himself had been blasted, although despite everything he did not abandon the latter ambition.

Why did Johnson lose to the Republicans? There were many reasons but basically they all came to this: Johnson believed, as did Seward, that the first priority—indeed that the sole important objective of the government—should be the restoration of the Union and that Northerners would not sacrifice this great and necessary goal to a hypocritical and impractical attempt to achieve equal rights for Negroes. At the end of the war, however, as William Brock has pointed out, Northerners did not want merely a reestablishment of the Union; they wanted a *more perfect Union*—one from which the spectre of Southern domination (through an alliance with Northern Copperhead Democrats) had been exorcised, one in which former slaves were guaranteed the fundamentals of freedom. Republicans, fighting for the preservation of their principles, party, and power, took up the cause of this more perfect Union. Johnson opposed it. Consequently the Republicans and not Johnson occupied the political center in the North, the area of decision in post–Civil War America, and so gained the victory.[39]

Yet, in spite of everything, at the outset of 1866 Johnson's cause was far from hopeless; indeed, his prospects for success were excellent. That he suffered the debacle he did during the fall of that year was mainly his own fault. No one realized this better than the Republicans. Following the election Governor Cox of Ohio, who as late as June had hoped to be able to continue supporting Johnson, wrote: "Had Mr. Johnson used the most ordinary discretion . . . we [the Republicans] would have been in a most critical condition during the late canvass, . . . but he succeeded in doing, with an absolutely incredible fatuity, the very things which were sure to ruin his plans, and the only things which could place our success beyond doubt."[40]

Or, as Wendell Phillips, who had opposed Johnson as early as May 1865, put it in a victory speech on November 7, 1866, "Let us pray to God that the President may continue to make mistakes. . . ."[41]

6

★★★★★

REPUBLICAN RECONSTRUCTION

On October 24—before the 1866 elections were over but after their outcome was evident—the Moderate Republican leader, Senator Grimes of Iowa, wrote Welles: "Now, the question is will the President accept the popular judgment. . . . The [Radical] party will spring up soon demanding stronger terms [for the South] than are now proposed and that party will be increased by the President's opposition to the present propositions"; by this Grimes meant the Fourteenth Amendment.[1]

Immediately following the elections Raymond urged Johnson in the pages of the *New York Times* "to forgo his own plans" and either help Congress secure Southern ratification of the Fourteenth Amendment or else step aside and let Congress reach a settlement with the South based on the amendment. Bennett's *Herald* expressed similar sentiments, advising Johnson that "his own favorite ideas of restoration" had been superseded and that he should "tack ship and sail with the wind."[2] And within Johnson's official family, Seward likewise sought to steer the president onto a conciliatory course. When Johnson asked the secretary to draft the annual message to Congress, Seward produced a speech which pleaded for the early admission of the ten Southern states still unrepresented in Washington; but it also acknowledged that Congress had the exclusive right to judge the eligibility of its own members, noted that six states had already approved the Fourteenth Amendment, and pledged the president's "cheerful concurrence and co-operation" in "all judicious and constitutional measures" aimed at restoring peace and unity to the nation.[3] In brief, Seward wanted Johnson to offer the Republicans a deal: presidential acquiescence in the Fourteenth Amendment in return for congressional acceptance of the Southern senators and representatives.

Raymond, Bennett, and Seward, however, were wasting both time and ink. Johnson had no intention of compromising with Congress. To him that would be surrender. Back in October, when it was clear that the election was going against him, the Democratic leader, Samuel S. Cox, had asked Johnson if there was any truth to rumors that he might moderate his opposition to the Fourteenth Amendment. Not only did the president answer with an emphatic "No!" but he "got ugly as the Devil," Cox reported. "He was regularly mad. . . . There's no budge in him."[4] Defeat in the elections, overwhelming as it was, affected Johnson the way defeat always had: It just made him all the more determined to continue fighting.

But there was more to Johnson's reaction to the 1866 debacle than mere pugnacious stubbornness. Furthermore, contrary to what some historians have suggested, he was not impelled by a blind prejudice—after all even the strongly racist Seward was willing to go along with the Fourteenth Amendment out of expediency. Instead, Johnson's decision to remain firm in his opposition to Congress and to the Fourteenth Amendment derived from a careful and quite plausible evaluation of the political situation.

At the end of 1866, despite their great victory, the Republicans were in a difficult predicament. Three border states—Delaware, Maryland, and Kentucky—had rejected the Fourteenth Amendment. Apart from Tennessee the Southern states had done, or would do, the same. Hence the three-fourth's majority of the states needed for ratification of the amendment would not be forthcoming unless Congress did one or both of two things: employ military coercion and/or enfranchise Negroes in order to establish Republican control of the South.

However, Johnson calculated that should the Republicans resort to such high-handed measures, public opinion in the North would turn against them. Duped by Radical propaganda, most Northerners might agree to civil rights for Negroes, but once the real issue became clear they would not support the imposition of black suffrage on their fellow whites in the South. Likewise they would refuse to tolerate the intensification or the indefinite continuation of bayonet rule in the Southern states. This was especially true after December 17 when the Supreme Court formally announced its decision in the case of *Ex Parte Milligan*. The Court held that military tribunals lacked constitutional authority, even in wartime, to try civilians in areas where the civil courts were functioning.

In essence, as Thurlow Weed put it, Johnson's strategy was to let the Republicans "hang themselves." It was for this reason that he ignored warnings that his continued opposition to the Fourteenth Amendment would drive Congress into an extreme position—that was precisely what he wanted to happen.

On the other hand, there was the possibility that the Republicans, unable to secure ratification of the amendment by ordinary means and afraid to use extraordinary ones, might abandon it. But then they would have no practical choice except to seat the Southern congressmen. And once that occurred Johnson would have no trouble keeping the Republicans in check with the veto. At the same time the foundation for Johnson's successful bid for the presidency in 1868 would have been laid. By holding on to the votes the National Union and Democratic candidates had received in the North in 1866 and adding the votes of the Southerners, Johnson could command a nationwide majority.

So when the Thirty-ninth Congress assembled on December 3 for its second session, Johnson faced it defiantly. To be sure, his message (delivered December 4) was conciliatory in language, but it conceded nothing of substance. Again he criticized Congress for not admitting the delegates from the ten unrepresented states; again he denounced the view that the South was "conquered territory." As for the most important issue of all, the Fourteenth Amendment, he mentioned it not at all. In effect he told Congress: I stand pat; the next move is yours.[5]

The Moderate Republicans hoped that Congress would not have to make another move—that the South, confronted with the results of the elections, would submit to the North's peace terms by ratifying the Fourteenth Amendment. On the other hand, the Radicals eagerly looked beyond the amendment to Negro suffrage. On the eve of the convening of Congress, Stevens jocularly proclaimed, "I was a Conservative in the last session of this Congress, but I mean to be a Radical henceforth."[6]

Even most Radicals, however, agreed that if the Southern states ratified the Fourteenth Amendment, then they would be restored to the Union. The big question, therefore, was what would the South do—accept or reject the amendment? When Congress had adopted it in June, Southerners had reacted with almost unanimous opposition. The granting of citizenship to Negroes outraged them; the reduction of their representation in the House unless they gave

101

Negroes the vote incensed them; and the disfranchisement of their ruling class enfuriated them—especially those who were members of that class. But, inspired by Johnson, the Democrats, and wishful thinking, Southerners also had been confident that the North itself would repudiate both the amendment and its authors in the 1866 elections.[7]

Of course the North did just the opposite. Hence, following the elections, a few Southern leaders—notably Alcorn in Mississippi and Governor Robert M. Patton of Alabama—began urging ratification as the only way both to obtain early readmission and to forestall even more drastic congressional measures. Moderate Republican leaders and newspapers gave the same advice; and Grant, both directly and indirectly, urged several Southern governors to seek approval of the amendment in their state legislatures. By December it seemed possible to both proponents and opponents of the amendment that at least Virginia, South Carolina, and Alabama might ratify it, perhaps leading to identical action by most, if not all, of the other Southern states.

At this juncture, however, Johnson intervened. First, and in secret, he used his influence to block ratification in Virginia. Next, shortly before Christmas he told a South Carolina legislator, who had traveled to Washington to solicit his views, that the Southern states should "steadfastly reject" the amendment. "Leo," the Washington correspondent of the *Charleston Courier*, learned of this interview and reported it in his paper, after which journals throughout the nation reprinted the story. Johnson angrily denied it—had he not often asserted that intervention by Washington in state affairs was wrong? The aforementioned legislator, however, informed his colleagues of what the president had said to him, whereupon they rejected the amendment with only one dissenting vote.

As for Alabama, on December 6 Governor Patton, hitherto opposed to the amendment, called for the legislature to approve it, declaring, "We should look our true condition full in the face." Learning of Patton's action, the former provisional governor of Alabama, Lewis E. Parsons, promptly sent a dispatch from Washington to Montgomery denouncing ratification. Believing, probably correctly, that Parsons spoke for Johnson, the Alabama legislature on December 7 almost unanimously voted down the amendment.

But this did not end the matter. Convinced that readmission under the Fourteenth Amendment was the best the South could hope for, Governor Patton campaigned to have the legislature reconsider its vote. He appeared to be making headway—so much so, in fact, that on January 17 Parsons, now back in Alabama, used the telegraph to alert Johnson: "Legislature in session. Efforts making [sic] to reconsider vote on constitutional amendment."[8] Johnson replied immediately:

> What possible good can be obtained by reconsidering the Constitutional amendment? I know of none in the present posture of affairs; and I do not believe the people of the whole country will sustain any set of individuals in attempts to change the whole character of our government. . . . I believe, on the contrary, that they will eventually uphold all who have patriotism and courage to stand by the Constitution, and who place their confidence in the people.[9]

No new vote on the Fourteenth Amendment took place in the Alabama legislature. And by February, every one of the other Southern states still outside the Union had also rejected it.

It would be easy to blame Johnson for the South's rejection of the Fourteenth Amendment. Indeed many historians have done exactly that. Nevertheless, although Johnson definitely did contribute to the Southern refusal to ratify, he was not solely or even mainly responsible. The Northern Democrats also had something—probably a lot—to do with the outcome.

After Appomattox many Southerners tended to take an ambiguous view of the Democratic party. On the one hand, they resented its failure to be of more help during the war; but on the other hand, they realized that the party was the South's chief ally in the North in the struggle against Republican domination. Therefore, Southern politicians and editors looked to Northern Democrats for guidance in responding to congressional Reconstruction policies. In particular they paid close attention to Barlow's *New York World*.

When the 1866 election results started coming in, Barlow considered recommending that the South accept the Fourteenth Amendment as an evil necessary to readmission. But he soon dropped this notion in favor of what became known among Democrats as the "dead-lock" concept. This was identical to Johnson's let-the-Republicans-hang-themselves strategy and probably helped inspire it. Like Johnson, Barlow and a majority of Democratic leaders reasoned that if Congress failed to secure Southern ratification of the Fourteenth Amendment, Congress would have to give up or resort to unconstitutional measures which would be overthrown by the Supreme Court and which would antagonize the North. Hence, following the elections the *World* and most other

Democratic journals strongly and repeatedly urged the South to defeat the amendment, promising that this was the road that would return the region to the Union and the Democratic party to power.

Southerners listened and believed. They believed because the Democrats told them what they wanted to hear, confirming what they already believed. As noted, following the 1866 elections a few Southerners advocated ratifying the Fourteenth Amendment in order to avoid worse terms. But the overwhelming majority of Southern leaders rejected such "weak-kneed" counsel. In some instances their response was purely emotional: Better the South suffer even more than stultify itself by accepting the Fourteenth Amendment. Also many Southerners, unable or unwilling to distinguish between Radicals and Moderates, were convinced that the real object of the Republicans was to secure Negro suffrage; that the Republicans would be satisfied with nothing less, since it was needed to keep them in power; and that therefore it would be useless—in fact self-defeating—to concede Negro citizenship, for that merely would encourage the "Radicals" to insist that Blacks must vote.

Most of the top leaders of the South, however, were motivated in their opposition to ratification by more subtle considerations. First, the Republicans had staked everything on the Fourteenth Amendment; if they failed to secure its ratification, internal differences would bring about the disintegration of the party. Second, should the Republicans manage to unite behind a Radical program, sooner or later the people of the North would tire of Radical excesses and refuse to support the Republicans. And third, even if neither event happened and the Radicals triumphed, whites would nevertheless retain the real power in the South because of their superior intelligence, courage, and socio-economic status. Hence, most leaders felt the best course for the South to follow was one of "masterly inactivity"—that is, a refusal to cooperate in any way with the vicious schemes of the Radical-dominated Congress. By so doing, the South would provide the president, the Democrats, and the Supreme Court with an opportunity to thwart the Republicans. But even if the Republicans were for the time being to prevail, Southerners would have the satisfaction of knowing that they had remained loyal to the cause of white supremacy—a cause which, unlike that of the Confederacy, could not and would not, in the long run, be lost.

Given their thinking, fears, and hopes, it is unlikely that Southerners would have agreed to the Fourteenth Amendment even if Johnson had urged them to. Certainly his earlier efforts to persuade the South, out of self-interest, to permit limited Negro suffrage, provide fair treatment for blacks, and elect non-Confederates had proved unavailing. To be sure these attempts had occurred before the 1866 elections, but as we have seen only a small minority of Southerners concluded after the elections that the South should acquiesce in the Fourteenth Amendment. More typical of Southern reaction to the elections was an editorial in the *Richmond* (Virginia) *Times* declaring, "We are not ready to eat dirt at the bidding of Northern majorities." This would be true, the *Richmond Times* added, even if the president ceased to oppose the amendment. Thus only a tremendous amount of pressure from Johnson might have persuaded the South to ratify the amendment. But it is more likely that such pressure would have caused Southerners once more to repudiate him as a traitor to his section.[10]

In any case, to assert, as some historians have, that Johnson should have advocated ratification in order to spare the nation—and especially the South—further travail is utterly pointless. It is to ask for a Johnson who did not believe in white supremacy, who did not cherish states rights, who was willing to concede victory to his enemies, and who did not have political ambition. No such Johnson existed.

As state after state in the South rejected the Fourteenth Amendment, a growing number of Moderate Republicans began to think that the Radicals were right—that something beyond the amendment was necessary. Prompting them to reach that conclusion were continued outrages in the South against Negroes, Northerners, and Unionists. Hardly a day went by without reports of such persons being threatened, beaten, or murdered. Worse, local authorities refused to arrest—or if they did, local courts failed to convict—the perpetrators of these deeds, no matter how flagrant their guilt. And to cap it all, Johnson himself, citing *Ex Parte Milligan*, intervened on several occasions to prevent military courts from punishing offenders. Thus it seemed as if there was neither security not justice for "loyal" people in the South—and especially for Negroes. How then, Republicans asked themselves, to remedy this intolerable situation?

Thad Stevens answered this question on January 3 when he introduced a bill calling, in effect, for a fresh start on Reconstruction: The present governments in the South were to be abolished as illegal; all former Confederate military and civilian officers were to forfeit their citizenship for at least five years; and new state constitutions were to be adopted providing for Negro suffrage. Only in this way, declared Stevens, could the South be kept "under the guardianship of loyal men" and Negroes and Unionists protected from the "barbarians who are now daily murdering them." Last, but not least, his bill would insure the ascendancy of the Republican party nationally by depriving the Democrats of their Southern bailiwicks. This "party purpose" Stevens did not hesitate to avow: "For I believe, on my conscience, that on the continued ascendancy of that party depends the safety of this great nation."[11]

Not all Republicans agreed with Stevens's proposal—far from it. Bingham in particular strongly denounced it, arguing that Congress was committed to the Fourteenth Amendment as its terms of Reconstruction and, furthermore, that it was still possible the South would ratify it. Nonetheless Stevens's contention that Negro suffrage was needed to protect Negro rights—and Republican dominance—held a powerful appeal for most of his colleagues. In fact, they already were coming to the same conclusion for the same reasons.

Before and during the 1866 elections, Republicans had emphasized civil rights for Negroes and, apart from the Radicals, had downplayed or ignored voting rights. Most Republicans feared an adverse reaction in the North if they did otherwise, few of them favored Negro suffrage as such. Their one-sided triumph in the elections, however, caused many Republicans to conclude that they need not fear the Democrats' appeal to racism and that the Northern public would accept Negro suffrage if presented as a means of safeguarding the Negro from rebel oppression. In addition the Republicans realized that despite the recent elections, their hold on national power was precarious as long as the Confederate-Democrats controlled the South; therefore it was highly desirable to displace them with "loyal" people (i.e., Republicans), which meant giving Southern blacks the vote.

The Republicans manifested their bolder attitude regarding Negro suffrage soon after Congress reassembled. In December they passed Stevens's earlier bill, which had been sidetracked in the previous session, granting the vote to adult male Negroes in the District of Columbia. Johnson, needless to say, vetoed it; but it was passed over his veto. Next, during January, the Republicans proceeded to establish Negro suffrage in all of the territories and to admit Nebraska and Colorado to the Union, also with Negro suffrage—notwithstanding the fact that the settlers in both territories overwhelmingly opposed it. Johnson did not bother to veto the territorial suffrage bill but he did send back the Nebraska and

Colorado bills. In the case of Colorado, he won because enough Republicans agreed with him that a population of some thirty thousand did not justify statehood, but he lost on Nebraska; thus, the Republicans gained two more senators and another state ratified the Fourteenth Amendment. In other actions the Republicans prevented the further enfranchisement of former Confederates by depriving the president of his power to restore the right to vote by pardons, and they made sure that no representative from the unreconstructed Southern states could enter the House without that body's explicit approval. Johnson allowed both of these measures to become law without his signature.[12]

Congress did not take immediate action on Stevens's bill to reorganize the Southern governments on the basis of Negro suffrage. But the South's rejection of the Fourteenth Amendment, its maltreatment of Negroes and Unionists, and the failure of anyone to offer a better solution—resulted in Stevens's bill becoming the starting point for a completely new Reconstruction program. For a while however, it seemed as if the bill would never become law. Bingham, Fessenden, and other Moderates did their best to kill it and nearly succeeded. Stevens himself abandoned it in favor of putting the South under total and indefinite military rule. But in the end, the Republicans, faced with disaster or at least humiliation if they did not come up with something, united behind what became known as the First Military Reconstruction Act.

Passed by the Senate on February 17 by a vote of 29 to 10 and by the House on February 20, 126 to 46, this measure provided for the total reordering of the South. First it divided the ten unreconstructed Southern states into five military districts, each under a commander empowered to employ military courts and troops to maintain order and enforce federal laws. Second, it directed that conventions, elected by black voters and eligible whites, be held in each of the ten states for the purpose of framing new constitutions which were to guarantee Negro suffrage and which would be submitted to the same voters for approval. Third, it stipulated that after a state had adopted its new constitution, it was to elect a governor and legislature; once the state ratified the Fourteenth Amendment and that amendment became part of the Constitution, the state would be entitled to congressional representation and no longer would be subject to military occupation. Finally, the measure barred from voting for and serving in the state constitutional conventions all persons guilty of violating an oath to uphold the United States Constitution by their voluntary participation in the rebellion.

This was—and still is—the single most drastic piece of legislation to emerge from Congress. It placed millions of citizens under military rule in peacetime, deprived hundreds of thousands of them of political rights, and enfranchised a race which the vast majority of Americans at the time considered unqualified to participate in the governmental process. Furthermore, the legislation by-passed the Constitution (which, to be sure, was not designed to apply to situations such as that created by the Civil War); defied the basic principle of the *Milligan* decision; and ignored the Supreme Court's rulings, announced January 14, in *Cummings* v. *Missouri* and *Ex Parte Garland*, which held disfranchisement by test oaths to be unconstitutional. Yet like the Freedmen's Bureau Bill, the Civil Rights Act, and the Fourteenth Amendment, this was predominantly a Moderate measure. Although it was originally Stevens's bill, Blaine, Sherman, and others of their outlook had more to do with its final contents than he did. In fact Stevens and Sumner ended up denouncing the measure, first, because it provided for the readmission of the Southern states following ratification of the Fourteenth Amendment and, second, because it failed to confiscate "rebel" lands and distribute them to Negroes; they voted for the bill only because it was the best that could be obtained for the time being. Moreover, the bill would have been less drastic had not the Democrats, in pursuance of their "dead-lock" strategy, sought to make it intolerable to Moderate Republicans by voting with the Radicals to pass certain provisions which otherwise would have failed![13]

When it became apparent that Congress was moving to formulate a new and (from his standpoint) totally unacceptable Reconstruction program, Johnson likewise attempted to exploit the division in the Republican ranks with a view to forestalling the enactment of this program. He did so by offering behind the scenes a so-called compromise known as the North Carolina Plan. Developed by a group of North Carolina politicians and advocated by a number of other Southern leaders who were in contact with the president, this plan proposed admitting the Southern states in return for their approving the Fourteenth Amendment minus its disfranchisement clause and for agreeing to limited Negro suffrage. On February 12 two go-betweens representing Johnson, George P. Este, and W. W. Warden, met with a group of mainly Moderate Republicans at the Metropolitan Club in Washington and offered just such a deal. The Republican spokesmen, however, insisted on the entire Fourteenth

Amendment and on universal Negro suffrage; the following day, Johnson himself informed them that neither he nor the South could accept that. Thus Johnson's scheme failed. In fact it was doomed from the start. The Republicans, having already decided to go beyond the Fourteenth Amendment, were not about to retreat from it. Moreover Southern backing for the North Carolina Plan came almost exclusively from its progenitors, most of whom were former provisional governors who had been elected to the Senate and were eager to take their seats. In all liklihood a majority of Southerners opposed the scheme because they felt that it conceded too much, namely limited Negro suffrage.[14]

Also Johnson considered, at least briefly, revamping his cabinet in an "effort to prevent the extreme measures proposed by the majority in Congress." On the morning of February 14 Representative Nathaniel P. Banks of Massachusetts, a leading Moderate, suggested during a White House visit that "there should be someone in the cabinet who could be approached by those who were in opposition to the President, and who could thus become a channel of communication between the Executive and Congress." Later that day, at lunch, Johnson told his private secretary, Colonel William G. Moore, that by appointing Grant as secretary of war, Farragut as secretary of the navy, Charles Francis Adams (the highly respected minister to Britain) as secretary of state, and Horace Greeley as postmaster general, he could "settle the question [of Reconstruction] in two hours." He added, however, "Such a course would occasion harsh feelings on the part of some of the Cabinet officers." Moore then asked "if there was no way in which he could carry out such plans?" According to Moore's diary, Johnson replied, "I do not know that there is." Moore believed that "the subject was evidently painful" to Johnson.[15]

Following passage of the Military Reconstruction Act, Frank Blair, Sr., urged Johnson to exercise the pocket veto, which would be possible because the president received the bill from Capitol Hill less than ten days before the scheduled expiration of the Thirty-ninth Congress on March 2. "It ought to be suffered," wrote Blair, "to slide into nonentity with the broken Congress that gave birth to the monster. . . ." On the other hand several Conservatives advised Johnson to sign it, arguing in the words of one of them, Henry Ward Beecher, that it was "regarded by people of all parties as the most sane and reasonable bill likely to be passed" and that vetoing it would only lead to passage of something worse. Likewise George Este, Johnson's contact with the Moderates, wrote him that "all the more moderate Radicals [i.e., Republicans] desire you to sign the bill. I mean those who don't wish to follow the lead of Stevens, Boutwell & Co. *They* say your signing of the bill will forever kill the extreme wing of the [Republican] party and give you control of the situation."[16]

Johnson, however, probably had decided on a veto even before the bill was passed. Rather than sign a measure depriving Americans of habeas corpus, he told his secretary, Colonel Moore, "I would sever my right arm from my body." And according to another (although rather suspect) source, Johnson declared that the purpose of the "Radicals" was to trample underfoot the people of the South in order "to protect niggers."[17] Soon after he received the bill, he asked Jeremiah S. Black, former attorney general and secretary of state under Buchanan and one of the nation's top lawyers, to prepare a veto message. For several days Black, assisted by Stanbery, worked on the document at the White House, with Johnson himself supervising. When it was finished, contrary to his previous practice, Johnson did not submit it to the cabinet for criticism— further evidence that his response to the Military Reconstruction Act was predetermined.[18]

In the opinion of the historian Michael Les Benedict, Johnson's decision to veto the bill was a blunder. Had he signed it, the president "could have put the Republican coalition under terrific stress" in the manner indicated by Este. Or at the very least, Benedict further contends, Johnson should have followed Blair's advice and pocket-vetoed the bill, thereby setting the stage for another "divisive contest" between the Moderates and Radicals over Reconstruction policy when the Fortieth Congress met.[19]

Benedict's analysis is worth considering but it is not convincing. For Johnson to have signed the military Reconstruction bill would have meant his reneging on everything he hitherto had said and done with respect to Reconstruction; and hence, it would have caused most Democrats, many Conservatives, and practically all Southerners to turn against him. As for a pocket veto, instead of dividing the Republicans, more likely it would have exasperated them, prompting repassage of the bill after the Fortieth Congress convened on March 4. On the other hand, a veto was in accordance with Johnson's basic political strategy: He hoped, indeed believed, that by returning the bill to Congress with a message which exposed the measure's revolutionary and oppressive character, he would arouse public sentiment in the North against the Republicans, thus tightening the noose which they had placed around their own necks by passing the bill.

On March 2 he sent the veto message to Capitol Hill. What Congress proposed, he stated, was unnecessary, unconstitutional, and un-American. The bill established an "absolute despotism" in the South; it reduced the people of ten states to "the most abject and degrading slavery"; it would "force the right of suffrage out of the hands of the white people and into the hands of the negros."

Congress listened calmly to the message, then just as calmly overrode the veto that same day by votes of 135 to 48 in the House and 38 to 10 in the Senate.[20] Furthermore, if press reaction provides reliable evidence, the veto message made little impact. It merely persuaded those who already agreed with the president, and that is all. As historian William Brock has observed, Johnson used "precisely those arguments which would stir up opposition" and ignored those which might have encouraged "a desire for second thoughts." In particular he failed to strike at the bill's most vulnerable point, namely its dubious practicality. Also he evaded the key issue of protecting Negroes and Unionists in the South by denying, in effect, that there was such an issue. In a private letter Grant called the message "ridiculous."[21] Quite likely the majority of Northerners reacted the same way—if they read it at all.

March 2 also saw Congress pass over Johnson's veto another momentous law: the Tenure of Office Act. This prohibited the president from removing any official appointed with the Senate's consent without that body's prior approval. In writing it, the Republicans vented their anger over the removals Johnson had already made and endeavored to protect incumbent officeholders from dismissal: During the "swing around the circle" Johnson had threatened to "kick them out just as fast I can." The Republicans, however, had difficulty agreeing on whether the measure should apply to cabinet members. Some, anxious to keep Stanton in his post, maintained it must, whereas others argued that a president, even Johnson, was entitled to name and unname his own ministers. In the end the Republicans adopted a vaguely worded clause stating that cabinet officers "shall hold their offices . . . during the term of the President by whom they may have been appointed, and for one month thereafter, subject to removal by and with the advice and consent of the Senate."

At once the question arose whether this meant that Johnson could dismiss a holdover from Lincoln's cabinet—like Stanton—without Senate approval. Yes, answered Senator Sherman. No, said other Republicans. But Sherman added that this would never be a problem in practice: "I take it that no case can arise when a Cabinet minister will attempt to hold on to his office after his Chief desires his removal." On that note the Senate on February 19 approved the measure, voting 22 to 10, and the House followed suit the next day by a vote of 112 to 41. [22] As any president would, Johnson considered the tenure bill an unconstitutional infringement by the legislature on executive power. His entire cabinet concurred —even Stanton. In fact, when Johnson brought up the subject on February 25, the secretary of war took the lead in denouncing the measure.

Stanton's attitude must have aroused Johnson's suspicion or at least his curiosity. It was common knowledge that in passing the tenure bill many Republicans sought to protect Stanton from removal. Moreover, Stanton continued to oppose the president and abet Congress. Thus, defying Johnson's expressed wish, he had furnished the Senate with a report on the enforcement of the Civil Rights Act which made excellent propaganda in support of the Military Reconstruction Act. Also, at a cabinet meeting on February 22, he alone had advocated approval of that legislation. To Johnson, this was further proof of Stanton's treachery. As the cabinet was gathering on February 25, Johnson took Welles aside and, according to Welles's account, "alluded to the . . . pitiful exhibition which Stanton made of himself [at the February 22 cabinet session], and wondered if he (S.) supposed he was not understood. The sparkle of the President's eyes and his whole manner betokened intense though suppressed feeling."[23]

Hence when Stanton attacked the tenure bill, Johnson seized the opportunity to embarrass him with his congressional allies by asking the secretary of war to draft a veto message. Realizing Johnson's purpose, Stanton quickly backed off. He claimed that he was extremely busy (which was true enough) and that rheumatism had crippled his writing arm (which, as one historian has punned, was a lame excuse). Seward thereupon volunteered to write the message if Stanton would assist him. Stanton agreed and did provide Seward with legal and historical materials in support of a veto.[24]

Was Stanton sincere in denouncing the tenure bill? That question, much discussed by the biographers of Johnson and of Stanton, is not only unanswerable but also of little consequence. More to the point is the fact that Stanton followed a safe course in opposing the bill: Johnson was sure to veto it, and Congress was sure to override the veto. On the other hand, had Stanton supported the measure, he might have provoked Johnson into dismissing him before the bill became law. Indeed, as it turned out that is exactly what Johnson should have done.

Seward and Stanton's collaboration produced a veto message filled with arguments and precedents that convinced most constitutional experts then (and since) that the tenure bill was a rape of presidential powers. But the message changed no minds in Congress, which promptly repassed the bill by the now customary lopsided partisan majority. In view of later events Johnson would have done better to have pocket-vetoed it. Then, possibly, the next Congress would not have reenacted it. Many Moderates, notably Fessenden and Sherman, disliked the bill and had gone along with it mostly to maintain party unity at that crucial time.

On Johnson's desk was still another piece of legislation which also curtailed his authority. This was the Army Appropriations Bill, to which Congress had tacked clauses requiring the president and the secretary of war to transmit all orders to military commanders through the General of the Army (Grant), forbidding the president to relieve, suspend, or transfer from Washington the General of the Army without the Senate's consent, and disbanding the Southern state militias. Unbeknownst to Johnson, these riders had been instigated and written by Stanton in December, acting with Grant's prior approval and in collaboration with Republican leaders. Originally the purpose had been to forestall the recurrence of anything like Johnson's attempt to send Grant to Mexico and to prevent the rearming of the South—in November Johnson had "suggested" to Grant that he issue ten thousand rifles to the Virginia militia, a suggestion which Grant had ignored. But by late February, when Congress passed the army bill, these provisions also served to guard against Johnson's sabotaging the congressional Reconstruction program. Although not yet sure of Grant's political sympathies (for in public he continued to be discreetly noncommittal), the Republicans counted on him to block or at least alert them to any hostile move by Johnson. After all—and apparently Johnson was not aware of this either—Grant had assisted in framing the Military Reconstruction Act.[25]

Johnson's impulse was to veto the army bill with its obnoxious and, he rightly believed, unconstitutional riders. At his request Browning prepared a message so doing. On the morning of March 4 Johnson met with the cabinet in the President's Room of the Capitol in order to dispose of last-minute legislation passed by Congress, which, by dint of holding back the official clock, continued in session beyond its March 2 expiration date. When Johnson asked for advice on the army bill everyone agreed that it should be vetoed except Seward and Stanton. They argued that this would demoralize the army by depriving it of funds. With great reluctance he thereupon decided to sign it, but also to protest the riders. Stanbery then wrote a protest, after which Johnson asked each cabinet member if he approved of it. When his turn came, Stanton said, "I make no objection to it." "But," pressed Johnson, "I wish to know whether you approve of a protest." "I approve your taking whatever course you may think best," replied Stanton, neatly avoiding being pinned down.[26]

At noon the Thirty-ninth Congress at last ceased to function, but immediately the Fortieth Congress commenced its first session. Most prominent among the new members was Ben Butler in the House. Although in his first term, he immediately assumed a position of leadership on the Radical side second only to that of Stevens. As bold as he was bald, Butler's brilliance was exceeded only by his cynical unscrupulousness.

Normally the new Congress would not have assembled until December. But the Republicans did not want to leave Johnson alone and unchecked in Washington. In particular they were worried that he might try to wreck military Reconstruction at the outset by refusing to appoint commanders for the districts into which the South had been divided. Should he resort to this tactic, a strong majority was prepared to impeach him. Already, in fact, the House Judiciary Committee, spurred by the ultra-Radicals, had sought grounds for impeachment but had found none, as it admitted in a report issued on March 3. Johnson's refusal to carry out the Reconstruction act, however, would alter that situation.

The danger of impeachment caused McCulloch on March 8 to urge Johnson to appoint the district commanders quickly. The president, recorded Browning in his diary, "got very angry and swore vehemently, and said that they might impeach and be damned—he was tired of being threatened—that he would not be influenced by any such considerations, but would go forward in the conscientious discharge of his duty without reference to Congress, and meet all the consequences."[27]

As always Johnson resented being pressured. Nevertheless he had no intention of engaging in a suicidal defiance of the Military Reconstruction Act. He asked and received from Grant recommendations for the district commanders. At the close of the cabinet meeting on March 12, the president took Stanton aside and talked privately with him for more than fifteen minutes. When the conversation ended, "Stanton was unusually jubilant, had a joke or two with McCulloch, and could not suppress his feelings."[28] Johnson had told him the names of the commanders: Schofield in the First District (Virginia), Sickles in the Second District (the Carolinas), John Pope in the Third District (Georgia, Florida, and Alabama), E. O. C. Ord in the Fourth District (Arkansas and Mississippi), and Sheridan in the Fifth District (Louisiana and Texas.).

Announcement of these appointees the following day relieved Republican fears that Johnson might try to block implementation of their Reconstruction program. That program, however, was encountering an obstacle for which Congress had only itself to blame. In the hectic process of formulating the Military Reconstruction Act, Congress had neglected to specify procedures for registering voters and for holding the new constitutional conventions in the South. As a result Southerners endeavored to forestall the conventions by refusing to register to vote and by employing intimidation to keep Negroes and Unionists from registering.

To remedy this situation Congress passed the Second Military Reconstruction Act. This bill authorized the district commanders to register black and eligible white voters, prescribed a stricter oath for whites, and placed the holding of conventions, and the referendums on the constitutions they produced, under military supervision. Declaring that "no consideration" could induce him to sign such a bill, Johnson vetoed it on March 23. That same day Congress overrode his veto. A week later, after agreeing to reconvene on July 3, Congress adjourned. Just before doing so, however, the House adopted a resolution instructing the Judiciary Committee to report to it, following the recess, on the subject of impeachment. This was a warning to Johnson not to try to wreck military Reconstruction while Congress was away from Washington.[29]

But probably most Republicans felt that they now had little to fear from the president, who according to one observer looked "very feeble & wretched."[30] During the past four months they had scrapped his Reconstruction program and replaced it with one of their own, stripped him of much of his authority over the civil service, the army, and even his own cabinet, and brushed aside his vetoes with contemptuous ease. In short, they had completely overwhelmed Johnson.

Or so it seemed.

7

★★★★★

THE PRESIDENT COUNTERATTACKS

Broadly speaking the power of the presidency is twofold: political and institutional. By the spring of 1867 Johnson had little political power left. Outside the Border states and the South he lacked popular support, his Republican enemies dominated Congress and his de facto alliance with the Democrats hurt more than it helped him. But despite the Tenure of Office Act and the riders to the Army Appropriations Act, he retained a good deal of institutional power. To the Republicans this was an awkward and potentially troublesome fact; they were ready, therefore, to resort to the ultimate weapon of impeachment if need be. But to Johnson institutional power provided the only effective means by which he could continue to combat the Republicans and their nefarious schemes, uphold his own policies and principles, and ultimately achieve political redemption and personal vindication. Hence he resolved to exploit those assets he still possessed. His efforts to do this constitute the best example in American history of the inherent strength of the presidency.

"The White House," Theodore Roosevelt once said, "is a bully pulpit." Johnson knew that too and tried to make the most of it with his messages, speeches, and above all press interviews. More than any of his predecessors Johnson endeavored to reach the people through reporters. On March 5, the day after the Thirty-ninth Congress ended and the Fortieth had begun, he did so again in an interview with Charles G. Halpine, who as "Miles O'Reilly" was one of the most influential journalists of the day.

A great new issue, Johnson told Halpine, soon would "swallow up all minor questions." This was the "financial issue, the issue of the national debt; whether it shall be paid or repudiated." Before the war, Johnson explained, the Southern aristocracy had dominated the nation, deriving its power from $3 billion in slave property. But now a new aristocracy, "based on over $2,500,000,000 of national securities, has arisen in the northern States, to assume that political control" formerly held by the "slave oligarchy." Moreover, Johnson said, instead of seeking to pay off the national debt this group wished to extend it, for it received $180 million in annual interest. And to make matters worse, he continued, Congress, sustained by "this plutocracy of the national debt," was appropriating excessive sums for veterans' bounties, internal improvements, and its own salaries while resisting every attempt to increase taxes to meet debt-related expenses out of a fear that higher taxes "might help to awaken the people from their false dream of prosperity under the sway of revolutionary and radical ideas." At the same time, Johnson said, the western farmers were clamoring for "further inflation of our inflated currency" whereas the "manufacturers and men of capital in the eastern States" favored a "contraction of the currency" and "prohibitory tariffs." Thus he warned that a "war of finance is the next war we have to fight," and left no doubt about its outcome. The East, which he characterized as "a mere strip or fringe on the broad mantle of our country," would be crushed by the broad and rapidly growing West; furthermore, he said, there soon would be a "great financial crash" from which will emerge a party which "will openly hoist the banner of repudiation." Johnson warned that the only way to save the country from this calamity was to repay the debt as quickly as possible, reduce government expenditures, restore the Southern states so they can "help us in bearing our heavy burden," and above all respect the Constitution. The president explained that his own battle to uphold the Constitution against "congressional usurpation" was, in truth, a struggle to prevent repudiation of the debt. To be sure, his efforts had been defeated by the "preponderating influence" of the "aristocracy of bonds and paper money" who were blind to their "true interests." Nevertheless he was confident of ultimate vindication: "Unless all the senses are deceptive, unless all truth be a lie, unless God has ceased to live, I tell you that the folly and fraud now dominating the councils of this distracted country in Congress cannot endure forever."[1]

In the Halpine interview Johnson attempted to open up a new front against the Republicans—the economic one. For some time, various advisers had urged him to do this. Also a number of Democratic leaders, following their party's dismal showing in 1866, had proposed shifting debate from Reconstruction to the financial question. In particular a group of Ohio Democrats had begun to advocate a scheme soon known as the "Ohio idea"—namely, to pay off the national debt with greenbacks, the quantity of which was to be increased rather than decreased. Some Republicans took the same stand, notably Ben Wade and Ben Butler. Drawing together these otherwise disparate elements was a steady decline in business and prices, highlighted by a stock market panic in January 1867. Many members of both parties blamed this situation on McCulloch's currency contraction policy. As a result, in February the House had passed a bill authorizing the secretary of the treasury to issue up to $100 million of additional greenbacks to redeem that portion of the national debt composed of interest-bearing legal tender notes. The measure failed, however, in the fiscally more conservative Senate, and eventually Congress adopted and Johnson signed (on March 2) a law empowering McCulloch to issue low interest temporary loan certificates rather than greenbacks.[2]

Clearly, economic issues had political potential. But in trying to exploit them, Johnson faced a problem: If he embraced monetary inflation (the essence of the "Ohio idea") he would be abandoning the fiscal policy of his own administration, as established by McCulloch, and would transform many conservative Eastern businessmen —who hitherto had been friendly or at least passive—into active opponents. On the other hand, if he adhered to monetary deflation (the essence of contraction) he would be throwing away an opportunity to win favor among the mainly Western greenbackers. For these reasons in his interview with Halpine the president tried to appeal to the inflationists by denouncing the "new aristocracy" of the East while simultaneously preserving his support among contractionists by warning against repudiation of the debt, which they equated with the "Ohio idea." Needless to say, Johnson left himself open to valid accusations of inconsistency and demagoguery—accusations all the more forceful in view of the fact that he had just signed the Wool and Woolens Act; it was precisely the sort of "prohibitory" tariff he had denounced to Halpine. As a result the Halpine interview, although widely published, gained few, if any, converts for this particular preacher in the White House. It merely demonstrated a rather desperate readiness to use any weapons that came handy.[3]

The Constitution assigns the president paramount power to conduct foreign relations. Johnson, in effect, had delegated this power to Seward. Nevertheless, the responsibility remained his as did the final decisions. Moreover, following the 1866 elections he had compelling reasons to try to offset domestic failure with diplomatic success. So too did Seward. Because of his support of Johnson Seward had lost many of his friends and most of his adherents, lost his dominance in New York, and lost his influence nationally. All he had left was his position as secretary of state—that and an obsessive desire to expand American territory and trade.[4]

Early in March 1867 an opportunity to do both presented itself. The Russian government had decided to unload Alaska. It was a financial and strategic liability; it might become a source of trouble should American settlers begin moving into the area, as they now gave signs of doing; and in any case, the Imperial treasury could use a transfusion of United States dollars. Hence the Russian minister to Washington, Baron Edouard de Stoeckl, received instructions to negotiate the sale.

Stoeckl, "a large man, large of face and figure, quite unconventional, and with easy pleasant manners,"[5] took an indirect approach, for he knew Seward and his expansionistic ambitions well. Through a mutual friend he sent word to Seward that he was interested in discussing Alaska. Seward invited him to a meeting which the secretary of state opened by inquiring about trade and fishing concessions for Americans in Alaska. Impossible, replied Stoeckl. Seward then asked if Russia would sell Alaska. That, answered Stoeckl, was possible.

During the next several days the two diplomats developed the terms of a treaty which called for the United States to purchase Alaska for $7 million in gold. This was $2 million more than Seward initially offered—and also $2 million more than the minimum price the Imperial government had instructed Stoeckl to obtain. But Seward was eager to complete the transaction while Congress was still in session, and Stoeckl, realizing this, took due advantage. Indeed, by raising some new issues after Johnson had approved the treaty draft, the Russian was able to get another $200,000. Then, using the transatlantic cable, which had been put into service in July 1866, he informed St. Petersburg of the bargain he had made; the czar telegraphed his approval.

On the evening of March 29 Stoeckl came to Seward's home

and told him that he had permission to sell Alaska for the stipulated price. They could draw up the formal treaty at the State Department in the morning.

"Why wait till tomorrow, Mr. Stoeckl?" responded Seward. "Let us make the treaty tonight."

"But your Department is closed. You have no clerk, and my secretaries are scattered about the town!"

"Never mind that," Seward replied. "If you can muster your legation together before midnight, you will find me waiting for you at the Department, which will be open and ready for business."[6]

At 4 A.M. on March 30 Seward and Stoeckl signed the completed treaty. At 10 A.M. Seward went with Johnson to the President's Room in the Capitol. Both hoped to have the Senate approve it before Congress adjourned at noon, but after talking with several senators they realized that this was out of the question. Therefore Johnson issued a proclamation stating that "an extraordinary occasion" required the Senate to meet on April 1.

Some Radical newspapers, notably the *New York Tribune,* derided the purchase as "Seward's folly," labeled Alaska "Johnson's polar bear garden," and accused the president and his secretary of state of seeking to hide their disgrace at home with fictitious exploits abroad. In addition a number of Republican senators told Stoeckl that they intended to vote against the treaty because they disliked Seward. Most of the press, however, reacted favorably to the purchase; Thad Stevens gave it his endorsement, thereby removing it from the partisan arena; Seward mounted an effective campaign of propaganda and senatorial lobbying; and most importantly of all, Sumner, after some hesitation, decided to support the treaty. Had he done otherwise, it certainly would have failed, for not only was he chairman of the Senate Foreign Relations Committee, but the rank-and-file Republican senators followed his lead when it came to diplomatic matters, about which (like most American politicians) they cared little and knew less. Consequently on April 9, following a speech by Sumner in which he extolled the potential value of Alaska and warned against offending our Russian friends, the Senate passed the treaty 37 to 2. (Fessenden cast one of the nay votes—he detested Sumner and despised Seward. Justin Morrill, a Republican from Vermont, cast the other.)

So Johnson's administration could (and did) claim a great diplomatic triumph—thanks to the czar and Charles Sumner. To be sure, Seward had agreed to pay more for Alaska than he need have, but no one knew that at the time except the Russians, who also knew that there was gold in Alaska—they just did not know exactly where. What was important was that a region twice the size of Texas had been added to the national domain; Russia had been removed from North America (the only time that country ever voluntarily relinquished territory); and, as Seward and Sumner saw it, a long stride had been taken towards squeezing Britain out of Canada, which they believed should, and someday would, join the United States.[7]

One of the most common arguments against acquiring Alaska was that the United States already had plenty of unsettled and undeveloped land. That was true, even though the Civil War had not slowed the American people's march westward. That march accelerated with peace, as thousands of Union and Confederate veterans followed Horace Greeley's famous advice and as the Irish workers of the Union Pacific pushed forward to meet the tracks being laid from California by the Chinese laborers of the Central Pacific. Vast areas of the Northwest, the Southwest, and the Central Plains remained largely vacant. Moreover, the Cheyenne, Sioux, Apache, and other warrior tribes harried the few settlers who had ventured into those regions, disrupting communication lines and threatening to block the further advance of whites.

Pleas, indeed demands, that the government do something to end the Indian menace poured into Washington. An effective response became a practical necessity—and also a possible political gain—for Johnson's administration. But how to achieve it? The army, with Sherman as its main spokesman, advocated using overwhelming force to subdue the hostiles and transferring the Bureau of Indian Affairs from the Interior Department to the War Department. The first course would bring peace, the second would preserve peace by putting the Indians under direct military control and would provide more honest and efficient supervision than was presently being exercised by the bureau's civilian agents, many of whom were either corrupt, or incompetent, or both.

Of course Interior Department officials and agents strongly objected. Backing them was a motley but powerful host of congressmen, who did not fancy losing the patronage provided by the Bureau of Indian Affairs, and some idealistic reformers who believed that the Indians were victims rather than victimizers. These reformers, mainly preachers and intellectuals concentrated in the East, argued that the way to establish peace in the West was to protect the Indians from "lawless white men," provide them with food and other necessities, and civilize them with Bibles and primers. The army, the reformers charged, merely provoked the Indians into war.

The debate between these opposing viewpoints came to a head following the Fetterman massacre on December 21, 1866: A large band of Sioux ambushed, killed, and mutilated eighty-one soldiers near Fort Phil Kearney in Wyoming. The entire frontier panicked, and Sherman, now commanding in the West, was incensed; in typically hyperbolic language he telegraphed Grant, "We must act with vindictive earnestness against the Sioux, even to their extermination, men, women, and children." With Grant's approval Sherman prepared to launch expeditions against the Indians in the spring. In January, however, a special congressional committee chaired by Senator Doolittle delivered a report on the condition of the Indians which took the reformers' side. At the same time, Browning vigorously fended off attempts by Stanton and Grant to have the Bureau of Indian Affairs transferred to the War Department. The rest of the cabinet, especially Welles and Stanbery, seconded him. What with Johnson's closest political friends backing a "peace" policy, it is little wonder that he decided to do the same. In February he appointed a commission, which was to report to Browning, to investigate the causes of the Fetterman massacre and to negotiate treaties with the Plains tribes.

While the commission made ready, Major General Winfield Scott Hancock, commander of the Department of the Missouri, marched army columns through western Kansas and eastern Colorado. His intent was to overawe the Indians. Instead he provoked them into an outbreak that put the settlers of the region under a virtual state of siege. This outcome compared poorly with the subsequent efforts of the commission, which in October signed a treaty with a number of tribes at Medicine Lodge, Kansas, by which they agreed to keep the peace and stay on reservations in exchange for rations and rifles—the weapons to be used solely for hunting, of course. In January 1868 the commission happily informed Browning that it had found the way to avoid war with the Indians—namely "to do no act of injustice" to them.

But then in August, discontented and restless bands of Cheyennes, Arapahoes, Kiowas, Commanches, and Sioux went on the warpath in Kansas. Scores of settlers lost their lives, hundreds fled. According to a telegram from the state's governor to Johnson, "Wounded women were ravished . . . in the presence of their own dying husbands and children." That fall a special army task force under Sheridan waged a campaign designed to crush the hostiles. It climaxed on November 27 when Custer's Seventh Cavalry attacked a Cheyenne village in the Washita Valley, killing (so he claimed) over one hundred braves; a number of women and children were also killed. Following a winter of relentless pursuit by the army, the Indians of the southern Plains agreed to return to their reservations.[8]

Thus the "peace policy" appeared to be a failure. Certainly it garnered no political benefits for Johnson: Westerners denounced it, Eastern reformers gave him no credit for it. Nevertheless, the basic approach to the Indians—seeking to protect and civilize them by establishing reservations—which started with Johnson, continued almost uninterrupted throughout the rest of the nineteenth century and well into the twentieth. If it ultimately fell far short of the success expected and predicted by its proponents, then so has every other "solution" which the government has adopted for what is, in fact, an insoluble problem.

Under the Constitution, the president is also commander in chief of the armed forces. With the enactment of military Reconstruction that power became crucial in the struggle between Johnson and the Republicans—which, as we have seen, was one of reasons Congress adopted the Tenure of Office Act and the riders to the Army Appropriations Act. Furthermore, in the original version of the Military Reconstruction Act the Republicans had empowered Grant to appoint the Southern district commanders; but in the end concern over possible legal and practical difficulties caused them to leave this function to the president. Then, after Johnson appointed the generals recommended by Grant, the Moderates concluded that he intended to cooperate, or at least not to be overtly obstructionist. Accordingly they repelled a Radical move, which Stanton and Grant secretly supported, to keep Congress in almost continuous session to guard against Johnson. The most the Moderates would agree to, prior to adjournment on March 30, was to assemble Congress again on July 3 if necessary, but otherwise not to reconvene until November. All Republicans believed that a July meeting was unlikely; only a few ultra-Radicals wanted one.[9]

On April 1 Connecticut held an election. The Democrats won the governorship and three of the four House seats. It was the first Democratic victory—and the first Republican defeat—in a Northern state since 1864.

The news from Connecticut elated Johnson. He saw it as "the turn of the current," proof that the strategy of letting the Republicans hang themselves was working.[10] It also strengthened his confidence and determination as he entered into the next phase of his war with Congress—namely, a campaign to limit the impact of military Reconstruction on the South and as much as possible to defeat its purposes.

During late March several generals requested official clarification of the disfranchisement provisions of the Reconstruction acts; Congress had left these clauses quite vague, either out of hasty carelessness or out of a desire to open the way for reducing the white conservative vote to a minimum. Soon, too, questions arose over the nature and extent of the powers possessed by the district commanders. The first and most important instance occurred in Sheridan's Fifth District. The thirty-six-year-old Sheridan ranked second only to Grant and Sherman as a Northern hero and was the protégé of Grant, who considered him a military genius. Moreover Sheridan possessed—or rather was possessed by—an intense anti-Southern bias which caused him to be an equally intense pro-Radical. Hence, on March 27, acting on his own initiative, he removed from their offices a Louisiana state judge, the mayor of New Orleans, and the Louisiana attorney general because of their complicity in the New Orleans riot. To Radicals—indeed, to most Republicans and Northerners—this was justice, but to Johnson it was tyranny. He demanded an explanation from Sheridan. Sheridan replied that he did not "deem it necessary to give any reasons" but supplied them nevertheless. Johnson thereupon ordered him to suspend further removals until Attorney General Stanbery delivered an opinion covering that subject and also the matter of disfranchisement.

Grant duly transmitted the president's order (which under the Army Appropriations Act had to go through him) to Sheridan. Privately, however, he warned Sheridan that Johnson was disposed to remove him from command, assured him that he and Stanton "will oppose any such move, as will the mass of the people," and advised Sheridan that although "Congress intended to give District Commanders entire control over the civil governments" in the South, it would be best to obey Johnson because "an opinion from the Attorney General should be weighed." More importantly, the "power of removing District Commanders undoubtedly exists with the President. . . ." Johnson's order and Grant's counsel caused Sheridan to postpone his next intended move—the removal of the governors of Louisiana and Texas. But at the same time, he was encouraged by Grant to believe that he could successfully defy Johnson in the event of a showdown.[11]

Through April and into May Stanbery labored at preparing

an interpretation of the Reconstruction acts. Completing this task became ever more imperative as other district commanders removed or threatened to depose state officials and problems concerning voter registration and disfranchisement multiplied. Finally, Stanbery presented his opinion in three installments as cabinet meetings held on May 14, 21, and 23. The district commanders, he stated, had no power to remove the officials or alter the laws of the Southern states; their basic function was to assist rather than supersede the state governments. The commanders, Stanbery said, could not deny the vote to anyone who took the required oath of eligibility: Only those Southerners who had voluntarily aided the Confederacy by overt acts in violation of an oath to uphold the Constitution could be disfranchised. Last but not least, in Stanbery's opinion, the president had the right and the duty to supervise execution of the Reconstruction acts. The interpretation drew a mixed response: Stanton opposed Stanbery's opinion, the rest of the cabinet backed it. Welles thought that the attorney general "had done as well as one could who was compelled to try to make sense out of nonsense, law out of illegality." Johnson, of course, endorsed Stanbery's handiwork. From his standpoint it could not have been better. To quote historian Michael Les Benedict, the interpretation "virtually emasculated the Reconstruction law."[12]

Johnson had Stanbery's opinion published in the press on May 27. He did not, however, send official copies of it to the district commanders. To have done so might have provoked the House Judiciary Committee into recommending his impeachment. This body had remained in Washington after Congress adjourned. Urged on by Stevens, Butler, and other ultras it spent the spring seeking evidence which would provide a credible excuse for impeaching Johnson. Among other things it examined his bank account, collected reports of his speeches, questioned members of the cabinet, including Seward and Stanton, and looked into such matters as Booth's death and the granting of presidential pardons. Also, after Jefferson Davis was released May 13 on bail by a federal court, the committee investigated why the Confederate president had not been brought to trial, hoping to find that Johnson was responsible. But all that it learned was that no one in the government was more eager than Johnson to try Davis. Likewise, the other lines of inquiry that the committee pursued failed to produce any evidence of an impeachable offense. Even so, four of its Radical members proposed drawing up charges against the president; however, the chairman, Moderate James F. Wilson of Iowa, backed by two other Republicans and the two Democratic members, voted them down. On June 3 the committee recessed its hearings.

All the time the committee was in session, Johnson kept himself posted on its proceedings through the work of detective Allan Pinkerton, who used a female agent to pump the committee's male secretary. Thus Johnson knew that only a bare majority of the members opposed impeaching him despite the lack of a valid cause. Furthermore, through volunteer informants he found out that Butler and James Ashley, a fanatical Radical from Ohio, were trying to implicate him in Lincoln's assassination by procuring false testimony both from Sanford Conover, a convicted perjurer, and from Booth's coconspirator, John Surratt, who recently had been apprehended and was lodged, like Conover, in the Old Capitol Prison. Hence it is understandable that the president moved cautiously in attempting to undermine the congressional Reconstruction program.[13]

Another probable reason that Johnson did not issue Stanbery's opinion at once as an official order was that he hoped that this would be unnecessary—that the district commanders would be guided by it in any event. Two of them, Schofield in Virginia and Ord in Arkansas and Mississippi, did follow it on the whole; but Sickles in the Carolinas ignored it, Pope sought to circumscribe it, and Sheridan defied it outright by leaving in effect some highly proscriptive disfranchisement regulations that he had promulgated. Again, Grant privately assured Sheridan that he approved. At the same time, Grant criticized Ord for putting Stanbery's opinion into effect in his district. The First Military Reconstruction Act, Grant wrote Ord, "makes district commanders their own interpreters of their power and duty under it. . . ."[14]

Early in June, accompanied by Seward and Randall, Johnson journeyed to North Carolina where he witnessed the unveiling of a monument to his father in Raleigh and attended the graduation ceremonies at the university in Chapel Hill. It was Johnson's first visit to his birthplace since leaving as an impoverished boy, and to return now as president of the United States was a deeply moving experience. It was also gratifying to be greeted as a hero by people who a few years ago had denounced him as a traitor.[15]

The great majority of Southerners had reacted to the black-based congressional Reconstruction program with a mixture of anger and dismay. "Masterly inactivity" obviously had failed. But what strategy should they adopt in its place? Some Southern leaders hoped to overturn the Reconstruction laws in the Supreme Court. Thus in April the Mississippi state government brought separate suits to prevent Johnson and Stanton from executing the laws. But a unanimous Supreme Court rejected both pleas on the grounds that it had no authority to enjoin the executive branch in the performance of its duties. Johnson himself took the same view: As much as he wanted to put down military Reconstruction, he believed that the prerogatives of the presidency must be upheld.[16]

By the time Johnson went to North Carolina most Southern leaders had decided to try "cooperation." They would participate in the forthcoming elections of constitutional conventions in hopes of controlling them. Although the Reconstruction acts had resulted in the disfranchisement of between eighty-five thousand and one hundred and twenty-five thousand Southerners, whites still constituted a majority of the electorate in Virginia, North Carolina, Georgia, Arkansas, and Texas. In the other states planters believed that they could secure a decisive portion of the Negro vote through personal influence and economic coercion. Stanbery's opinion, by limiting the impact of disfranchisement, abetted the "cooperationist" strategy.[17]

While Johnson was in North Carolina, Sheridan again kicked up his heels in Louisiana. Back in May, he had dismissed the Louisiana Levee Commission in order to "relieve the State . . . from the incubus of the quarrel" that had broken out between Governor Wells and the legislature over how a $4 million flood-control appropriation was to be spent. Wells had appealed this action to Johnson, who before leaving Washington had directed Sheridan to suspend the dismissals. On June 3 Sheridan complied, but at the same time he ordered the removal of Governor Wells himself. Confident of being sustained by Stanton, by Grant, and by Congress, Sheridan deliberately and flagrantly flouted Stanbery's opinion and the president's authority.[18]

Johnson returned to Washington on June 8. Three days later he met with the cabinet. Stanbery read a new exegesis on the Reconstruction acts. Again he held that the district commanders could not supplant civil officers or be the sole judge of their powers under the acts. As before, Stanton and Stanton alone opposed this interpretation. The argument continued at subsequent cabinet sessions. On June 18 Johnson declared that he wanted to reach a definite decision on the matter. It was important, he added, to have an unanimous cabinet. Stanbery thereupon proposed that a record be kept of each member's views. Welles said that he preferred to submit a written opinion but Johnson directed that Stanbery's proposal be instituted. Most likely Welles was correct in suspecting that Stanbery and Johnson had "concocted" this arrangement before hand. It had the effect of pressuring Stanton to go along with the rest of the cabinet by making it impossible for him ever to deny that he was a minority of one. Indeed, it might even drive him into resigning.

Stanton, however, was not to be so easily intimidated. During the remainder of the June 18 session, which lasted all afternoon and into the evening, he persistently dissented on all important points in Stanbery's opinion. Then the next day Johnson distributed to the cabinet copies of a printed list of nineteen "interrogatories" concerning the Reconstruction acts. As he did so he again spoke of the need for a uniformity of opinion in the cabinet. Stanton promptly protested this "string of general questions" to which "gentlemen were required to make immediate answer." Stanbery, who had prepared the list, retorted that they were plain and simple enough to answer on the spot. McCulloch and Seward agreed with him. Stanton then read a statement supporting congressional control over Reconstruction and the independence of the district commanders. He ignored attempts by Johnson and Stanbery to interrupt him, and after he finished made no reply to criticisms of his views. As for the nineteen "interrogatories," Stanton finally assented to twelve of the questions dealing with minor matters, but he was the only one in the room who disagreed with the remaining seven, all of which were of major consequence.

Culmination of the long wrangle came on June 20. Johnson submitted a set of special questions to Stanton. They were to be answered yes or no and were designed to force Stanton either to admit that the president retained full authority over the district commanders or else to assert that he had no control whatsoever over them. But again Stanton avoided the trap. He declared that the commanders must obey the president's orders—but only if those orders complied with the Reconstruction acts (something which the commanders themselves would judge).

Johnson then proposed sending Stanbery's opinion to the district commanders with a preamble stating that the cabinet had approved it. At once Stanton saw that Johnson wanted to give the district commanders the impression that Stanton endorsed the opinion, thereby making it more likely that they would go along with it. Hence Stanton asserted that the cabinet had not agreed to it. Did not a majority vote constitute agreement? asked Johnson. Not in the cabinet, replied Stanton, who went on to argue that the head of one department could not be bound by the opinions of other cabinet officers. On this point, Seward supported Stanton. Thus encouraged, Stanton warned that he would refuse to transmit the preamble proposed by the president. Johnson thereupon backed off and asked Stanton and Stanbery to draft a new preamble. Each presented a different version. Johnson accepted Stanton's but with the addition of an amendment suggested by Randall. It stated that Stanbery's opinion represented what the president, "following discussion with the Cabinet," had "concluded" as the "correct and practical interpretation" of the Reconstruction acts.[19]

On June 21 the War Department sent the attorney general's opinion and the preamble to the district commanders. That same day the newspapers published the record of the cabinet votes on the opinion, Johnson and Seward left Washington to dedicate a Masonic temple in Boston, and Stanton took to his bed in a condition of physical collapse. Rumors circulated that he was on the point of death or resignation. But as Horace Greeley commented in the *New York Tribune*, the secretary of war belonged to a "breed who rarely die and never resign."[20] The perceptiveness of the latter part of Greeley's statement would soon be demonstrated.

Sheridan, whose temper was as short as his stature, boiled over with range when he received his copy of the attorney general's opinion. "Mr. Stanbery's interpretation," he telegraphed Grant from New Orleans, "is practically . . . opening a broad macadamized road for perjury and fraud to travel on" as regards the registration of Southern voters. Hardly had he sent this message when the *New York Herald*, the most enterprising newspaper of the day, published it. According to Stanton's biographers, Johnson's "friends in the War Department supplied him with a copy" and Johnson "released it to the Democratic press"; Thomas and Hyman, however, cite no sources that support their contention. Welles, on the other hand, suspected that Sheridan himself leaked the message. In any case, Sheridan's language was insolent if not insubordinate; even Stanton stated that Grant should rebuke him.[21]

Grant, however, did nothing of the kind. Instead, on June 24, he counseled his favorite general to procrastinate in complying with Stanbery's opinion: "In the meantime Congress may give an interpretation of its own, differing possibly from those [sic] given by the Attorney General." Then on June 28, after Sheridan asked whether Stanbery's opinion should be regarded as an order, Grant told him: "Enforce your own construction of the military bill until ordered to do otherwise. The opinion of the Attorney General has not been distributed to district commanders in language or manner entitling it to the force of an order. Nor can I suppose that the President intended it to have such force."[22] Grant also sent identical instructions to Pope.

In the estimation of one recent historian, "For the first time Grant had resorted to subterfuge to counter the President's wishes."[23] Whether it was the first time, or whether it was even subterfuge, are debatable points. But certainly Grant was performing the role assigned him by the riders to the Army Appropriations Act: He was holding the fort, so to speak, until Congress could take counteraction against the president. And that was precisely what Congress proposed to do: On July 3, in accordance with the Republican contingency plan, it reconvened.

Johnson had realized the Stanbery's opinion might cause this to happen. The prospect, recorded Welles, made the president "nervous and apprehensive."[24] But he also felt that he could not permit generals like Sheridan to ride roughshod over the South. They had to be restrained, and if the Republicans retaliated with further legislation—or even impeachment—so be it. They merely would be taking another step towards their political scaffold. He was sure of that, especially after the friendly receptions he had received during his journey to Boston, from whence he returned on June 29.

As for the Republicans, most of them did not relish a sojourn in Washington during hot and humid July. Yet something had to be done about Stanbery's opinion. If allowed to stand, at the very least, it would cripple—and at the worst, would wreck—military Reconstruction. Justice for the Negro and power for the Republicans required that neither be allowed to happen.

On July 13 the House, by a vote of 112 to 22, and the Senate, voting 31 to 6, passed the Third Military Reconstruction Act. It overruled Stanbery on every important point. District commanders could remove and appoint state officials; they could, in effect, deny the vote to anyone they pleased and give it to everyone they desired; both they and their subordinates need not heed "any opinion of any civil officer of the United States"; finally, "all provisions of this act and of the acts to which this is supplementary shall be construed liberally. . . ." On July 19, denouncing the measure as unconstitutional, Johnson vetoed it. The same day Congress overrode his veto, and the next day it went home.[25]

Johnson was right. The Third Military Reconstruction Act did violate the Constitution by depriving the president of administrative control over that portion of the army occupying the South and by placing millions of United States citizens under uncontrolled power. Most of the Republicans knew this. But what else could they do if their Reconstruction program was to succeed? The only alternative was to remove Johnson from the White House and install in his place Ben Wade, who as president pro tem of the Senate was next in line under the existing law of succession. At this point, only the Radical minority wanted to go so far. That quickly became clear: On July 5 the Republican caucus voted to limit the business of the special session to supplementing the Reconstruction acts; and later the Moderates defeated a Radical proposal to reconvene in October for the purpose of considering impeachment. Instead the caucus adopted a resolution to have Congress meet again on November 21. When the session ended the majority of Republicans hoped that Johnson had learned his lesson and that he would cease combatting implementation of their Reconstruction program.

They hoped in vain. At the end of July, confident that he now could proceed with impunity, Sheridan removed the governor of Texas and appointed a man with practically no popular support. Simultaneously Johnson discovered for a fact what he had long suspected as a probability—that Stanton was collaborating with Congress to the extent of having drafted the Third Military Reconstruction Act. Sheridan's impudence and Stanton's treachery, the president decided, no longer could be tolerated. He would dismiss them both and make Grant secretary of war.[26]

Why Grant? Johnson was aware that he favored military Reconstruction—the general had not attempted to conceal that fact. Johnson also sensed that Grant, like Stanton, was cooperating with his Republican enemies, although to what degree and in what ways the president did not know. Probably he calculated that replacing Stanton with Grant would curtail adverse reaction to Stanton's removal and make it appear that the hero of Appomattox supported the administration. Furthermore, Johnson may have hoped to win Grant over to his side, or at least to manipulate him, once he was in the cabinet. By so doing Johnson could then jam the wheels of congressional Reconstruction: No district commander would dare disobey an order from Grant. Finally, it is possible that Johnson sought, by naming Grant as secretary of war, to impair or wreck the general's presidential prospects by creating doubt among Republicans as to his allegiance and reliability.[27]

In any case, on the morning of August 1 Johnson summoned Grant to the White House. He told him that he intended to remove Stanton and relieve Sheridan and asked Grant to accept an interim appointment as secretary of war. Surprised, Grant warned that deposing these two heroes of the North would be highly unpopular, but Grant stated that he would not "shrink from the performance of any public duty that may be imposed on me." He then left. Later in the day, however, he wrote a letter to Johnson asserting that the Tenure of Office Act protected Stanton, that the president should have dismissed him while Congress was still in session, and that "the removal of the able commander of the fifth military district" would offend the "loyal people of this country."[28] This message caused Johnson to hold the note he had already written Stanton requesting his resignation.

The next day, following a regular meeting of the cabinet and after Stanton left the White House, Johnson asked the remaining cabinet members for their advice on relieving Sheridan of his command—but the president did not reveal his intention to dismiss Stanton. McCulloch thought that it would be "injudicious" to remove Sheridan: It would "strengthen the extreme Radicals, who really wanted the President to take this step in order that they might make successful war against him," and "discourage the conservative portion" of the Republican party (i.e., the Moderates). Browning seconded this view, saying that the Moderates were "already sick" of Radical measures. Welles on the other hand made a passionate speech in which he declared that duty and self-respect demanded Sheridan's removal. Randall likewise advocated turning "the little fellow out." While Welles spoke, Johnson "warmed up," and following Randall's comment his "eyes flashed" as he asked:

> What have we to expect from long keeping quiet? Will the Republicans, the conservative portion of them, come into our views? They are always promising, but they never perform. It may be said this will enrage them and that they will then go forward and impeach me. If they would impeach me for ordering away an officer who I believe is doing wrong—afflicting and oppressing the people instead of protecting and sustaining them—if I am to be impeached for this, I am prepared.[29]

This informal conference ended with an understanding "that Sheridan's case would be delayed for the moment." Early the next morning McCulloch, "very much exercised in regard to the removal of Sheridan," came to Welles and asked him to prevent the president from taking "hasty action." Welles repeated his arguments in favor of dismissing the general but promised to talk to Johnson. Later that day he went to the White House and told Johnson that he could understand why it might be inexpedient to make the removal, for "it would undoubtedly lead to a violent assault on him" by the "extreme Radicals." "What," Johnson responded,

> have I to fear, what to gain or lose by keeping this man who delights in opposing and counteracting my views in this position? It is said that the weak Radicals—the conservative ones—will join the ultras to impeach me. If Congress can bring themselves to impeach me, because in my judgment a turbulent and unfit man should be removed and because I, in the honest discharge of my duty to my country and the Constitution, exercise my judgment and remove him, let them do it. I shall not shun the trial, and if the people can sanction such a proceeding, I shall not lament the loss of a position held by such a tenure.[30]

Welles then remarked that Sheridan was "really but a secondary personage after all in the business. He would never have pursued the course he has if not prompted and encouraged by others to whom he looked, from whom he received advice, if not orders. Little would be obtained, if only he were taken in hand." At this point Johnson informed Welles of his decision to dismiss Stanton, related his conversation with Grant, and showed him Grant's letter opposing the removal of Stanton and Sheridan. Welles, after reading the letter, commented: "Grant is going over."

Johnson answered, "Yes, I am aware of it. I have no doubt that most of these offensive measures have emanated from the War Department."

"It is unfortunate, perhaps," continued Welles, "that you did not remove all of the Cabinet soon after your Administration commenced—certainly some who have made it a business to thwart and defeat your measures ought to have been changed."

With "some emotion" Johnson agreed. Still, he doubted whether he could have gotten rid of Stanton and observed that it would have been very unpleasant to have tried and failed. As for Grant, Johnson said he presumed that Grant had informed Stanton of his impending dismissal and that Stanton was behind Grant's letter of protest. Johnson then announced his intention "to bring this matter to a conclusion in a few days."[31]

Welles's interview with Johnson took place on a Saturday. The Sunday morning papers contained sensational news from the trial of John Surratt, which was in progress. In rebutting a defense charge that Johnson had not seen the petition for clemency for Surratt's mother, the prosecution had stated that the president had "signed the warrant for her death with the [clemency] paper right before his eyes." When Johnson read this, he was astonished—and outraged. Not only had he no recollection of seeing the clemency petition, this was the first time, he claimed, that he even had heard of it! Holt, he declared, had deliberately withheld it from him. And behind Holt, Johnson was certain, was Stanton.[32]

Monday morning he instructed Moore to deliver to Stanton the dismissal notification (which was redated August 5). It read:

Sir: Public considerations of a high character constrain me to say that your resignation as Secretary of War will be accepted. Very respectfully yours,

Andrew Johnson
The President of the United States[33]

Shortly before noon the following day Johnson received Stanton's reply:

Sir: Your note this day has been received, stating that public considerations of a high character constrain you to say that my resignation as Secretary of War will be accepted.

In reply, I have the honor to say that public considerations of a high character, which alone have induced me to continue at the head of this department, constrain me not to resign the office of Secretary of War before the next meeting of Congress.

Edwin M. Stanton
Secretary of War[34]

Stanton was not the first cabinet officer to refuse a presidential request (tantamount to a command) to resign: Secretary of State Timothy Pickering had so defied John Adams in 1800 and Secretary of the Treasury William Duane had likewise refused Andrew Jackson in 1833. Both of those men, however, had forthwith been dismissed, and thus they established no valid precedent for Stanton, whose conduct, to say the least, was both exceptional and extraordinary, regardless of whatever meaning might be squeezed out of the Tenure of Office Act. Stanton's friendly biographers justify his recalcitrance on the grounds that he was resisting an attempt by Johnson to override the will of Congress, of the Northern people, and of God (i.e., racial equality). Stanton himself professed to be doing the first two, and no doubt he was filled with the sincerity that usually accompanies hatred. Yet it should be noted that he had been a cabinet member for most of the past seven years, first under

Buchanan, then Lincoln, now Johnson; it had become a way of life for him. It also was a livelihood, and given his poor health it would be difficult to find a better one. But Stanton calculated that there would be no need to. Congress would not permit his removal, and if Johnson attempted it he would be impeached. Believing that Johnson himself realized this, Stanton was confident that he would remain in office.

Welles had predicted that Stanton, although "very tenacious of his place," would resign if asked. We do not know if Johnson thought the same. But according to Moore, when the president read Stanton's refusal he "did not evince much, if any surprise." Instead Johnson remarked that Stanton would find it difficult to justify his course before the country and then said, "I will leave Mr. Stanton hanging on the sharp hooks of uncertainty for a few days and then suspend him from his office."[35]

Johnson, however, faced an uncertainty: Would Grant agree to serve in Stanton's place? He had not said no, but neither had he said yes. During the next several days Johnson scouted other possibilities. Welles suggested Frank Blair, Jr.: Were he appointed, said Welles, "Stanton, who though a blusterer is a coward, would fly out of one door as Frank entered at the other." Johnson laughed and concurred. On August 10 he saw Montgomery Blair at the White House and asked him where his brother could be found. Not in Washington, replied Blair, who thought the president looked "very unhappy." What should he do regarding Stanton? Johnson then asked him. Send for Grant, Blair advised.[36]

The following day Johnson did so. He told Grant that he had decided to suspend Stanton from office pending the convening of Congress. Would Grant serve as acting secretary of war? Since he was Commanding General of the Army, a post he would retain, Johnson said Grant understood the needs of the service better than anyone else and so was the logical choice for a temporary replacement. As Johnson himself later described it to Moore, Grant answered with "the hectic smirk peculiar to him, 'I will, of course, obey orders.'" Was there, Johnson next inquired, "anything between us"—he had "heard it intimated that there was" and would like to know. Nothing personal, said Grant—simply and frankly a difference of opinion regarding Reconstruction. Grant then left, "pleased," so it seemed to Johnson, "with the proposed arrangement."[37]

Johnson also was pleased—so much so that he told Moore that he might have him rephrase the already prepared order suspending Stanton to include the words "removed from office" as well. But he left the order unchanged and the next day Moore delivered it to Stanton. "I will send an answer," said Stanton. The previous evening Grant had notified Stanton that he had agreed to serve as acting secretary of war. This news had surprised and upset Stanton, for as the days had gone by he had become evermore convinced that Johnson would not dare supplant him. It also had caused him to doubt Grant's trustworthiness. After a while he handed Moore the answer: He denied the president's right to suspend him without prior Senate approval, thereby appealing for protection to the Tenure of Office Act—the same law he earlier had condemned as unconstitutional. Stanton closed by stating, "I have no alternative but to submit, under protest, to superior force," which was his snide way of implying that Johnson (and Grant too) had threatened to hoist him out of his office on the points of bayonets.

Johnson frowned as he read Stanton's letter. Then, "with an expression of feeling in his face" beyond anything Moore had seen before, he said to his secretary: "The turning point has at last come; the Rubicon is crossed. You do not know what Mr. Stanton has said and done against me."[38]

8

★★★★★

JOHNSON VERSUS GRANT

Stanton was gone—now for Sheridan. On August 17 Johnson dictated an order replacing Sheridan with George H. Thomas, who as commander in Tennessee had displayed restraint and impartiality. The president then sent the order to Grant with a note stating that he "would be pleased to hear any suggestions you may deem necessary respecting the assignment" of Thomas to the Fifth District.

Grant, on taking over the War Department, had expected Johnson to remove Sheridan immediately. When this failed to happen he sent word to Sheridan that "the President has about given up the idea of relieving you." Hence Johnson's order surprised as well as angered Grant. His first act was to alert Sheridan to the president's intention and to assure him that he would "receive the entire support of these Headquarters." His next was to write a letter to Johnson protesting Sheridan's removal "in the name of a patriotic people who have sacrificed thousands of loyal lives and thousands of millions of treasure to preserve the integrity and union of this country. . . ." It was, he continued, "the expressed wish of the country that General Sheridan not be removed from his present command. This is a republic where the will of the people is the law of the land. I beg that their voice may be heard."[1]

Johnson wasted no time and had no difficulty in responding to Grant. Sheridan's tenure, he pointed out, had never been "submitted to the people themselves for determination." His conduct as district commander had "in fact been one of absolute tyranny." And although this was a government of the people, it was one based on a

139

written Constitution which made the president commander-in-chief of the armed forces and directed him to "take care that the laws be faithfully executed."[2]

The reply did not change Grant's mind but he sensed that he had been out-argued. Therefore on August 19 he went to the White House, told Johnson that he acquiesced in Sheridan's removal, but asked that the young general be assigned to the West. Johnson readily agreed—fighting Indians was just the thing for Sheridan. Thomas, however, asked not to be transferred to the Fifth District, on the grounds that the New Orleans climate would be bad for his health. Johnson thereupon appointed Major General Winfield Scott Hancock to the command. Hancock was a Democrat who could be counted on to administer military Reconstruction with all possible leniency. Also, as the "victor at Gettysburg," he had great prestige in the army and in the North.[3]

Next Johnson turned his attention to General Sickles. An excitable eccentric with one leg (he had lost the other one at Gettysburg where he also nearly lost the battle for the Union side), Sickles as military overlord of the Carolinas had nearly equaled Sheridan in high-handedness. Then, early in August, Sickles surpassed Sheridan by defying a court order issued by no less a personage than Chief Justice Chase, acting in the capacity of circuit judge. On August 13 Grant, attending his first cabinet meeting as secretary of war, declared that Sickles had exceeded his authority and that he would instruct him accordingly, which he did. Sickles, however, replied on August 17 that "if the United States Courts in the rebel States be allowed to control the military authorities, the execution of the Reconstruction Acts will for obvious reasons soon become impracticable." Grant's initial reaction to this was to order Sickles to cease obstructing the court. But then he telegraphed him: "Follow the course of action indicated by you as right."[4]

Johnson meanwhile showed Sickles's letter of August 17 to Welles, who advised him "to make short work with King Sickles." That precisely was what the president intended to do. On August 23 he took up Sickles's case with the cabinet. Assistant Attorney General J. M. Binckley, substituting for Stanbery, who was out of town, expressed surprise that Sickles, a lawyer by prewar profession, "should put himself in opposition to the Chief Justice." Grant thereupon reported that he had countermanded his order to Sickles to cease obstructing the court order, explaining that since "there are always two sides to a question" he wanted to give Sickles "an opportunity to be heard." Congress, Grant added in justification of his conduct, had put in his hands the execution of the Reconstruction acts. To this Binckley replied that he supposed "the General expected to execute it in subordination to law and authority."[5]

On August 26 Johnson signed an order replacing Sickles with Major General Edward R. S. Canby, a much more moderate officer politically and personally. At the cabinet meeting on the following day Grant voiced no objection to this action, but he did revive the argument over Sheridan's removal, the order for which he had not yet issued. In addition Grant repeated his contention that he possessed paramount authority to administer the Reconstruction acts. "The President," recorded Welles, "was very cool, calm, and deliberate in his reply. . . ." General Grant, stated Johnson, "must understand it is my duty to see the laws are executed, and also that when I assign officers to their duty my orders must be obeyed." Grant, according to Welles, "was humbled by his great rebuke." In a "subdued manner" he remarked that "while it is proper I should discharge the duties *ad interim* of Secretary of War, I am no politician and prefer not to be mixed up in political questions." He then asked to be excused from further cabinet meetings so as to avoid involvement in political discussions. Johnson answered that the choice was his.[6] Thereupon Grant left the room.

At 3 o'clock that afternoon, however, Johnson received from Grant a long letter which was nothing more than a political discussion. In it Grant asserted that he had certain powers under the Reconstruction acts which he intended to exercise. Admittedly the president had the right to assign district commanders; nonetheless, rightly or not, the country deemed the displacement of Sheridan an attempt by the president to "defeat the laws of Congress for restoring peace, union, and representation to the ten States not now represented." The people, Grant concluded, were tired of Reconstruction and wanted an end to the controversy over it so that they could "meet the great financial issues before us."[7]

The letter greatly excited Johnson. He considered it insubordinate. But also, as he commented to Moore, it left Grant quite vulnerable—"If it were ever published naked and alone, it would, in the minds of all sensible persons, condemn the author." The next morning, August 28, he sent for the general. When Grant arrived Johnson told him that, "without meaning any offense, he wished to speak plainly to him." He then reminded him that at yesterday's cabinet meeting he had "asked to be excused from attending cabinet sessions, as he did not wish to participate in political discussions. . . ." But now, Johnson continued sternly, it seemed that even while Grant was so asking, "this very letter, which amounts to a sort of political essay, was being copied for his signature at army headquarters." Johnson then proceeded to point out various fallacies in the letter, making it clear as he did so that its publication would expose Grant to devastating rebuttal. Realizing that he had blundered, Grant requested permission to withdraw the letter. Johnson said that he could do as he pleased but kept the letter on the desk in front of him. Grant thereupon reached across the desk, folded down the letter, and picked it up. As he did so he promised to send a note withdrawing it, but he said that he would like to take it with him now. Later that day, Grant sent the note. Furthermore, the following day he transmitted, under date of August 27, the orders relieving Sheridan and Sickles and assigning Hancock and Canby in their stead.[8]

Thus Johnson prevailed over Grant. But was it a Pyrrhic victory? For a while it seemed as if it might be. The suspension of Stanton elicited cries of outrage from the Republicans; the removal of Sheridan and of Sickles intensified the criticism; and amongst all of this were strident demands for impeachment, some of which came from men hitherto opposed to such a step. Writing to McCulloch on September 2, Fessenden stated that when Congress had adjourned, few people in New England supported impeachment, but now he knew of "no man who is not in favor of impeachment if any decent pretense for it can be found." And in Ohio one of Johnson's staunchest supporters, former Senator Thomas Ewing, Sr., the father-in-law of General Sherman, gloomily predicted that it was "almost certain that the President will be impeached this winter."[9]

After a few weeks, however, most of the Republicans calmed down. They realized that Johnson had done nothing definitely illegal, hence nothing that was clearly impeachable. By October only a few Radical newspapers and leaders continued to call for impeachment—and they had been doing that anyway.

Potentially—and, as it turned out, actually—the most damaging consequence for Johnson of his actions against Stanton, Sheridan, and Sickles lay in their effect on Grant. The suspension of Stanton did not particularly bother Grant; although he had cooperated with Stanton in endeavoring to check Johnson, like most of the generals Grant cared little personally for the rude and officious "Carnot of the North." But the dismissal of Sheridan deeply offended him, and it would be surprising if he did not resent the way in which Johnson had trampled over his protests and arguments. The experience could only have been humiliating to a man whose first two initials had come to stand for Unconditional Surrender by the enemy.

In agreeing to serve as interim secretary of war, Grant's primary motive had been to prevent Johnson from undermining military Reconstruction. Grant believed that this program represented the will of the Northern people, that it was necessary to secure the results of the war, and that Congress had empowered him and the army to implement it. Hence he regarded Johnson's continued opposition as pig-headed, unlawful, and calculated to keep the nation in turmoil. Last, but not necessarily least, Grant thought that Johnson's obstructionism might defeat or badly impair the Republicans' Reconstruction policies. Should that happen, Grant's own political future would be jeopardized.

Grant realized, like everyone else, that he was practically assured of the Republican presidential nomination in 1868. The prospect did not dismay him. On the contrary he found it rather attractive, especially since nomination by the Republicans would be almost equivalent to election—provided, that is, that their Reconstruction program succeeded. Should it fail, then they probably would lose strength in the North and certainly would not gain power in the South. Thus Grant had a personal stake in making military Reconstruction work. Little wonder then that he encouraged the district commanders who, like Sheridan, sought to promote the Republican party in the South but was annoyed with those who, like Ord in his district, displayed more restraint. Indeed, when Hancock passed through Washington to take over at New Orleans, Grant tried to persuade him to continue Sheridan's policies. Then, after failing to accomplish this, Grant issued an order on September 2 to all district commanders forbidding them to reinstate any civil officers removed by their predecessors, his obvious objective being to keep Sheridan's and also Sickles's appointees in place. Commenting on the order in his diary, Welles stated, "General Grant is more intensely partisan than I was aware." He was more so than most historians have been aware.[10]

During their August 18 White House discussion of Grant's "political essay," Johnson remarked that he was not a candidate for president; Grant answered that neither was he.[11] Both men were lying and both men knew it. The very fact that Johnson made his remark and that Grant responded to it as he did makes it evident that the two looked upon each other as rivals. It was, however, a muted rivalry, for reasons particular to each man. In Grant's case overt defiance of the president would expose him to a legitimate charge of insubordination and make it difficult for him to continue in his wisely chosen role of the hero who was above petty politics. As for Johnson, he needed to retain the general as at least a nominal member of his administration; removing or publicly reprimanding Grant might provoke impeachment and might also cost the Democrats the forthcoming fall elections, which Johnson hoped, even expected, them to win, thereby deflating Republican sails. So for the time being the two remained outwardly cordial. But inwardly Johnson looked forward to replacing Grant in the War Department with someone more trustworthy; and in private Grant assured Republican leaders that in agreeing to take over from Stanton, his sole purpose was to keep the president in check.[12]

Stanton's suspension and the advent of the elections produced rumors that Johnson intended to remodel the entire cabinet. Meanwhile, the Democrats pressed him to dismiss Seward, Randall, and McCulloch: The first because, as ever, they hated him; the other two because, as always, they hungered for the patronage of the Post Office and Treasury departments.

Noting the predictions of a cabinet shake-up—the *National Intelligencer*, Johnson's organ, was one of the newspapers making them—Seward decided to force the issue. On August 23 he secretly submitted his resignation to Johnson. Promptly and just as secretly Johnson rejected it. Although Seward was, as Johnson himself put it, "rather a dead carcass" politically, he had been loyal and had suffered for that loyalty.[13] In addition Johnson continued to value Seward's counsel even when (usually to his own detriment) he had failed to follow it. But above all Seward had provided the Johnson administration with its single outstanding accomplishment, the acquisition of Alaska, and it would be nearly impossible to find anyone else who matched Seward's experience and expertise in diplomacy.

For his part Seward did not really wish to resign, and he would have been dismayed if Johnson had accepted his offer to do so. Stimulated by his Alaska coup, he was busy with a great variety of new diplomatic ventures: a treaty to purchase the Danish West Indies (present-day Virgin Islands), negotiations to obtain Samana Bay in the Dominican Republic, a scheme to intervene in Panama with the ultimate object of constructing a canal there, an indirect attempt via a trade treaty to annex Hawaii, and inquiries regarding the availability of Tiger Island in the Gulf of Fonseca as well as Cuba, Puerto Rico, Iceland, Greenland, and the Fiji Islands! In addition he proposed seizing a naval base on Formosa where on June 13, 1867, two United States warships bombarded a town in retaliation for the massacre of American sailors; and he also was initiating preparations for an expedition to Korea to "open it up" à la Perry in Japan. According to a recent historian, Ernest N. Paolino, Seward was motivated by a grand vision of achieving "global commercial supremacy" for the United States, an aspiration which also was manifested by American participation during the summer of 1867 in an international monetary conference at Paris and by plans to build a telegraph line through Siberia. All other historians who have dealt with Seward's diplomacy, however, take the view that he was prompted simply by a desire to pick up overseas real estate whenever and wherever the opportunity presented itself. This orthodox interpretation seems to be supported by Seward's failure to make any effort to promote the rebuilding of the war-shattered United States merchant marine. Moreover, there is no indication that Johnson, the cabinet, or such key congressional leaders as Sumner and Stevens (with whom Seward cultivated friendly personal relations) knew that the secretary of state had any master plan for United States economic expansion. Welles, for one, considered Seward a "monomaniac" on the subject of territorial acquisition, that being "the hobby on which he expects to be a candidate for President." Welles, however, always took a jaundiced view of Seward. Also it is worth noting that Welles himself did a little acquiring when, per his instructions, a naval vessel took possession early in 1867 of the uninhabited and unclaimed island of Midway. In addition, at Seward's behest the Navy Department sold the former Confederate cruiser *Stonewall* to Japan in the summer of 1867. Since the Japanese lacked the know-how to navigate this ship across the Pacific, Welles assigned an American crew to deliver it to Japan. On the way it passed Pearl Harbor and Midway.[14]

Unlike Seward, McCulloch did not tender his resignation. Had he done so, Johnson might have accepted it. In a largely successful effort to keep the Treasury Department free of the battle over Reconstruction, McCulloch had kept on many antiadministration Republicans and also had preserved close contact with Senators Sherman and Fessenden, whose cooperation on fiscal matters he rightly considered vital. As a result some of Johnson's adherents complained to him, with reason, that Treasury officials were aiding the "Radicals." In addition many people, especially the Greenbackers, blamed McCulloch's hard-money policy for the nation's economic problems. Finally, Johnson thought that McCulloch had displayed weakness in arguing against the removal of Stanton, and he erroneously suspected McCulloch of harboring presidential ambitions. But although Johnson told Moore on August 14 that "there was a man out west [Democrat William S. Groesbeck of Ohio] who could do infinitely better as Secretary of the Treasury than the present incumbent," he did not ask McCulloch to step down, for a number of reasons.[15] First of all, disturbed by reports that the president was considering replacing him, McCulloch wrote Johnson a letter affirming his loyalty; then the Democratic congressmen from Indiana interceded on his behalf; and most importantly numerous businessmen and Conservatives urged that McCulloch be retained, implying that otherwise they would go over to the Republicans. Hence Johnson concluded that dismissing McCulloch would lose him more support than it would gain.[16]

Early in September the Northern states began holding their elections. The first state to vote was California. There the Democrats carried two of the three congressional districts and won control of the legislature. A few days later Maine counted its ballots: although the Democrats did not win—that would have required a miracle—the Republican majority fell from twenty-eight thousand in 1866 to only eleven thousand.

The crucial test, however, of which way the political wind was blowing took place on October 8 in Ohio and Pennsylvania. The results, wrote a happy Welles in his diary, "indicate the overthrow of the Radicals." In Pennsylvania, Republicans retained the legislature but the Democrats gained most of the executive and judicial offices. In Ohio, Republicans lost the legislature and their gubernatorial candidate, Rutherford B. Hayes, squeaked by with a mere 3,000-vote margin out of the 484,000 votes cast. Also the Ohioans overwhelmingly rejected Negro suffrage. The results in Ohio and Pennsylvania, along with those in California and Maine, were additional reasons why most Republicans ceased to talk of impeaching Johnson.

A month passed, then in November voters in the rest of the North and the Border states went to the polls. They put Democrats in power in New York and New Jersey and reelected them by increased majorities in Maryland and Kentucky. At the same time the voters decisively defeated Negro suffrage proposals in Minnesota, New Jersey, and Kansas—in the latter state by a two-to-one ratio. Even where the Republicans won, they usually did so by greatly reduced majorities. Overall, excluding the eleven former Confederate states, the Democrats garnered 1,628,183 votes, the Republicans, 1,578,748.[17]

Various factors accounted for the Republican reversals, including the economic situation. Ben Wade, however, provided the best as well as the bluntest explanation: "The nigger whipped us." Unlike 1866, when most Republican candidates carefully avoided the issue, in 1867 they came out in favor of Negro suffrage. Some did so out of idealistic conviction, others because they were conscious of the inconsistency, not to say hypocrisy, of imposing Negro suffrage on the South while it was generally nonexistent in the North. Nearly all of them believed, or at least hoped, that the Northern people were now prepared to accept it as the just and necessary completion of the process of emancipation. In response, Democrats accused Republicans of seeking to establish "Negro supremacy" and made blatant appeals to racial prejudice. "Any Democrat," wrote the French newspaper correspondent Georges Clemenceau, "who did not manage to hint in his speech that the negro is a degenerate gorilla, would be considered lacking in enthusiasm." The election results made it clear that this time the Democrats, not the Republicans, were in tune with popular sentiment. As a Republican politician in Illinois put it, "Negro suffrage hurt us here very considerable [sic]. A great many of our party here are mean enough to want it in the South, and not in the North."[18]

To Johnson the elections meant that his strategy of holding firm while the Republicans destroyed themselves with their own excesses had worked. When the returns from Ohio arrived, he telegraphed the Democratic Executive Committee there: "Ohio has done its duty and done it in time. God bless Ohio." And on November 13 he told serenaders at the White House: "I am gratified, but not surprised at the result of the recent elections. . . . I had still an abiding confidence in the people and felt assured that they in their might would come to the rescue. They have come, and thank God, they have come."[19]

The Democrats likewise were elated: they scented a return to power in 1868. But only a few of them gave Johnson any credit for what had happened. On the contrary the *New York World* and the *Chicago Times* declared that the victory belonged solely to the Democratic party. And in fact during the campaign most Democratic state conventions and candidates refrained from endorsing or defending Johnson. They solicited patronage from him but otherwise deemed him a political liability because of his unpopularity in the North. In the words of one of their leaders, they had no desire to take stock in Johnson himself—they were interested only in "administering on his estate."[20]

To the South the elections in the North were a welcome ray of hope. During the summer the cooperation strategy had failed miserably. The great mass of Negroes ignored the cajolings of their former masters and aligned themselves with their Republican liberators. At the same time large numbers of whites who retained the right to vote refrained from exercising it, whether out of apathy, repugnance at going to the polls with Negroes, or a feeling that it was useless to struggle against the congressional Reconstruction program. As a result, the Republicans had succeeded in obtaining majorities in favor of holding the constitutional conventions, the first step in the process of reorganizing Southern state governments, and in electing a majority of the delegates who would sit in these conventions. In the face of this defeat, most Southern leaders now urged whites to abstain from voting in the referendums that would be held on the constitutions to be produced by the conventions. By this tactic they sought to prevent the constitutions from going into effect, for under the provisions of the First Military Reconstruction Act a majority of all registered voters had to participate in ratifying them. This of course would mean continuation of military rule, but to most Southerners that was preferable to black rule. Meanwhile they would, and did, hope that the anti-Radical reaction in the North would increase, that the Democrats would overthrow the Republicans in 1868, and that then home rule and white supremacy would be restored to the South.[21]

As for the Republicans, they were disappointed but by no means dismayed by their setback. After all, they still controlled Congress and most of the North. In the estimation of the dominant Moderates, they could preserve their party's hold on national power by doing three things. First, they must back off from the extremism of the Radical "wild men," whom they blamed for antagonizing the Northern public with their agitation for Negro equality and impeachment. Second, the party must nominate Grant for president. Prior to the elections Moderates had considered this merely desirable; now they regarded it as necessary, for none of the other conceivable Republican candidates began to match his popularity in the North. Third, they must push ahead with military Reconstruction so that whatever gains the Democrats made in the North would be offset by the Republican takeover of the South.[22]

All Republicans concurred on this last objective. They also agreed that it would have to be achieved by means of the Negro vote. Efforts by Republican leaders during the summer to attract white support in the South had been no more successful than the attempt of Southerners to enlist blacks. Except in a few cases, Southern white Republicans remained, and were doomed to remain, a beleagured minority, dependent on the Negroes for political power and on the occupation troops for physical security.[23]

On the other hand many of the Radicals looked askance at nominating Grant. Some of them, notably Greeley and Butler, opposed the general for personal reasons—in Butler's case because Grant had publicly criticized his own inept performance as a general during the war. Others, such as Sumner and Stevens, doubted Grant's commitment to equal rights for the Negro and distrusted him because of his association and, as they saw it, cooperation with Johnson. At a Republican meeting in Washington, however, Sumner's plea not to bypass the party's political leaders in favor of the general fell on deaf ears. Like Galusha Grow of Illinois, the vast majority of Republicans believed that with Grant "as our candidate our success in the [1868] elections would be beyond doubt."[24]

Furthermore, despite the Democratic resurgence and the North's rejection of Negro suffrage, the Radicals refused to concede the need for moderation. "I thank God," declared Stevens, "for our late defeat. The Republicans have been acting a coward's part and have met a coward's fate." Along with Boutwell he announced his intention to press for impeachment and national Negro suffrage when Congress convened. Sumner did likewise. The elections, he stated, "only show more imperatively the necessity for impeachment." And Butler and Ashley continued to scurry about for evidence that might support impeachment charges.[25]

Johnson himself did not believe that the danger of impeachment had passed. Like certain historians, but with more justification, he exaggerated the power of Sumner, Stevens, Butler, and their ilk, thus believing that Radicals dominated the Republican party. He also feared that defeat would make the Republicans all the more desperate to deprive him of office and that they might even attempt an armed coup or place him under arrest. Consequently, like the year before when he was similarly alarmed, he summoned Sherman from St. Louis and, on October 7, asked him if he would be willing to serve as secretary of war or at least to remain in Washington; but again, as in 1866, Sherman's reaction was negative.

Following a regular cabinet meeting on October 8 (the day of the Ohio and Pennsylvania elections), Johnson discussed "the condition of affairs" with Stanbery, Browning, and Welles. Browning predicted that Congress would impeach Johnson when it convened. Furthermore, he asked what Grant would do if Congress passed a law ordering that the president be put under arrest while on trial. Johnson, who obviously had been pondering that very question, replied that Grant would obey it. Johnson added, however, that since the Supreme Court would be in session, the law could be declared unconstitutional immediately and that Grant would abide by the Court's decision. Browning was not so sure, and he suggested that Grant be replaced as secretary of war *ad interim* by Jacob Cox of Ohio. Welles, expressing doubt that Cox could be relied upon to "stand by the President against Congress," proposed instead Frank Blair, Jr. Then, after Browning and Stanbery left, Welles also mentioned Thomas Ewing, Sr., as a possibility. Ewing, he pointed out, "might have influence with Sherman, who had been his ward and who had married his daughter." On the other hand, Welles continued, it was unlikely that Ewing "would detach Sherman from Grant." This drew from Johnson the observation that Sherman had a "superior intellect to Grant." Welles agreed, but added that he lacked the "firmness, persistence, and stubborn will" of Grant, "and if there were to be antagonism with Grant, the President might have to depend on some other man than Sherman." Johnson then concluded the discussion by stating that "Grant had gone entirely over to the Radicals, and was with Congress"—an opinion Welles shared.[26]

Two days later Welles again advised Johnson not to depend on Sherman "as his reliable friend for such an emergency as was anticipated." Instead, Johnson should have a "frank and unreserved conversation with Grant," for it still might be possible to win him back from the "Radicals," in which case Congress "could do nothing." Johnson listened attentively, then thanked Welles for his views, and assured him that he would talk to Grant as soon as possible. Sherman, who left Washington on October 11, also urged Johnson to discuss matters with Grant.

On October 12 Johnson went to the War Department and bluntly asked Grant what he would do should an attempt be made to depose or arrest Johnson before a trial or conviction, or "if impeachment was attempted." Grant replied that he would obey the president's orders, but that should he "change his mind he would advise the President in season, that he might have time to make arrangements." Satisfied with this response, Johnson did not press the point further. Later he informed Welles of the interview and stated that he thought he "might rely on General Grant."[27]

Nevertheless, Johnson still would have preferred Sherman as secretary of war. And Grant for his part remained uncooperative in his dealings with Johnson. Thus when Johnson asked him to investigate a newspaper report that two regiments of Negro veterans were armed and drilling in the District of Columbia, Grant returned the president's request with the sarcastic endorsement: "In addition to military organization here reported, I understand there are four companies of white military in the District raised by the authority of the Government." The general's reply, Johnson remarked to Moore, "showed an unkind feeling."[28]

An even more unkind feeling was displayed by the House Judiciary Committee. On November 15 it resumed its efforts to locate a plausible excuse for impeachment, but the results were nil. The crackpot Radical, Congressman Ashley, admitted as much. When asked by a committee member whether he had any evidence to support his charge that Johnson had plotted Lincoln's assassination, Ashley replied that "it was not that kind of evidence which would satisfy the great mass of men, especially men who do not concur with me in my theory about this matter." What was his theory? It was that all vice-presidents who had become president had done so through murder. Nevertheless, on November 25 the committee voted 5 to 4 to submit a report recommending Johnson's impeachment. Representative John C. Churchill of New York, hitherto opposed to impeachment, had joined Boutwell and the other Radical members. He gave as his reasons Stanton's suspension and the removal of Sheridan and of Sickles. Welles believed, however, that he had been bribed by Wall Street speculators who (mistakenly) "expected that a resolution for impeachment would cause a sudden rise in gold."[29]

Johnson received advance notice of the committee's action on November 21. He remarked, "So let it be." His main fear continued to be that Congress would try to suspend him from office or arrest him prior to a trial. On November 30 he met with the cabinet, Grant included. After Moore read the draft of the annual message, to which nobody voiced any objection, Johnson presented a memorandum, drafted by Jeremiah Black and then revised by himself, which set forth the constitutional issues involved in possible congressional actions seeking to remove or replace him as president. All of the cabinet members agreed that Johnson should submit to being tried under the articles of impeachment voted by the House, but that he should not allow himself to be suspended or arrested before conviction. Grant, in expressing his views, said that it "would be clearly *ex post facto* to pass a law for suspension in the case of the President, and unless the Supreme Court sustained, it ought not to be submitted to." He also stated that he thought "a mere law of Congress would not justify suspension or authorize it, but that there should be an amendment to the Constitution to effect it." Johnson, Moore noted, "was much gratified" by the cabinet's response. After the meeting adjourned the president declared: "The day has produced great results. The time for mere defense is now past and I can stand on the offensive in behalf of the Constitution and the country."[30]

On December 3 the offensive began. That day Johnson sent his message to Congress. Written primarily by Black (Johnson rejected a conciliatory draft prepared by Seward), it contained two sections of special significance. The first, which followed a denunciation of military Reconstruction as unconstitutional and tyrannical, employed the same technique so successfully used by the Democrats in the recent elections—an appeal to white radical fears and prejudice:

> The blacks in the South are entitled to be well and humanely governed, and to have the protection of just laws for all their rights of person and property. . . . [If, however,] it were practicable at this time to give them a Government exclusively their own . . . it would become a grave question whether we ought to do so, or whether common humanity would not require us to save them from themselves. But under the circumstances this is only a speculative point. It is not proposed merely that they shall govern themselves, but that they shall rule the white race, make and administer State laws, elect Presidents and members of Congress, and shape to a greater or less extent the future destiny of the whole country. Would such a trust and power be safe in such hands?
>
> The peculiar qualities which should characterize any people who are fit to decide upon the management of public affairs for a great state have seldom been combined. It is the glory of white men to know that they have had these qualities in sufficient measure to build upon this continent a great political fabric and to preserve its stability for more than ninety years, while in every other part of the world all similar experiments have failed. But if anything can be proved by known facts, if all reasoning upon evidence is not abandoned, it must be acknowledged that in the progress of nations negroes have shown less capacity for government than any other race or people. No independent government of any form has ever been successful in their hands. On the contrary, wherever they have been left to their own devices they have shown a constant tendency to relapse into barbarism.[31]

The second section was an implicit but clear warning that Johnson would forcibly resist any attempt to deprive him of office without an impeachment trial:

> How far the duty of the President "to preserve, protect, and defend the Constitution" requires him to go in opposing an unconstitutional act of Congress is a very serious and important question. . . . Where an act has been passed according to the forms of the Constitution by the supreme legislative authority . . . Executive resistance to it, especially in times of high party excitement, would be likely to produce violent collision between the respective adherents of the two branches of the Government. This would be simply civil war, and civil war must be restored to only as the last remedy for the worst of evils. Whatever might tend to provoke it should be most carefully avoided. A faithful and conscientious magistrate will concede very much to honest error. . . . [However] cases may occur in which the Executive would be compelled to stand on its rights, and maintain them regardless of all consequences. If Congress should pass an act which is not only in palpable confl.ct with the Constitution, but will certainly, if carried out, produce immediate and irreparable injury to the organic structure of the Government, and if there be neither judicial remedy for the wrongs it inflicts nor power in the people to protect themselves without the official aid of their elected defender—if, or instance, the legislative department should pass an act . . . to abolish a co-ordinate department of the Government—in such a case the President must take the high responsibilities of his office and save the life of the nation at all hazards.[32]

The "so-called reconstruction acts," Johnson continued, although "plainly unconstitutional," were not in the category which required the president to resist them by force:

> The people were not wholly disarmed of the power of self-defense. In all the Northern States they still held in their hands the sacred right of the ballot, and it was safe to believe that in due time they would come to the rescue of their own institutions. It gives me pleasure to add that the appeal to our common constituents was not taken in vain, and that my confidence in their wisdom and virtue seems not to have been misplaced.[33]

The message, no doubt as Johnson intended, caused the Radicals to boil with rage. It was, asserted Sumner, "an incendiary document calculated to stimulate the rebellion once more and to provoke civil war." It also intensified their desire to impeach the president. On December 5 Boutwell moved that the House adopt the Judiciary Committee's report calling for impeachment. But Wilson, the committee's chairman, countered with a minority report stating that there was no legal basis for such action. After acrimonious debate between Moderates and Radicals, the House on December 7 rejected Boutwell's report by a vote of 108 to 57. Sixty-six Republicans joined 42 Democrats in the negative. They agreed with Garfield that Boutwell had "not made out a case."[34]

Johnson's organ, the *National Intelligencer*, in support of Johnson promptly proclaimed "The Death of Impeachment." The *New York Times* echoed, with a headline proclaiming, "End of the Impeachment Folly." Even the *Chicago Tribune* declared that Congress deserved well of the country for defeating "this source of mischief." In contrast the Radical leader Julian of Indiana thought it was "pitiful" the way "Congress backed down on impeachment," and Wendell Phillips gave a lecture entitled "The Surrender of Congress."[35]

On December 12, in accordance with the Tenure of Office Act, Johnson transmitted to the Senate a message giving the reasons why he had suspended Stanton. It ably and accurately described Stanton's obstructionist conduct. It also revealed publicly for the first time Stanton's withholding of Baird's telegram prior to the New Orleans riot and Stanton's support of the veto of the tenure act.[36] As a result only the most fanatical Radicals could now claim that the president lacked just grievances against Stanton.

Six days later Johnson dispatched yet another message to Capitol Hill. This time he asked Congress to commend General Hancock, who on assuming command of the Fifth District had announced that he intended to uphold the "civil authorities in the faithful execution of the laws." The Republicans greeted the president's proposal with laughter but Johnson did not care. He merely was displaying his own contempt for the Republicans, who recently had passed a resolution praising Sheridan and Sickles and deploring their removal.[37]

Hancock's conduct pleased Johnson; that of General Pope, commanding the Third District of Georgia, Alabama, and Florida, did not. Early in December Pope climaxed a long series of actions avowedly designed to abet the Republicans by issuing an order requiring the state treasurer of Georgia to pay the expenses of the Radical-dominated constitutional convention and then threatened to remove him if he did not comply. In addition, at about the same time Johnson received a letter from John Forsyth, editor of a Mobile paper, declaring that if Pope were out of the way, Republican-Negro domination of Alabama could be prevented. Johnson, who hitherto had refrained from dismissing Pope out of expediency, waited no longer. On December 27 he directed Grant to replace Pope with Major General George G. Meade, the apolitical victor of Gettysburg. Johnson also acceded to Ord's request, which had been seconded by Grant, to be relieved as commander of the Fourth District. Grant did not concur in Pope's being supplanted but neither did he object. On December 28, therefore, he issued orders transferring both Pope and Ord to new posts. Of the five original district commanders, only Schofield in Virginia now remained.[38]

The removal of Pope and of Ord caused the *Chicago Tribune* to ask in exasperation, "Cannot Congress devise some means of checkmating the villainous conspiracy of Johnson & Co. to defeat the restoration [i.e., the Republican takeover] . . . of the Southern States?"[39] The answer, as 1868 got underway, seemed to be no. On December 18 the House had passed a bill sponsored by Stevens that was designed to defeat the new Southern tactic of nonparticipation in the constitutional referendums by requiring only a majority of the votes cast to put a constitution into effect. The Senate, however, had failed to take any action on the measure. Likewise that body had blocked another House bill which gave Grant the sole power to appoint or remove military commanders in the South and authorized him to replace Southern civil officials. Last, but most importantly of all, the Republican majority had been unable to agree on how to cope with the political force potentially more dangerous than even the president—namely, the Supreme Court.

In November 1867 General Ord had arrested William H. McCardle, editor of the *Vicksburg* (Mississippi) *Times*, and ordered that he be tried before a military commission on the charges of violating the military Reconstruction laws and of libeling General Ord. Taking ironic advantage of a congressional act intended to protect Negroes from Southern injustice, McCardle had applied to a federal district judge for a writ of habeas corpus. The judge had denied the writ, but McCardle had then appealed to the Supreme Court. Should the Court take his case, and should it follow the precedent set by *Ex Parte Milligan*, then the military Reconstruction acts would be declared unconstitutional! The Republicans knew this and furthermore they knew that Johnson knew it: His confidant, Jeremiah Black, had agreed to represent McCardle before the Court.[40]

Therefore, early in December the House had passed a bill prohibiting the Supreme Court from declaring any federal law unconstitutional by less than a 6 to 3 majority (the Radicals had wanted to require unanaminity). Since only five of the justices had joined in the *Milligan* decision, the intent of this measure was only too obvious. But for the more conservative members of the Senate it also was too drastic. Hence they took no action on it and instead endeavored through Trumbull, who was serving as Ord's attorney, to persuade the Supreme Court to turn down McCardle's appeal. On January 21, however, after listening to a plea from Black to expedite proceedings, the Court announced that it would hear the case on March 1; furthermore, on February 17 it rejected a desperation argument by Trumbull that the Court lacked jurisdiction over the matter.

The Republican's failure to repel promptly Johnson's assault on military Reconstruction and the collapse of the impeachment movement caused Thomas Ewing, Sr., to assert that "the President has Congress on the hip." Boutwell agreed; if things went on as they were, he predicted on January 17, Johnson and the South would prevent Negroes from voting in the upcoming presidential election. As a consequence the Southern states would go to the Democratic candidate and a year hence, "this country will be brought again to the extremity of civil war, or we shall be compelled to surrender . . . to the rebels . . . who are yet struggling through their alliance with the Executive to destroy the Government."[41]

There was one thing, however, on which the Republicans had no trouble agreeing and acting: Johnson must not be allowed to displace Stanton. If that happened, the Tenure of Office Act would become a dead letter and Johnson would be free to name a secretary of war who would cooperate in dismantling military Reconstruction. This the Republicans could not permit: It would mean the loss of their power in the South and eventually in the nation.

Accordingly, on January 7 Jacob Howard of Michigan, chairman of the Senate Military Affairs Committee to which Johnson's message on Stanton's suspension had been referred, laid before the committee a report written with Stanton's aid. It contained a deliberate falsehood designed to clear Stanton of any blame for the New Orleans riot and concluded that Stanton's suspension was unjustified. Simultaneously Howard leaked the report to the press, thus making Johnson cognizant of its contents. At once Johnson instructed Moore to prepare both a letter dismissing (not merely suspending) Stanton and a message to the Senate informing it of that action. Johnson wanted these documents ready, he explained, "for signature at any moment." Moore called his attention to published stories that "Grant had expressed an intention to transfer the War Office to Mr. Stanton, in case the Senate should decide in the latter's favor." Johnson answered that Grant had promised him "that his actions would be limited to withdrawing from the Department and leaving it in the hands of the President." (Johnson presumably was referring to his October 12 interview with Grant.) Indeed, continued Johnson, "Perhaps it would be well for the Senate to reinstate the Secretary, as he could at once be removed, and in the meantime General Grant [could] be gotten rid of. . . ." For "Grant has served the purpose for which he had been selected, and it is desirable that he should be superseded in the War Office by another."[42]

On Friday, January 10, Howard presented his report to the full Senate, then moved the adoption of a resolution of nonconcurrence in Stanton's suspension. Democratic opposition, however, prevented the Republicans from taking action either that day or on Saturday, with the result that the matter had to be carried over until Monday. Meanwhile, on Saturday, at the War Department, Grant discussed the situation with Sherman, who had returned to Washington on routine army business. Grant told Sherman that he had decided to relinquish the office of secretary of war if the Senate disapproved of Stanton's suspension. Sherman thereupon advised Grant to inform the president of his decision.

Later that day Grant visited Johnson at the White House. For the first time ever, the general asserted, he had read the Tenure of Office Act. On doing so he had discovered that if he remained on as secretary of war after the Senate refused to concur in the suspension of Stanton, he would be subject to fine and imprisonment! Hence, Grant said, if the Senate so acted he would surrender the post.

It is conceivable that Grant hitherto had not read the tenure act—although earlier he had seen fit to lecture Johnson on its terms. His claim that he was afraid of being fined or imprisoned, however, was preposterous: The chance of the Republicans doing either to the North's number one hero and their prospective presidential candidate was nil. Knowing this, Johnson countered with a preposterous proposal of his own: If Grant would remain at the War Department, Johnson himself would pay his fine or go to jail in his place! But Grant need not worry about the Tenure of Office Act,

Johnson added; Stanton had been suspended under the president's constitutional authority and Grant appointed interim secretary of war by virtue of the same. The unconstitutional tenure act, Johnson concluded, did not apply. Grant replied that he was nevertheless bound by the act until the courts declared it unconstitutional. For an hour Johnson argued with him. Finally he asked Grant to return to the White House on Monday and continue the discussion. The president understood Grant to say that he would. To Johnson this meant that Grant would adhere to his promise not to vacate the War Department without prior notice.[43]

On Sunday a "greatly concerned" Grant again sought Sherman's counsel. He told Sherman that he still planned to relinquish his post as secretary of war if the Senate refused to concur in Stanton's suspension, but that he "felt that . . . the workings of the government would be needlessly thwarted by the intrusion of an unwelcome Cabinet officer upon the Head of State." Sherman thereupon suggested that the solution would be for Johnson to appoint Jacob Cox to the position. Presumably, Sherman reasoned, this very moderate Republican, who also had been an excellent general during the war, would be acceptable to the Senate and tolerable to the president. Grant liked the idea and asked Sherman to propose it to Johnson. On Monday Sherman did so. Meanwhile, at Sherman's behest Reverdy Johnson and Thomas Ewing, Sr., likewise urged Johnson to appoint Cox. Ewing wrote President Johnson on Sunday that he had "assurance" that if Cox was nominated on Monday morning, "he will be confirmed at once, and no direct vote will be taken on Stanton—indirectly this will sanction his removal." But, warned Ewing, "It must be done tomorrow morning, or the occasion will have gone by. It will avoid unpleasant complications, of which we have had as many as the country can well endure."[44]

Monday, January 13, passed. Johnson did not send to the Senate the nomination of Cox or anyone else as secretary of war. Obviously, despite the promptings of Sherman, Reverdy Johnson, and Ewing, the president did not consider the matter urgent. Apparently, too, he resented others telling him in effect whom to select for his cabinet.

The day also went by without Grant visiting the White House as he had promised. Either he forgot, which is unlikely, or else—and this is probable—he decided it would serve no useful purpose to talk further with Johnson. Late that afternoon the Senate adopted Howard's resolution by a vote of 36 to 6. Stanton held a celebration at his house. Grant, on learning of the Senate's action, wrote a letter resigning as secretary of war. He then went to a White House reception. Johnson greeted him but did not ask him why he had failed to see him during the day. Grant for his part did not mention his letter of resignation.

At nine o'clock Tuesday morning, Grant entered the War Department building, locked the secretary of war's office, and gave the key to Acting Adjutant General Edward D. Townsend. An hour later a beaming Stanton arrived, obtained the key from Townsend, and entered his old office. His first act was to draw $3,000 in pay. Next he sent an orderly across the street to army headquarters to fetch Grant. The general was annoyed at being summoned in so cavalier a fashion. Also, he claimed afterwards to have been surprised and offended by the manner in which Stanton reoccupied the War Office. He had, Grant subsequently asserted, expected Stanton to request in writing the return of the office, whereupon he had planned to notify Johnson that he had relinquished it and thus give the president an opportunity to take control of it.[45]

Grant probably told the truth about his expectations and intentions.[46] But why then did he give the office key to Townsend? When Grant did that, in effect, he gave up the office. His dominant desire, obviously, was to avoid being caught in the impending collision between the president and Congress. Although he did not conspire with Stanton, neither did he act as he knew Johnson, whether reasonably or not, expected him to.

Despite his irritation at Stanton's summons, Grant went over to see him. First, however, he sent one of his aides, General Cyrus B. Comstock, to the White House with his letter of resignation and a copy of the Senate's resolution of nonconcurrence in Stanton's suspension. Under the circumstances it was the least Grant could do.

After Johnson read Grant's letter, he told Comstock that he "supposed General Grant would be very soon at the cabinet meeting." Then, as soon as Comstock left, Johnson indignantly denounced "Grant's duplicity." No later than last Saturday, he told Moore, "Grant had distinctly told him" that if he found himself unable to stand against the Senate's determination to reject Stanton's suspension, he would give the president the opportunity to appoint someone else secretary of war. Johnson appeared calm, however, when the cabinet assembled a short time later. Grant, who interpreted Johnson's statement to Comstock as an invitation to attend, was present. Johnson followed the regular order of business. When the War Department's turn came, he asked Grant if he had any matters to report. Grant answered that he no longer was secretary of war.

Johnson maintained "perfect self-control" but his voice was cold as he began firing questions at Grant. Back in October, he asked, had Grant not agreed to remain at the head of the War Department until the courts determined the legal issues involved in Stanton's suspension, or at least to leave any subsequent appointment to the office at the president's disposal?

Grant admitted that this was so, but again resorted to the nonsensical excuse that he had made the agreement before learning of the penalties to which he was exposed under the Tenure of Office Act.

Why, persisted Johnson, had Grant failed to discuss the matter with him on Monday, as agreed?

Grant said he had been "busy with General Sherman, and had a good many little matters to attend to." Besides, he "did not suppose the Senate intended to act so soon." (This was more nonsense on Grant's part, for everybody knew that the Senate intended to act as soon as possible.)

"Was not our understanding—did you not assure me some time ago, and again on Saturday, that if you did not hold on to the office yourself, you would place it in my hands that I might select another?" asked Johnson.

"That," replied Grant, "was my intention. I thought some satisfactory arrangement would be made to dispose of the subject. . . . I sent General Sherman yesterday after talking the matter over. Didn't you see Sherman?"

Johnson said that he had seen him but that this was beside the point. "Why did you give up the keys to Mr. Stanton and leave the Department?" he asked.

Grant answered that he "gave the key to the Adjutant General and sent word to the President by General Comstock."

Johnson then reminded Grant that "that, you know, was not our understanding."

According to Welles, Grant "attempted some further apologies about being very busy, stammered, hesitated, said Sherman had taken up a great deal of his time, but he had intended to call on the President on Monday." He then asked to be excused and left. Johnson subsequently described Grant as having "an abashed look never to be forgotten." Welles thought "his manner, never very commanding, was almost abject." McCulloch believed that Grant was drunk.[47]

The next morning the *National Intelligencer* carried an article which accused Grant of betraying the president and of lying during the previous day's cabinet meeting. The obvious assumption is that the article had been planted by Johnson or at least appeared with his knowledge. If so, and probably it was so, Johnson was giving vent to his resentment over what he considered to be Grant's treachery and also possibly seeking to ruin Grant's presidential prospects by ruining his reputation.

As might be expected the article upset Grant. Accompanied by Sherman, he went to the White House. Johnson received them, in Sherman's words, "promptly and kindly." "Mr. President," Grant began, "whoever gave the facts for the article of the *Intelligencer* this morning has made some serious mistakes." Johnson thereupon said, "General Grant, let me interrupt you just there. I have not seen the *Intelligencer* of this morning, and have no knowledge of the content of any article therein." Probably Grant did not believe this, but he was not prepared to call the president a liar to his face. So he simply repeated his denial of having broken his word to Johnson: Instead of Stanton's sending him a written demand for the War Office, as he had anticipated, "Stanton was in the office before he knew it."

Johnson seemed to be placated by the general's explanation and, according to Sherman, the two "entered into a general friendly conversation, both parties professing to be satisfied." Indeed, after a while Grant offered to urge Stanton to resign for the "good of the service." Moreover, as he and Sherman were leaving, Grant also said, "Mr. President, you should make some order that we of the army are not bound to obey the orders of Mr. Stanton as Secretary of War." Johnson indicated that he would do this. Then, after the two generals left, he asked Moore to read him the *Intelligencer* article. (Without his glasses, which he rarely wore except when alone, Johnson had trouble reading small print.) After Moore finished, Johnson commented that the article was "substantially true." Later that day he told Welles that Grant and Sherman had been to see him, that "Grant attempted to explain," but "only reaffirmed the fact that he had not been true to the understanding and his pledged word."[48]

On January 18 Grant again visited the White House. According to Johnson's account as recorded by Moore, he "spoke of the insignificance to which Mr. Stanton could be reduced in his present position" and declared that he "would not obey Mr. Stanton's orders unless he knew they emanated from the President." Johnson thereupon gave Grant verbal instructions to disregard Stanton. Grant in turn once more stated that he would urge Stanton to resign.[49]

The next day Grant called on Stanton. But Stanton, perceiving Grant's purpose, adopted an "imperious and angry look" as he launched into a "loud and violent" tirade against his enemies. Grant, as he reported to Sherman later that day, "soon found that to recommend resignation to Mr. Stanton would have no effect, unless it was to incur further his displeasure." Welles, when he learned of the "interview" via the Washington grapevine, was not far off the mark when he commented that Stanton had "overawed" Grant.[50]

Grant likewise failed to carry out Johnson's instructions to ignore Stanton's orders, realizing that it would be very risky without written authorization. Also his anger at Johnson had been revived —or rather intensified—by the embarrassing accounts of the January 14 cabinet meeting which continued to appear in the press. Hence on January 24 he wrote Johnson asking that the president's instructions regarding Stanton be put in writing. Johnson, however, did not comply with his request. According to Moore, Johnson remarked that Grant "had been very restive under Mr. Stanton, had evidently been very glad to get rid of him, had now put him back in the War Department, and he [Johnson] thought he would let them fight it out."[51]

On January 28 Grant repeated his request for written instructions; he desired them, he wrote, because of "the many and gross misrepresentations affecting my personal honor" which were being circulated in the press and which purported to "come from the President." Then, in great detail, Grant proceeded again to deny that he had broken his promise to Johnson with respect to retaining control of the War Department.

Grant's letter exasperated Johnson. "I have tried to be decent," he declared to Moore. "I know my nature and I will be damned if some things have not gone about as far as they are to go." Taking Grant's January 24 note, he sent it back to the general with the endorsement: "As requested in this communication, General Grant is instructed in writing, not to obey any orders from the War Department [i.e., Stanton] . . . unless such order is known by the General commanding the armies of the United States to have been authorized by the Executive."[52] Then, aided by Moore, he set to work preparing a reply to Grant's latest attempt to defend his recent conduct.

On January 30 Grant again wrote Johnson, this time with reference to the endorsement instructing him to ignore Stanton's orders:

"I am informed by the Secretary of War that he has not received from the Executive any order or instructions limiting or impairing his authority to issue orders to the army. . . . While this authority to the War Department is not countermanded, it will be satisfactory evidence to me that any orders issued from the War Department . . . are authorized by the Executive."[53] In other words, Grant would not obey the president's instructions (which he himself had solicited) to disregard Stanton's orders unless Johnson also commanded Stanton not to issue orders to Grant! Nothing could have been more absurd, but it served Grant's purpose, which was to wiggle free of his agreement with Johnson to reduce Stanton to "insignificance."

On January 31 Johnson, after incorporating some changes suggested by the cabinet, sent his reply to Grant's January 28 letter. Again he accused Grant of failing to keep faith and stated that five members of the cabinet concurred in the "general accuracy" of the *Intelligencer* article. Three days later Grant responded with a letter that had been written by his chief of staff, General John A. Rawlins, in lieu of Grant's original rejoinder which Rawlins had found to contain some damaging admissions. In the message Grant repeated his now-standard defense of his conduct, then closed by declaring: "And now, Mr. President, when my honor as a soldier and integrity as a man have been so violently assailed, pardon me for saying that I can but regard this whole matter, from the beginning to the end, as an attempt to involve me in the resistance of law . . . and thus [to] destroy my character before the country"—and also, Rawlins might have added, to wreck Grant's presidential prospects.[54]

That same day, February 3, the House passed a resolution, introduced by a friend of Stanton's, calling on the secretary of war to produce the correspondence between Grant and the president. Stanton, of course, promptly furnished copies of all the letters recently exchanged between the two, including Grant's latest. This confirmed the belief held by Johnson and his inner circle that Grant had conspired with Stanton all along. When Johnson had his correspondence with Grant read to the cabinet on February 4, all the members except Seward, who kept silent, joined in condemning the general. The following day Johnson showed Stanbery and Welles the draft of a reply to Grant's February 3 communication. Both advised against sending it; but after Johnson said he believed it best to reply, Stanbery proposed that since "the question was now one of veracity between the President and the General, the members of the Cabinet who were present at the Cabinet meeting of the 14th ultimo should be called upon for a statement respecting the conversation which then took place." Johnson accepted this suggestion and asked all of the cabinet members to furnish him with such statements. On February 10 he sent his reply, backed by the cabinet's testimony, to Grant. Even Seward, who obviously wished to avoid offending the general, stated that during the January 14 cabinet meeting Grant did not "insist" that he had told Johnson that he planned to surrender the War Department to Stanton without first notifying Johnson and that Grant had "admitted that it was his expectation or purpose" to visit Johnson on the Monday prior to Stanton's takeover.[55]

Grant responded, very feebly, on February 11, thus ending the great epistolary altercation between the president and the commanding general. Soon the newspapers published the letters, and at once debate broke out over who was lying—a debate historians have continued. Suffice to say that Thad Stevens was probably correct when he declared, "They both do lie a little, though the President has the weight of evidence on his side. . . ."[56]

Grant's conduct, and his consequent prevarications, can be explained—if not excused—by his fear of offending the Republicans by appearing to be Johnson's cat's-paw in preventing Stanton from recovering control of the War Department. (Of course, that is just the role the president had in mind.) Then, after publication of the *Intelligencer* article and the subsequent newspaper assaults on his truthfulness, Grant concluded—with good cause—that Johnson sought to ruin him personally and politically.[57] Therefore, he deliberately picked a public quarrel with Johnson in order to signal his total break with the president and allegiance to the Republicans. As a result even the Radicals dropped their suspicions of Grant. "Won't it do now," a Radical asked Stevens "to let Grant into our church?" "Yes," replied Stevens, "open the doors and let him in. He is a bolder man than I thought him to be."[58]

Johnson himself made the best comment on Grant's conduct. Writing to a friend some eight months later, the president stated, "Grant did the proper thing to save Grant, but it pretty nearly ruined me." Then he added: "I might have done the same thing under the same circumstances. At any rate, most men would. . . ."[59]

As so often before, Johnson had himself largely to blame for being "pretty nearly ruined" by Grant. He first blundered by relying on Grant to aid him in keeping Stanton out of the War Department and in getting the whole issue before the courts. Johnson had ample reason to distrust Grant, and in effect Grant himself warned the president not to rely upon him in this matter. What the president should have done was to have secured Grant's resignation as secretary of war on January 11 and replaced him with someone who was dependable. Apparently, however, Johnson still felt that he needed Grant—or, to be more exact, could make use of him.

Johnson blundered again by not following the advice of Sherman, Ewing, and Reverdy Johnson to nominate Cox as secretary of war. Almost surely this would have led Grant, Sherman, and the Moderates to exert irresistable pressure on Stanton to resign, thereby ending the whole controversy.

Finally Johnson blundered by attacking Grant in the newspapers. To be sure he had suffered great provocation and the truth was largely on his side. But by thus indulging his wrath, he caused Grant, who obviously felt at least somewhat ashamed of his conduct, to back off from his promise to urge Stanton to resign, to break his agreement to ignore Stanton's orders, and to become an overt and embittered personal enemy. Moreover, when Johnson, the most unpopular man in the North, accused the nation's most popular man of lying, the majority of Northerners believed the hero of Appomattox rather than the drunken tailor. It was Johnson, not Grant, who got hurt.

But this was just the beginning of the consequences Johnson would suffer from his mishandling of the Stanton affair. More disastrous results were soon to follow.

9

★★★★★

IMPEACHMENT

Once it became evident that Grant indeed had "gone over," Johnson turned, as he had twice before, to Sherman. He was aware that Sherman passionately desired to stay clear of politics, and he had been warned repeatedly by Welles that Sherman never would oppose Grant. Even so Johnson believed—or perhaps desperately hoped—that Sherman could be prevailed upon to serve as the instrument for prying Stanton loose from the War Department. After all, Sherman had in private sharply criticized the congressional Reconstruction program; he was Thomas Ewing's son-in-law; and above all he detested Stanton.

On January 24 (the day he received Grant's request for written authorization to ignore Stanton's orders) Johnson offered Sherman an appointment as interim secretary of war. Sherman politely declined, citing family obligations. At the same time he gave Johnson a letter from his father-in-law in which Ewing stated that "it is not expedient for the President to take any action now in the case of Stanton." By attempting to dislodge him, Ewing argued, Johnson merely would expose himself to impeachment. On the other hand, Ewing felt that if Stanton was "left to perform his clerical duties," then the Republicans would have to "bear the odium which is already upon them for placing him where he is."[1]

Despite Sherman's refusal and Ewing's advice, on January 30 Johnson asked Sherman to take command of a military department to be created in the East with headquarters at Washington, after which he would assume the duties of secretary of war. Again Sherman said no, this time most emphatically. Neverthless Johnson adhered to this scheme. When Welles asked the president on February 5 what he would do if Congress, backed by Grant, tried to arrest him, Johnson "became somewhat excited, arose, and walked the room," then "suggested that Washington might be made a military department and Sherman ordered to it. Sherman, he knew, would take it." Accordingly, the next day Johnson issued an order establishing the Military Division of the Atlantic and directing Sherman, who had returned to St. Louis, to come to Washington "as early as may be practicable." This, he remarked to Moore, would "set some persons to thinking."[2]

But then on February 7 Johnson withdrew the order. Presumably he had had some second thoughts. Three days later, however, the House transferred its impeachment investigation from the Judiciary Committee to Thad Stevens's Committee on Reconstruction. Also, at about the same time Senator George F. Edmunds of Vermont presented a bill providing for the suspension of the president in case he was impeached. On February 12, faced with these ominous moves by his enemies, Johnson renewed the order, supplementing it by promoting Sherman to full general, the same rank Grant held.

If Johnson thought that the higher rank would induce Sherman to come to Washington and to his assistance, he soon learned otherwise. Sherman not only protested Johnson's order, he even threatened to resign from the army and telegraphed his brother to oppose Senate confirmation of his promotion. He was quite sincere in his wish to avoid political entanglements, and Welles was correct in predicting that Sherman never would go counter to Grant. In a letter to Ewing asking him to intercede with Johnson, Sherman stated that "Grant and I were bound by such ties during the war . . . that I would be mean indeed to allow myself to be used against him in the few short months remaining to President Johnson." He also observed in the same letter that although he regarded Johnson's original efforts to reconstruct the South "nearer right than have since been attempted" by Congress, he had no intention of going "into the wilderness" with the president: "He never heeds any advice. He attempts to govern after he has lost the means to govern. He is like a general fighting without an army—he is like Lear roaring at the wild storm, bareheaded and helpless."[3]

Sherman's strenuous, almost frantic, objections left Johnson with no choice except to withdraw the order creating the Atlantic Division and Sherman's nomination to full general. Besides, all of a sudden there no longer seemed to be any pressing need for Sherman's presence in Washington. On February 14 Stevens had presented to the Committee on Reconstruction a resolution recommending Johnson's impeachment on the grounds that he had conspired to violate the Tenure of Office Act by attempting to induce Grant to withhold the War Department from Stanton. Since Johnson obviously had failed to gain Grant's cooperation, however, the committee had rejected the resolution by a vote of 6 to 3. Stevens, Boutwell, and another Radical formed the minority; four other Republicans joined two Democrats in the majority. Disgusted, Stevens had denounced his fellow Republicans as cowards and declared, "I shall never bring up this question of impeachment again."[4]

Thus in mid February Johnson could feel, and probably did feel, that he had weathered the storm caused by his quarrel with Grant. Yet, Stanton remained secretary of war. Of course, as Ewing, Sherman, and others pointed out, Stanton was confined to transacting petty bureaucratic business; and not even he possessed the temerity to show up for a cabinet meeting. Had he done so, quite likely and quite literally Johnson would have kicked him out of the White House. But all the same, his continued presence in the War Department was intolerable to Johnson. It represented a personal defeat and a personal insult; it constituted defiance of his lawful authority as president; and it stood as an obstacle to further progress in his counteroffensive against military Reconstruction, which recently had scored a major victory in Alabama. There the whites, by staying away from the polls, had prevented ratification of the Republican-made constitution by denying it the needed majority of registered voters.

Hence, as soon as it became apparent that Sherman would not serve the purpose, Johnson began to look around for someone else to perform the dual function of getting Stanton out of office and the tenure act into the courts, where he was confident that it would be declared unconstitutional. In so doing he deliberately disregarded the advice of Sherman and Ewing, which Stanbery seconded, to leave Stanton alone and thus avoid a potentially disastrous confrontation with Congress. On Sunday morning, February 16, after attending church, the president had Moore read to him from Addison's drama *Cato*, then commented that "Cato was a man who would not compromise with wrong but being right, died before he would yield."[5]

The next day, acting on Johnson's instructions, Moore offered John Potts, chief clerk of the War Department, the interim post of secretary of war. Since Potts was designated by law as custodian of all official War Department papers in case of a vacancy in the office of secretary of war, Johnson considered him the appropriate person to replace Stanton until a regular appointment could be made. Moore explained to Potts that his primary task would be to demand the papers from Stanton and, if Stanton refused to surrender them, to take the issue to the courts. But, in Moore's words, "Mr. Potts shrank from this." Stanton, he whimpered, had appointed him chief clerk and would fire him if he asked for the papers. In any case, Potts did not want to offend Stanton, who had done him personal favors. So Moore returned to the White House and reported the failure of his mission. Johnson "seemed displeased" and said that "if he could only get the proper man, he would settle the matter this morning."[6]

But who was the proper man? Johnson pondered the problem for a couple of days, then decided on Major General Lorenzo P. Thomas. Recently, at Welles's prompting, Johnson had ordered Thomas, after a long absence from Washington, to assume his former post as adjutant general of the army (thus superseding Townsend, the officer who had handed over the keys of the War Office to Stanton). Thomas, to be sure, was old, rather weak in mind and character, and unpopular in the army. Like Potts, however, his official position suited him for taking over temporarily as secretary of war; he was known to hold a grudge against Stanton for exiling him from Washington; and in Johnson's opinion he was "right minded"—that is, he supported the president against Congress.[7]

On February 19 Johnson discussed with Moore the expediency of naming Thomas as secretary of war. Moore asked if Thomas's appointment "would carry with it any weight." Johnson admitted that it would not. Even so, in Moore's words, he was "determined to remove Stanton. Self respect demanded it and if the people did not respect their Chief Magistrate enough to sustain him in such a measure, the President ought to resign."[8]

Johnson, however, hesitated another day. Then on February 21 he acted with abrupt decisiveness. Entering his office early in the morning, he instructed Moore first to prepare an order removing Stanton and appointing Thomas as interim secretary of war; second, to write a letter notifying Stanton of his dismissal; third, to ask Seward to bring the cabinet the nomination of George B. McClellan as minister to England (presumably to ensure Democratic support); and finally, to send the Senate the nomination of George H. Thomas as a full general. (Probably Johnson intended to place the "Rock of Chickamauga" in the role originally cast for Sherman.)

Next Johnson sent for Lorenzo Thomas. Earlier, on February 18, he had asked Thomas to serve temporarily as secretary of war and Thomas had agreed. When Thomas arrived at the White House, about 9 A.M., Johnson handed him the order naming him to that position and also the letter dismissing Stanton. He then showed him the laws pertaining to cabinet appointments and removals and advised him to take along a witness to the War Department. Thomas said he would do so and that he would report back in person to the president.[9]

Shortly before 11 A.M. Thomas entered the War Department and, accompanied by one of his staff officers, knocked on the door of the secretary of war's office. Stanton told him to come in. Walking across the room, Thomas handed Stanton the president's dismissal notice. Probably it did not surprise Stanton. Two days before, War Department clerks had observed Thomas looking up the provisions of the Tenure of Office Act; also Thomas had "confidentially" informed Townsend that soon he would replace Stanton.

After reading the notice, Stanton asked Thomas, "Do you wish me to vacate at once, or am I to be permitted to stay long enough to remove my property?" Thomas answered, "Certainly, at your pleasure." He then showed Stanton the order naming himself as interim secretary. As he did so, Grant entered the room and Thomas showed him the order too.

Stanton then asked if he could have a copy of the order. Thomas agreed and went downstairs to the adjutant general's office to have it made. While he was gone Grant and Stanton hastily conferred. Stanton, they agreed, should not vacate the office. Hence, when Thomas returned and gave Stanton the copy, Stanton declared: "I want some little time for reflection. I do not know whether I'll obey your instructions or whether I will resist them." Thomas thereupon announced his intention of issuing orders as secretary of war. Stanton commanded him not to do so. At this Thomas left the War Department after warning that he would "most certainly, at all hazards, take possession of the war office on the following Monday"—that is, on February 24, three days hence. He returned to the White House and reported on what had happened to Johnson. "Very well," said Johnson, "go and take charge of the office and perform the duties."[10]

Johnson, however, did not instruct Thomas to do this at once, indicating that he felt no sense of urgency and was willing to wait until Monday for Thomas to take over the department. Apparently he expected Stanton to vacate his office simply because he had received a piece of paper dismissing him. If so, the president was guilty of naive optimism.

Later that afternoon Johnson sent the Senate a notification of Stanton's dismissal and Thomas's appointment. Then he met with the cabinet to whom he conveyed, for the first time, the same information. Welles promptly inquired "if Stanton had surrendered up the place and General Thomas taken possession." Johnson replied that Thomas had told him that Stanton "seemed calm and submissive." (If this was true, then Thomas had badly misinformed Johnson.) Both Welles and McCulloch expressed doubt that Stanton would give up his office. That evening Welles wrote in his diary: "The President is vigorous and active, but [it is] too late. . . ."[11]

Meanwhile, shortly before 2:30 P.M., the Senate received Johnson's notification. Simultaneously a note from Stanton stating that the president was attempting to oust him reached the House. The Republicans in both chambers exploded with anger. Johnson had committed the ultimate effrontery, he had defied Congress intolerably. He had to be removed from office.

There was, however, more to the Republicans' reaction than mere exasperation, although that had a lot to do with it. They saw their whole Reconstruction program in acute danger—and with it their own power. During the winter, as we have seen, Johnson had waged a campaign designed to undermine the military Reconstruction acts. His efforts had been sufficiently effective to draw from Southern Republicans numerous pleas for help and predictions of disaster unless something was done soon to counter the president. More recently, Johnson had pilloried the party's intended presidential candidate before the public as a liar and betrayer. Now he was deliberately and contemptuously flouting the law in an attempt to install as secretary of war a man who would serve as his pliant tool in further sabotaging military Reconstruction. "If you don't kill the beast," proclaimed Stevens, "it will kill you." Now even Moderates hitherto as staunchly opposed to impeachment as Bingham and James Wilson concurred: Self-preservation left no choice except to replace Johnson with Wade. Then, as Wade had said to Johnson back in April 1865, "By the gods, there will be no trouble running the government." Nor would there be any trouble in securing Negro-based Republican domination of the South and in electing Grant as president in the fall.

Two hours after Stanton's note arrived, the House voted without a single Republican dissenting to refer to Stevens's Committee on Reconstruction a resolution, introduced by Radical John Covode of Pennsylvania, calling for the impeachment of Johnson for "high crimes and misdemeanors." It took the Senate longer, however, to agree on the proper response to Johnson's attempt to displace Stanton. While it debated, leading Republicans sent messages to Stanton urging him to, as Sumner put it with uncustomary brevity, "Stick!" Emboldened by these manifestations of support, Stanton wrote an order for Grant to arrest Thomas, but then tore it up after Grant advised against it. Finally, at 9:30 that night, the Senate adopted by a 28-to-6 count a resolution declaring that the president had no legal or constitutional power "to remove the Secretary of War and to designate any other officer to perform the duties" of that office. Among the majority were a number of Moderates, notably Trumbull. On the other hand Fessenden, Grimes, Sherman, and several other Moderates did not vote at all.[12]

While Congress thus moved towards impeaching Johnson, his chosen agent, General Thomas, spent the afternoon telling various friends and reporters that he intended to take over the secretary of war's office even if he had to break down the door. Then, that evening, he attended a masquerade ball, drank heavily, and boasted that he would kick Stanton out if necessary. Exaggerated reports of his "threats" soon reached Stanton, who remained in his office throughout the day and night. Stanton's first reaction was to issue a secret order to the troops on duty at the War Department not to offer any resistance should Thomas use military force—he wanted no blood spilled on his account, Stanton declared. But later he had another idea. Even though it was midnight, he sent for the chief justice of the Supreme Court of the District of Columbia, David K. Cartter, and asked him to issue a warrant for the arrest of Thomas on the charge of violating the Tenure of Office Act. Cartter, who was a personal friend of Stanton's, readily complied and directed a court marshal to serve the warrant on Thomas.[13]

At 8 o'clock in the morning the marshal did so, just after Thomas arose from bed and before he had eaten breakfast. Thomas asked permission to see the president. The marshal agreed and accompanied him to the White House, where Thomas told Johnson of his arrest. Johnson was not surprised; during the night he had been informed that Stanton intended to have Thomas arrested and so had ordered Moore to go to Thomas's residence in the morning to advise him in case it happened. Nor was Johnson upset to learn that Thomas already had been arrested. On the contrary he was pleased: "Very well," he said to Thomas, "that is the place where

I want it in—the courts." He then instructed Thomas to see Stanbery.[14]

Still accompanied by the marshal, Thomas went to the hotel where Stanbery lived. Soon after Thomas had left, Moore arrived back at the White House and reported to Johnson that he had gone to see Thomas but found that he was too late. Johnson answered that Thomas had come to see him and then had gone to obtain advice from Stanbery, the plan being for Thomas to post bail and stand trial. Moore thereupon suggested that it would be better if Thomas "should refuse to give bail, submit to arrest, and then sue for a writ of habeas corpus and thus bring the case immediately before the courts for decision."

Johnson immediately perceived the advantage of this approach —it would place the legal initiative in Thomas's hands—and so asked Moore to see Stanberry. Again, however, Moore arrived too late: Thomas had departed with the marshal after Stanbery, instead of offering to represent him before Judge Cartter, had merely told him to go on to the court. Moore followed Thomas to the court, arriving in time to see Cartter order Thomas to post a $5,000 bond and to appear for trial on February 26. Moore then took Thomas back to the White House where the general informed Johnson that he had paid the bail money. Again Johnson simply said, "Very well; we want it in the courts."[15]

Thomas's adventures, however, were not over yet. Apparently angered at having been arrested, he decided in a befuddled way to supplant Stanton that very day instead of waiting until Monday. Proceeding to the War Department, he entered but found the door to the adjutant general's office locked. He asked an orderly for the key. The orderly replied that Stanton had taken all of the keys. Thomas thereupon went to Stanton's office. He found the secretary with eight Republican congressmen. Thomas offered to go away and come back later, but Stanton asked him what he wanted; the secretary of war's office, he answered. Stanton ordered him to return to the (locked) adjutant general's office. Thomas twice more demanded that Stanton turn over the secretary of war's office, and Stanton twice refused. Thomas then went across the hall to another room where he issued orders under the title of secretary of war to Townsend and to Brigadier General Edmund Schriver, another member of the adjutant's staff. Stanton, on being informed of this, came into the room, followed by two congressmen, and commanded the two officers to disregard Thomas. Then he again ordered Thomas downstairs to the adjutant's office. But Thomas remained where he was; and after listening to some further verbal exchanges, the two congressmen left the room. Thomas then said to Stanton, "The next time you have me arrested, please do not do it before I get something to eat." Also, added Thomas, he had not had anything to drink since morning—and it was now noontime.

Stanton, sensing he had triumphed, put his arm around Thomas's neck, then ran his hand through Thomas's hair as he turned to Schriver and said, "Schriver, you have got a bottle here; bring it out." Schriver produced a small flask of whiskey, Stanton poured two glasses, and Thomas and he each gulped down the contents. This being barely enough to wet their whistles, Stanton sent for a full bottle. When it arrived, he shared some more whiskey with Thomas. "Now," he laughed, "this at least is neutral ground." A short time afterwards Thomas left the War Department.[16]

While Thomas and Stanton were drinking, Stevens was endeavoring to secure adoption of Covode's resolution impeaching the president. Stevens hoped to have it passed that day, because it was both Washington's Birthday and the second anniversary of Johnson's White House harrangue denouncing Sumner, Phillips, and himself as traitors. But there were too many Republicans who wished to make speeches denouncing the president as a traitor. Not even by resorting to the expedient of turning back the legislative clock could Stevens bring the resolution to a vote. At last, well after midnight, he gave up and the House adjourned until Monday.

Also during the day, rumors of an impending armed clash between president and Congress swirled through Washington's muddy streets. The stories had begun the previous evening when orderlies sent by Major General William H. Emory, commander of the District of Columbia, appeared at a party held at the home of a Washington socialite and summoned all officers of the garrison to report immediately for duty. Welles's son Edgar, who was present, told his father what had happened; and fearing that the long-dreaded attempt to arrest the president was about to be made, Welles sent Edgar on to the White House. He was unable, however, to see Johnson, who was at a state dinner. The next morning Welles himself informed Johnson of what had occurred at the party. Johnson said that he had not ordered any troop movements. "Some one has," Welles observed ominously, asking, "Who is it? and what does it indicate?" Johnson decided to find out. He sent for Emory and asked him for an explanation. Emory replied that Grant had alerted the Washington garrison because of the excitement prevailing in the city. All orders to the army, Emory added, had to come through

Grant, even those from the president; it was the law of Congress, and all military officers had to obey it, constitutional or not. "The object of the law is evident," Johnson said in disgust, after which he told Emory he could leave.[17]

Emory at once reported his conversation with the president to various persons, giving the impression that Johnson had tried to induce him to defy Grant's orders. Some of the Republicans jumped to the conclusion that Johnson was planning to use force to extract Stanton from the War Department. Stanton himself told a reporter that Johnson, having failed to get Emory's cooperation, had asked Welles for a company of marines! At Stanton's urgent request Grant stationed extra troops at the War Department; in addition Senator Chandler and Representative John A. Logan posted over one hundred volunteers in the basement of that building. Logan also notified one of the "generals" of the Grand Army of the Republic, of which he was the leading spirit, warning, "It Seems that the city is filling up with Suspicious Class of men. That may mean harm tho' no demonstration *has been made*. . . . I hope you will quietly and secretly organize all of our boys, So that they Can assemble to protect the Congress. . . ."[18]

Despite all of the rumors and alarms, Sunday passed without incident. On Monday, February 24, Johnson sent to the Senate the nomination of Thomas Ewing, Sr., as secretary of war, along with a reply to the resolution condemning him for violating the Tenure of Office Act. He might as well not have bothered. The Senate ignored the first, which was a belated attempt to soften the impact of the attempt to remove Stanton, and it paid no heed to the second, which asserted that the dismissal of Stanton was designed to test the act's constitutionality in the courts. The attention of the senators, like everyone else's, was focused on the House of Representatives.

There the Republicans spent the day continuing to vie with one another in denouncing Johnson. Ultimately, however, their appetite for vituperation was sated. At 5 P.M. they passed by a vote of 126 to 47 Covode's resolution declaring "That Andrew Johnson, President of the United States, be impeached of high crimes and misdemeanors." Every Republican present, including Speaker Colfax, voted yea and all of the Democrats who were on hand nay. For the first—and so far the only—time in American history a president had been impeached. Inside the House chamber there was applause. Outside wind and rain beat on the Capitol dome. Wrote the French correspondent Clemenceau: "The dark cloud has finally broken. The President called upon the lightning, and the lightning came."[19]

The following day at 1:10 P.M., Stevens and Bingham entered the Senate, a Radical and a Moderate united in support of impeachment. Stevens, pale and corpse-like, leaned on Bingham. The doorkeeper announced "A message from the House of Representatives." Stevens pulled himself erect, threw his hat on the floor, handed his cane to the doorkeeper, and drew a paper from his pocket. In solemn tones he read:

> "In the name of the House of Representatives and of all the people of the United States we do impeach Andrew Johnson, President of the United States, of high crimes and misdemeanors in office; and we further inform the Senate that the House of Representatives will in due time exhibit particular articles of impeachment against him and make good the same; and in their name we demand that the Senate take order for the appearance of the said Andrew Johnson to answer said impeachment."

"The Senate will take order in the premises," responded Ben Wade, president pro tem of the Senate—and, so it seemed, soon to be president of the United States.[20]

That same day Lorenzo Thomas again entered the War Department and demanded that Stanton vacate the secretary's office. Again Stanton refused, and again Thomas went away. On the morning of February 26 Thomas, now supported by two lawyers, appeared before Judge Cartter and surrendered himself into the custody of the court. His lawyers then petitioned for a writ of habeas corpus. Stanton, however, had realized that Thomas's arrest was playing into Johnson's hands. Therefore on February 25 he had arranged with Cartter to drop the charges against Thomas. As a result Cartter now released Thomas, thus making it impossible for him to make an appeal to the Supreme Court.[21]

Thus it was that Johnson failed both to supplant Stanton and to secure a judicial test of the Tenure of Office Act. Instead he found himself impeached and faced with the prospect of removal from office. For this dismal outcome he once more had himself mainly to blame. As observed previously, he should have dismissed Stanton at least as soon as he learned of his treachery in connection with the New Orleans riot, and not later than the initial passage of the tenure act. After that he needed to proceed against Stanton, if proceed at all, with great care and greater skill. But, as we have seen, he did neither. Instead, to quote Welles, "by a final hasty move, without preparation, without advising with anybody [except, apparently, Moore], he took a step which consolidated the [Republicans] of every stripe . . . and brought down a mountain of trouble on himself."[22]

Johnson knew that he was risking impeachment when he attempted to supplant Stanton with Thomas. When it came, he "took the matter," according to Moore, "very cooly and was not at all excited." Johnson may have made mistakes—he admitted his error in employing a bumbler like Thomas for such a difficult mission—but he had no doubt that he had done what his official position and his personal self-respect demanded: "If I cannot be President in fact," he told Moore, "I will not be President in name alone."[23]

In the weeks to come he would learn whether he was to remain either.

10

★★★★★

TRIAL AND ESCAPE

The House had impeached Johnson for "high crimes and misdemeanors" but had not specified what they were. To that end Speaker Colfax appointed a committee (Stevens, Bingham, Wilson, and Boutwell were among the seven members) to draft articles of impeachment against the president. On March 2 the House adopted nine articles presented by the committee. The first eight were variations on the charge that Johnson had violated the tenure act, the ninth alleged that he had tried to suborn General Emory. Also the Republican representatives chose four Radicals—Stevens, Butler, Boutwell, and Logan—and three Moderates—Bingham, Wilson, and Thomas Williams of Pennsylvania to serve as the House's "managers" (i.e., prosecutors) in presenting the articles to the Senate; under the Constitution, that body would sit as a court and try the president. By threatening resignation Bingham became chairman of the managers. Butler, however, through the sheer force of his personality, soon emerged as "the life, soul, body, boots and breeches of impeachment."[1] Stevens, who visibly was tottering towards the grave, could do little more than serve as its symbol.

On March 3 the House, at the behest of the managers, added the tenth and eleventh article of impeachment. The former, written by Butler, accused Johnson of defaming Congress in public speeches. The latter, which was primarily Stevens's handiwork, rehashed the preceding charges. Dubbed the "omnibus article," its purpose was to induce senators who might have qualms about specific charges against Johnson to vote him guilty on general grounds.

At 1 P.M., March 4, the managers entered the Senate chamber and Bingham read the articles of impeachment. Wade thereupon appointed a committee to request the chief justice of the Supreme Court, who under the Constitution presides over a presidential impeachment trial, to be present in the Senate at 1 P.M. on the morrow. At the designated time Salmon P. Chase appeared, mounted the rostrum, and proceeded to administer to each senator an oath, which he himself took first, to "do impartial justice according to the Constitution and the laws." Wade took the oath along with the rest, despite a protest from Democratic Senator Hendricks that he could not possibly be impartial. The Senate thus having formed itself into a "High Court of Impeachment," the House managers then demanded that the president be brought before it. In turn the Senate ordered that Johnson be summoned to stand trial beginning March 13. Two days later the sergeant-at-arms of the Senate delivered the summons to the White House. Personally and solemnly Johnson accepted it.

During the previous two weeks the president had received many letters offering armed assistance in resisting the congressional "usurpation." He ignored them—which was wise. The overwhelming majority of Northerners supported impeachment. For them the latest attempt to remove Stanton had been the final straw. It convinced them that there would be no peace in the nation as long as Johnson occupied the White House. They wanted him out, both for what he had done and for what they feared he might do. Had he resorted to force to stay in, the consequences would have been suicidal—and probably farcical besides.

It was to lawyers and not to soldiers that Johnson looked for defense. Consulting with the cabinet, he chose five attorneys to represent him in the impeachment trial: Stanbery, Benjamin C. Curtis, William M. Evarts, Thomas A. R. Nelson, and Jeremiah Black. So that he could concentrate on the president's case and avoid the charge of defending Johnson at public expense, Stanbery resigned as attorney general; his duties were assumed by Browning. Curtis of Boston was a former Supreme Court justice and one of the two dissenters in the *Dred Scott* decision. Evarts, a star of the New York Bar, was a friend of Seward's, who suggested Evarts despite the fact he had delivered an anti-Johnson speech at a Republican rally in October. Johnson himself selected Nelson, a Tennessee Whig and a Unionist whom the president had long known. Likewise a combination of personal considerations and his great ability dictated the choice of Black. On March 19, however,

Black left the defense team, blaming—with good cause—Seward's influence with Johnson for the government's refusal to support the just claims of one of his clients against Santo Domingo. Johnson replaced Black, whom he unfairly but understandably believed had deserted him, with William Groesbeck of Cincinnati, the man whom the president considered better qualified than McCulloch to be secretary of the treasury.[2]

Stanbery's first act after taking over Johnson's defense was to insist that the president place himself completely in the hands of counsel and that he stop talking to reporters. The reason was a presidential interview which the *New York World* published on March 10. In it Johnson had set forth some of the main arguments which Stanbery planned to use in his behalf, thus tipping House prosecutors as to what to expect. Johnson promised to do as Stanbery desired, a promise he kept (apart from a couple of lapses in April when the trial was drawing to a close). Nevertheless, it went against his grain to be silent, especially when he was attacked. Ever confident of his oratorical powers, Johnson more than once proposed stating his case in person to the Senate. Fortunately his attorneys dissuaded him from this folly.

As scheduled, the Senate convened, with Chase presiding, to begin the trial on March 13. "Andrew Johnson, President of the United States; Andrew Johnson, President of the United States, appear and answer the Articles of Impeachment exhibited against you by the House of Representatives of the United States," cried the sergeant-at-arms. There was silence, and then laughter as Ben Butler, blinking owlishly, entered the chamber. But following him came Stanbery, Curtis, and Nelson. They were there, announced Stanbery, to represent the president. Would the Senate grant them forty days in which to prepare an answer to the impeachment articles? "Forty days!" exclaimed Butler. "As long as it took God to destroy the world by flood." Both he and Bingham insisted that the trial must begin at once. Two hours of debate ensued. Finally the Senate agreed to a ten-day postponement. On March 23 Johnson's lawyers again appeared and again asked for more time; they got another six days. These delays were a setback and a disappointment for Sumner and other ultras, for they had hoped to have Johnson out of the White House by now.

Meanwhile, however, there were things that could be—and that were being—done to defeat Johnson's offensive against military Reconstruction. The first was passage by the Senate on February 25 of the bill, previously adopted by the House, declaring that a majority of votes cast sufficed to ratify constitutions in states under-going Reconstruction. In this way the Alabama voter boycott used to defeat the Republican-designed constitution was overcome, and other Southern states were forestalled from resorting to the same tactic. This measure, known as the Fourth Reconstruction Act, became law on March 12 without Johnson's signature.[3]

Grant likewise acted to frustrate the president's attempt to aid Southerners in the struggle against Republican domination—and also to revenge the replacement of Sheridan by Hancock. In January Hancock had removed seven New Orleans aldermen (several of whom were Negroes, all of whom were Republicans) for violating a decree issued by Sheridan a year before and holding an election for a minor city office. Grant, ignoring the fact that he himself had directed Hancock to enforce his predecessor's regulations, restored the aldermen to office. Furthermore, Grant reinstated the Republi-can street commissioner of New Orleans after Hancock had deposed him for corruption. Late in February, rightly perceiving that Grant was deliberately humiliating him, Hancock asked to be relieved as commander of the Fifth District. Johnson complied and appointed him to the command of newly established Atlantic Division. (In the meantime, like Sherman, George H. Thomas had declined both that post and promotion to full general.) Major General Robert C. Buchanan, a nonenity who could be counted on to do just what Grant told him to do, replaced Hancock in New Orleans.[4]

A third and far more important Republican countermeasure was directed at the Supreme Court. Between March 2 and March 9 the Court heard arguments on the *McCardle* case. Black, represent-ing the plaintiff (and, in fact, Johnson), professed to be "extremely embarrassed" by having to advocate such an obvious proposition that the military Reconstruction acts were unconstitutional in light of the *Milligan* precedent. Trumbull, appearing on behalf of the "government" (meaning Congress), asserted that the Court could not pass on the constitutionality of the Reconstruction laws because they were a political not a judicial matter. At the close of the arguments all observers believed that a majority of the justices would favor Black's contention.

No one was more confident of that outcome than Johnson, just as no one stood to gain more than he: Congressional Reconstruction would be destroyed, he would be vindicated, and the continuation of the impeachment proceedings would be rendered impossible. In the aforementioned *New York World* interview, Johnson had made known his happy expectations.[5] When the reporter remarked that it would be a "fortunate thing" if the Court could deliver its opinion in the *McCardle* case before the impeachment trial began, Johnson replied:

> Too short a time for such a decision, I am afraid. But, I suppose the Court would feel itself bound, in consideration of the importance of the case, to render a decision upon it within three weeks, and that might occur during the interval between the answer to the summons and the day set for the commencement of the trial.

"True; what a grace that would be, also," affirmed the reporter:

> It is even hinted that if the decision of the Supreme Court should be against the constitutionality of the reconstruction acts, the President might find himself authorized to remove, at his discretion, the military despotism from the South, and let the Southern people enjoy what would be the luxury of governing themselves.

"That might seem to be the natural duty of the President," Johnson responded. Then, for form's sake, he added a tongue-in-cheek disclaimer: "Do not understand me, however, as intending to express a premature opinion upon what is likely to happen either in the Supreme Court or elsewhere." With an equal amount of polite hypocrisy, the reporter replied:

> Certainly not, sir, I alluded to the McCardle case because it suggested some possibilities which may be discreetly convassed. For instance, a decision upon that case adverse to the reconstruction acts would render pretty certain that some remaining laws, including the Civil Tenure act, will not stand a judicial test. In that event, would not the conviction of the President [in the impeachment trial] . . . look still more doubtful?

Johnson did not answer this question directly. He did, however, launch into a denunciation of the Tenure of Office Act, making it clear that he agreed that if the Court declared the military Reconstruction acts unconstitutional, that law would not survive very long either and the impeachment proceedings thus would collapse.

The *New York World* interview took place on March 8 and was published two days later, one day after the Supreme Court finished hearing arguments in the *McCardle* case. On March 11, Senate Republicans passed what seemed to be a routine bill to correct an oversight in an act of July 13, 1866, having to do with Supreme Court review of judgments under the internal revenue laws. The next day in the House, without the Democrats realizing what was happening, Wilson tacked onto it an amendment which repealed that part of the 1867 Habeas Corpus Act under which McCardle had appealed to the Supreme Court. The House then passed the bill as amended and returned it to the Senate which approved it that same day over the belated objections of the Democrats.[6]

The Republicans had used surreptitious means but they did not attempt to conceal their end: to prevent the Supreme Court from deciding the *McCardle* case. Alerted by Johnson himself in the *World* interview, they feared, in the words of Colfax, that "a Majority of the Supreme Court are evidently determined to overthrow all our Reconstruction laws."

In the past Congress had exercised its constitutional power to restrict the Court's appellate jurisdiction. But never had it done this with respect to a case already before the Court. Would the justices be deterred? Or would they hasten to render judgment, taking advantage of the fact that unless the president signed it (an impossibility) the bill could not become law until March 27? Johnson and his friends fervently hoped that they would do the latter. Thus, not until March 20 did Johnson ask Browning to draft a veto message, which he did with the assistance of Thomas Ewing, Sr.

On March 21 the justices met in conference. Following very solemn—and possibly, at times, heated—discussion, the majority decided to postpone consideration of the *McCardle* case. It would be unseemly, they maintained, for the Court to engage in a race against Congress. In saying this they no doubt were sincere and possibly justified. But most likely too the justices had an unexpressed deeper motive: fear that if they went ahead with the case, Congress would resort to even more drastic measures. Thus Trumbull had ready and waiting a resolution flatly denying the Court's jurisdiction over any of the Reconstruction acts; and in the House, bills had been introduced to require a two-thirds, even a unanimous, vote by the Court to overturn any law of Congress. Only two of the judges —Robert C. Grier, a Democratic holdover from the Taney days, and Stephen J. Field, a War Democrat appointed by Lincoln—wished to proceed with the case regardless of recent congressional actions, arguing that otherwise the Court would be dodging its responsibility.

News of the justices' decision soon became public. Welles, writing in his diary for March 23, expressed the reaction of Johnson and his circle: "The Judges of the Supreme Court have caved in, fallen through, failed in the McCardle case. Only Grier and Field have held out like men, patriots, judges of nerve and honest independence." On March 25 Johnson sent the Browning-Ewing veto message, "very much diluted" in Browning's opinion, to Congress. By stripping the Supreme Court of jurisdiction in the *McCardle* case, Johnson declared, Congress had deprived citizens retroactively of a vital right, weakened the judicial branch, and, in effect, admitted the unconstitutionality of the military Reconstruction acts. The following day the Senate overrode his veto by a vote of 33 to 9, and on March 27 the House did likewise, voting 114 to 34.

There still remained a chance, however, that the Court might deal with McCardle's plea despite congressional action. Accordingly, on March 30 Black asked the justices to take up at once the question of whether they retained jurisdiction over the case; in his opinion they did. But again, with only Grier and Field disagreeing, the Court chose discretion as the better part of valor and decided to postpone consideration of this issue until its next term. That did not begin until December—by which time, obviously, Johnson's fate would be determined. Ultimately, on April 12, 1869, the Court concluded that indeed it no longer had jurisdiction in the *McCardle* case. Also on that date, in the case of *Texas* v. *White*, the Court in effect bowed to the congressional contention that Reconstruction was a political question by refusing to consider the constitutionality of the Reconstruction acts. By then, of course, Grant was president and most of the Southern states were back in the Union. All in all, the *McCardle* case is a classic example of the Supreme Court not merely following but also anticipating the "iliction returns."[7]

On March 30, the day Black vainly urged the justices to defy Congress with regard to *McCardle*, Johnson's impeachment trial finally got underway. It lasted one and a half months—far longer than expected or desired by the impeachers, who rightly feared that the passage of time would calm public feeling, cause Senators to have second thoughts about removing Johnson, and so favor the president.[8]

Johnson's attorneys presented five basic answers to the main charge against him, violation of the Tenure of Office Act. First, the act was unconstitutional. Second, even if it were constitutional, it did not protect Stanton since he had been appointed by Lincoln, not by Johnson. Third, the president had not actually violated it in any event, for obviously Stanton still remained in office. Fourth, Johnson's attempt to replace Stanton was not motivated by criminal intent but rather by a legitimate desire to test the act's constitutionality in the courts. Finally, they argued, impeachment was a judicial and not a political process; hence having committed no indictable offense, Johnson was innocent of "high crimes and misdemeanors" in seeking to remove Stanton. As for the other charges against him, his attorneys contended that Johnson had merely questioned Emory about his orders and had not tried to induce him to violate them, adding that the president's speeches criticizing Congress were normal and valid exercises of freedom of speech.

On their side, the managers asserted that the tenure act was constitutional, that it did cover Stanton, that Johnson had violated it, that his intent in so doing was irrelevant, and that of necessity impeachment was political. Otherwise, how could the nation be protected against an unfit president unless he was obliging enough, as Butler sarcastically pointed out, to allow himself to be caught "robbing a chicken house" or committing some other statutory crime? With regard to Emory the managers resorted to innuendo and distortion, and to prove the charge that Johnson had slandered Congress, they cited quotations from his speeches.

Both defense and prosecution supported their cases with documents, witnesses, and long-winded oratory—Evarts's summation alone occupied four entire days. Most of the spectators who crowded the galleries agreed that Johnson's counselors outmatched and outperformed their rivals, a judgment ratified by historians. Butler, who had declared that he intended to "try the case as I should a horse case," did exactly that. The trouble was that he also made an ass of himself as he bullied witnesses, engaged in nasty invective, and employed agents to break into Evarts's hotel room in quest of incriminating documents. The managers also made a poor impression by trying unsuccessfully to prevent Sherman and Welles from testifying that Johnson's intent in dismissing Stanton was to test the Tenure of Office Act before the Supreme Court. Throughout the trial Chase presided with an impartiality that had the effect of benefiting the defense and therefore irritated the impeachers. Not only did Chase consider Johnson innocent but he also was angling for the Democratic presidential nomination now that Grant had clinched the Republican one.[9]

Under the Constitution, the concurrence of at least two-thirds of the Senate was needed to convict the president. This two-thirds would have to come from the Senate's forty-two Republican members: the ten Democrats and two Johnsonites (Dixon and Doolittle) were bound to support acquittal. Hence the task of the managers was to convince—and to keep convinced—a minimum of thirty-six Republican senators that Johnson should be removed from office. On the other hand, the defense needed to persuade no fewer than seven Republicans to join the Democrats and Johnsonites in declaring the president innocent. Johnson's lawyers had this as their objective. Apparently their arguments and eloquence carried the day, for all seven Republican senators who ultimately did vote to acquit Johnson asserted that they did so because they believed that the charges against him lacked legal foundation, and there is no reason to doubt their sincerity. Nevertheless, factors other than the merits of the case and the skill of Johnson's lawyers likewise influenced the decisions of these men.

Impeachment occurred, as we have noted, because Johnson's inept attempt to remove Stanton had aroused the wrath and fear of the Moderates and caused them to unite with the Radicals for the purposes of punishing him, of safeguarding military Reconstruction, and of preserving Republican power. Johnson sensed this. He also realized that without Republican votes in the Senate, he could not escape conviction, and these votes would have to come from Moderates. Therefore, following impeachment, he endeavored to placate the Moderates by ceasing his efforts to circumscribe Grant's administration of military rule in the South, by instructing Lorenzo Thomas to drop plans to obtain a court order instructing Stanton to vacate the War Department, and by refraining from provocative public pronouncements. Also, and more importantly, he made a couple of behind-the-scenes deals.

The first was with the key Moderate senators, Fessenden and Grimes. From the outset these two had strong misgivings about impeachment. They doubted its legal justification, feared that deposing Johnson ultimately would injure the Republican party, and, in common with many other Moderates, disliked the prospect of Wade (whom they considered a vulgar demagogue) becoming president. Consequently in mid April they informed Evarts that they would be more favorably disposed towards Johnson if he would nominate General Schofield, who had steered a middle course between Radicals and Conservatives as commander in Virginia, to be secretary of war. By so doing the president would assure them that he no longer would interfere with the congressional Reconstruction program. Evarts delivered their message to Johnson. Although Johnson considered Schofield a "cold and selfish man," he perceived that his appointment as secretary of war would, as the president put it to Moore, "relieve some of the Senators of the opposition." Hence Johnson authorized Evarts to ask Schofield if he would accept the war office. Schofield said he would, provided that Grant did not object and that Johnson henceforth would refrain from attempts to cripple the enforcement of the military Reconstruction acts. Evarts assured him on the latter point and Grant gave his permission, confident that Johnson would be removed in any event. Schofield thereupon agreed to take the post if confirmed; and on April 24 Johnson sent his nomination to the Senate, at the same time withdrawing Ewing's. Of course, while the impeachment trial was still in progress there was no chance that the Senate would act on the nomination. But, noted Moore, it "created considerable interest."[10]

Johnson's second deal was with Senator Edmund G. Ross of Kansas. Ross was a newspaper editor who had entered the Senate following the suicide of James H. Lane in July 1866. (There were those who asserted, without any basis in fact, that both Lane and Preston King took their own lives out of remorse over stopping Mrs. Surratt's daughter from seeing Johnson.) In general, Ross had voted with the Radicals, but according to his own account he had strong doubts about impeachment. Also it is possible that Kansas's overwhelming rejection of Negro suffrage in 1867 influenced him. In any case, on May 4 Ross sent one of his friends to talk to Browning. The friend told Browning that if the president would demonstrate his acceptance of congressional Reconstruction by forwarding to the Senate the newly drafted Republican constitutions of South Carolina and Arkansas, Ross "and others would then vote against impeachment." The next day at the urging of Browning and Stanbery, Johnson did exactly that.[11]

Had he wanted to, Johnson also could have made a deal of a different sort with Kansas's other senator, Samuel C. Pomeroy. "Pom the Pious," as he was known, based his political career on hypocrisy and bribery: He was always willing to buy and to be bought. In April 1867 he had indirectly approached Johnson, offering to support him should he "get into trouble, even if it be impeachment," in return for having one of his Kansas henchmen appointed postmaster of Leavenworth.[12] Then, in March 1868 he came several times to the White House, obviously hoping to be taken up on this proposal. Johnson, however, had vowed not "to use any unfair means" to escape conviction. "How would I feel after acquittal if I had bought it?" he rhetorically asked Moore. "How would I feel if my conscience told me I owed my acquittal to bribery?" Hence he ignored Pomeroy (whom he may also have suspected of laying a trap for him). Moreover, although he considered it, he did not use Pomeroy's April 1867 offer (for which the president had documentary evidence) to discredit the senator.[13] As for Pomeroy, after being spurned by Johnson he became one of the most outspoken advocates of impeachment. In addition he pressured Ross to vote against Johnson when he discovered that his colleague might do otherwise.

Johnson's less pugnacious and more cooperative attitude helped allay the apprehension of some Republicans that if acquitted he would, in the words of a Bostonian, "act like a mad elephant who had a fight with his keepers, and had conquered." Thus the *Chicago Tribune* observed on May 14 that "Andrew Johnson has been a changed man. The country has been at peace. The great obstruction to the law has been virtually suspended. . . ."[14] But would fewer than thirty-six Republican senators vote against his conviction? As the trial neared its end, that was the question which increasingly filled everyone's mind, none more so than Johnson's.

Immediately following impeachment, and throughout March and most of April, Johnson took a pessimistic view of his prospects. On February 26 he offered to obtain another post in the government for Moore. On March 14 Welles noted in his diary that the president appeared "uncomfortable and uncertain." Two days later Moore wrote that he "feels deeply on the subject of Impeachment, his only words generally are 'Too bad! too bad!'" And on April 15—the third anniversary of his presidency—Johnson seemed to Moore "unwell and gloomy."

Contributing to Johnson's depression was poor health. Late in February he suffered a recurrence of the gravel which forced him at times to lie on a couch in his office, and during mid March he had a severe cold. Moreover, after the trial got underway he became displeased with the conduct of his defense and expressed regret that he had not gone before the Senate in person. On April 19, in a conversation with Moore, Johnson was especially critical of Evarts, complaining that the New Yorker had failed to respond adequately to a "tirade of abuse" from Butler. The president also talked wildly of appealing to the Supreme Court if the Senate pronounced him guilty. The following day he was still worried and remarked to Moore that "things seem to manage us instead of us managing them. I don't like it."

But then his mood started to improve. On April 24—the day Schofield's nomination went to the Senate—Curtis sent him word that "during the last twenty-four hours impeachment has gone rapidly astern." A few days later Johnson felt sufficiently confident about the future to boast to Moore that he would "get hold" of Grant after the impeachment was over—words which, had they been heard by Fessenden, Grimes, and other Moderates, would have guaranteed his conviction. And by May 2 he was "in excellent spirits," "expressed himself well satisfied with the manner in which his case had been conducted," and was "greatly pleased with Evarts' efforts."[15] The deal with Ross two days later could only have added to his optimism, as presumably did the fact that ten Republican senators were voting most of the time with the Democrats on procedural issues during the trial.

On May 7 Bingham made the closing speech for the prosecution, and on the following day the Senate set May 12 for a vote on the articles of impeachment. By then Johnson, his lawyers, and all of the cabinet except Welles and Browning were confident of an acquittal. Browning considered the senators "cowards" who would convict the president in order to escape "the party lash." Welles believed that "more than one half of the Senators are demagogues and blockheads."[16]

On May 11 the Senate met to discuss the evidence before voting the next day. Fessenden, Grimes, and Trumbull (who originally had supported impeachment but who had changed his mind for the same reasons as the other two) announced that they intended to vote not guilty. Sherman declared that in view of his having said at the time of its passage that the tenure act did not cover cabinet members, he could not now vote for the first article of impeachment; Van Winkle, Willey, and Timothy Otis Howe of Wisconsin echoed him. John B. Henderson of Missouri and Joseph F. Fowler of Tennessee, both of whom were nominal Republicans, made it clear that they leaned towards acquittal. Several other senators who definitely were Republican refused to commit themselves, among them William Sprague of New Jersey, the son-in-law of Chief Justice Chase. Ross remained silent.

News of the dissension and uncertainty among the Republicans increased the optimism in Johnson's camp. Johnson himself was "gratified." Groesbeck stated that "the work was accomplished." McCulloch declared that "there is no question of acquittal." Randall predicted that the vote would be at least 22 to 32. Welles, still skeptical but becoming hopeful, remarked in his diary that he had no cause to question Randall's accuracy "except he is not an accurate man."[17]

In contrast rage and near-panic gripped the impeachers. Was Johnson to escape them after all? Certainly they needed every guilty vote they had or could get. Hence, on the morning of May 12 when Senator Howard reported himself sick, they had the Senate postpone the vote until Saturday, May 16.

Johnson, recorded Welles, was "more disturbed by the post-ponement than I have ever seen him, but he soon rallied." Browning, who like Welles had become hopeful, believed that "there is but little doubt the President would have been acquitted had the vote been taken today—doubtful what the result will be Saturday. Enough [Republican Senators] may be bought and dragooned into obedience to secure conviction."[18]

During the next three days the impeachers possibly tried to buy and most certainly endeavored to dragoon support. Republican state committees, Union League chapters, and the General Conference of the Methodist Church all sent resolutions to the Senate calling for Johnson's removal. The *New York Tribune* and most of other Radical newspapers denounced the "Judases"—Fessenden, Trumbull, and Grimes. Much to the alarm of the Johnsonites, Grimes fell ill. Would he be able to vote on the sixteenth? Butler, Stevens, and other top Radicals cajoled and threatened the doubtful senators; the Republican House delegations from their states did the same; and Pomeroy redoubled his efforts to persuade Ross to see the light. Ross also received a telegram signed by D. R. Anthony, a leading Kansas Radical, and "1,000 others of our truest and best men" which declared that "Kansas has heard the evidence and demands the conviction of the President." Even Grant, fighting Johnson with the same persistence as he had Lee, urged Trumbull, Fessenden, Henderson, and Frederick T. Frelinghuysen of New Jersey, another uncertain Republican senator, to vote guilty.[19]

At noon on May 16 the Senate assembled. Every member was present except Howard and Grimes. George H. Williams of Oregon moved that the eleventh article be voted on first. He did so on behalf of the Republican caucus, which had decided that in view of the announcements by Sherman, Howe, Van Winkle, and Willey, there would be a better chance of securing conviction on this catch-all charge. By a 34-to-19 count the Senate so ordered. As this vote took place, Howard entered and added his yea. After it ended, Edmunds moved that the Senate proceed to judgment. Fessenden asked for more time, then Reverdy Johnson announced that Grimes was in the building. A few minutes later Grimes, haggard and weak, was half-carried to his seat. Chase thereupon had the clerk read the eleventh article. Then, rising, he commanded, "Call the roll."

Johnson awaited the outcome in the company of McCulloch, Welles, Lorenzo Thomas, and Moore. A telegraph line had been strung from the Capitol to Willard's Hotel; from there an aide, William H. Crook, brought word of developments to the White

House, two blocks away. First Crook arrived with the news that Williams's motion had been passed, then with the nay count on that. Finally, panting from having run the whole distance from Willard's, he handed Johnson a dispatch stating that the Senate had voted 35 to 19 on the eleventh article. The dispatch also bore the names of the seven Republicans who had voted nay: Fessenden, Fowler, Grimes, Henderson, Ross, Trumbull, and Van Winkle. By the narrowest possible margin Johnson had escaped conviction.

"The President," recorded Moore, "took the matter very cooly, exhibiting no excitement. . . ." He had expected this outcome. Furthermore, elation would have been premature. Following the failure to convict, Senator Williams moved that further consideration of the impeachment articles be postponed until May 26 so that the Republicans could attend their upcoming national convention. Chase declared the motion out of order, but was overruled by the Republican majority which then passed the motion. Thus the possibility of conviction remained.[20]

It was, however, a remote one. If conviction could not succeed on the eleventh article, it was unlikely to do so on any of the others. The impeachers realized this. "The country is going to the devil," cried Stevens in disgust. Nevertheless, during the next ten days they labored furiously and sometimes viciously to reverse their defeat. They concentrated most of their attention on Ross. Radicals in Kansas accused him of being bribed, and Sumner and Butler believed the same. "Tell the damned scoundrel," snarled Butler, "that if he wants money, there is a bushel of it here to be had!" Telegrams and letters from angry constituents bombarded Ross, warning him of political death if he again voted nay. One writer even suggested that Ross follow Lane's example and shoot himself.[21]

Meanwhile the Republicans held their convention in Chicago. On the first ballot they unanimously chose Grant as their presidential candidate; it took them a little longer to pick Colfax as his running mate. Significantly, their platform proposed Negro suffrage only in the South. They had not forgotten what had happened in the 1867 elections. Indeed, Michigan's rejection of Negro suffrage by a huge majority in April kept it fresh in everyone's mind.[22]

At noon, May 26, the Senate reconvened. Again Johnson, this time with the entire cabinet, waited for a courier to bring the messages from Willard's. The first one stated, "They have refused to proceed with a vote upon the articles in their order"; the second said that "they have resolved to take a vote on the second article." Along with it was word that Ross had voted with the majority:

"This," noted Welles, "was for a few minutes a damper. . . ." But then came the third dispatch: "The vote is being taken. Ross stands firm and has voted right." Next the fourth: "The article is beaten 35 to 19." And the fifth: "They are voting on the third article. The vote is closed and the article beaten 35 to 19." And finally: "A motion had been made to adjourn the court *sine die*. The motion has prevailed and the court is dissolved."

As the tidings of his victory were delivered to Johnson, Browning watched him. "He was calm, dignified, placid and self possessed with no outward sign of agitation, what ever passions may have glowed in his breast. When the final results were announced . . . he received the congratulations of his cabinet with . . . serenity and self possession. . . ."[23]

And so Johnson would remain in the White House. How close did he come to being forced to leave it? The obvious answer is, as close as was possible. And, as is rather often the case, the obvious answer is probably the correct one. To be sure, Johnson wrote newspaper correspondent Benjamin Truman on August 3, 1868, that Senator Morgan would have voted for acquittal rather than permit Wade to become president.[24] Johnson, however, probably was expressing more of an opinion than a fact—and the fact is that Morgan voted guilty. Likewise the assertion made by many historians that Willey, Sprague, and James W. Nye of Nevada stood ready to switch their votes if necessary derives from sources which are, at best, secondhand and, at worst, unreliable. Thus the authority for the intent of Willey and of Sprague is Senator Henderson, who made the allegation more than thirty years later to historian William A. Dunning and to Horace White, editor of the *Chicago Tribune* during Reconstruction and subsequently Trumbull's biographer.[25] Since Henderson's account of his own role in the impeachment is filled with errors and exaggerations, his testimony concerning others must be viewed skeptically, especially as regards Sprague.[26] For if Sprague had voted for Johnson, as many expected him to do because of the supposed influence of his father-in-law, then he would have been taking a great risk: Stanton held evidence revealing Sprague's part in an illegal and treasonable Civil War scheme.[27] Perhaps, this explains why he voted against Johnson. As for Nye's supposed readiness to switch, this assertion is based on the September 23, 1868, entry in the diary of John Bigelow, former United States minister to France, and is mere hearsay which is contradicted by other and much stronger evidence.[28]

In any case, the fact remains that the votes of seven Republicans saved Johnson. As such each vote, of course, was equally important. But the decision of Fessenden not to support conviction was crucial. Given his prestige and influence, had he decided otherwise, so probably would have Grimes, Trumbull, and most of the other "recusants."[29] Furthermore, Ross deserves the credit traditionally given him. His motives may not have been altogether pure and idealistic; conceivably he thought that he would promote his own political future; and certainly after the impeachment trial he wasted no time asking Johnson for choice patronage plums. Nevertheless, he experienced and resisted much more pressure than any of the others who voted for acquittal.[30]

Was Johnson guilty? Should he have been removed? Thirty-five senators said yes, but the vast majority of historians and legal authorities say no. They hold with Johnson's lawyers that the tenure act was unconstitutional (the Supreme Court rendered the same judgment ex post facto in 1926), that it did not apply to Stanton in any event, and that Johnson had a right to test it in the courts. They also agree with Trumbull that "to convict and depose the Chief Magistrate of a great nation, when his guilt was not made palpable by the record, and for insufficient cause," would have been wrong in itself and set a dangerous precedent. It is doubtful, however, whether Johnson's removal would have permanently altered the balance of power between the executive and legislative branches in favor of Congress. Only extremely unusual circumstances, unlikely to recur, caused Johnson to become as weak and vulnerable as he was with respect to Congress; and the factors which have fostered the rise of presidential power since his time would have operated regardless of the outcome of the impeachment trial.[31]

The only noteworthy dissent to the conclusion that Johnson's conviction would have been both unjust and unfortunate comes from a few modern-day neo-Radicals. Like the Radicals, they consider Johnson a bad man who deserved punishment. Like Sumner and Stevens, they contend that Johnson was guilty of more and worse crimes than those with which he was charged. And one of them, Michael Les Benedict, even maintains that the articles having to do with the Tenure of Office Act were legally sound, that the House managers were correct in claiming that impeachment is properly and primarily a political process, and that the failure of impeachment in 1868 means that "the only effective recourse against a president who ignores the will of Congress or exceeds his powers is a democratic removal at the polls." (Benedict wrote before Watergate.) But the neo-Radical arguments, although stimulating, are not convincing.[32] Significantly, many of the impeachers themselves later acknowledged that they had been mistaken, that they had been motivated more by emotion than by reason, and that it was best that they had been unsuccessful.[33]

At 3:25 P.M., May 26, Johnson received a letter from Stanton in which he "relinquished" his post as secretary of war. Four days later the Senate approved Schofield's appointment. On May 31 Johnson accompanied Schofield to the War Department. The president entered the secretary of war's office, laughed, and said, "It is some time since I was in this room before."[34]

11

★★★★★

JOHNSON FINISHES HIS PRESIDENCY

Most Republicans, although disappointed, soon reconciled themselves to the outcome of the impeachment trial. After all, Johnson had only a brief time remaining to serve. It was unlikely he could cause any serious trouble, and if he tried, they would deal with him. In any event, Republicans felt it was less important to depose Johnson than it was to elect Grant. Even before the trial ended a Boston newspaper observed, "It is surprising to see how far the whole subject of impeachment seems to have been thrown into the background" by the approaching presidential campaign.

Johnson himself contributed to pacifying the Republicans. Realizing that it would be both useless and dangerous to do otherwise, he kept his promise not to interfere with the army's implementation of Reconstruction. Consequently he no longer posed a serious threat to Republican political control of the South; to that extent impeachment was a success.

Sumner, Stevens, and a few other embittered Radicals talked of impeaching Johnson again, but hardly anyone listened. On the contrary, some of the leading Republican journals actually praised the seven "recusants" for their courage in voting their convictions and for saving the party from a bad blunder. Before long Fessenden, Grimes, and Trumbull regained most of the influence their nay votes had cost them in the Senate.[1]

Johnson's enforced abandonment of his campaign to wreck the congressional Reconstruction program did not mean, however, that he intended to sit out the remainder of his term quietly and quiescently. Far from it. He believed that he deserved the Democratic nomination for president. Furthermore, he believed that if nominated he would defeat Grant: Had he not already humiliated the general on the issue of veracity and frustrated him with regard to impeachment? To win the election would mean more than victory: For Johnson it would mean vindication—and more than vindication, it would mean vengeance.

So as soon as he escaped conviction by the Republicans, Johnson began seeking the Democratic nomination. On June 20 he sent Congress a message vetoing and denouncing a bill which readmitted Arkansas under a constitution that not only provided for Negro suffrage but that also required all voters to take an oath affirming that they believed in racial equality—a provision clearly designed to discourage whites from going to the polls. Next, five days later, he likewise vetoed a so-called omnibus bill restoring six more Republican-controlled Southern states (North Carolina, South Carolina, Florida, Georgia, Alabama, and Louisiana). Of course—as he no doubt expected—Congress promptly overrode both vetoes. Nevertheless he demonstrated to the Democrats and to the South that he had not surrendered, that he was still battling against Republican iniquity; for the obvious purpose behind bringing these states back into the Union at that particular time was to provide Grant with seventy additional electoral votes.[2]

Next, on July 2, Johnson published a response to ten New York citizens who had inquired, probably by prearrangement, whether he would permit his name to be put forward as a candidate for the presidency at the Democratic convention:

> I am not ambitious of further service—I may say, indeed, of further endurance in that elevated and responsible position, unless by a call so general and unequivocal that it would be an endorsement by the people of my endeavors to defend the Constitution and the reserved rights of the several commonwealths composing what was once in fact the Federal Union. Of such approval, in the present temper of parties, I can, perhaps, have no reasonable expectations.[3]

The key word in this statement was "perhaps." Like many other politicians before and since, while seeming to say no, Johnson, was actually saying yes.

Finally, on July 4, the day the Democratic convention opened, the president issued a proclamation of general amnesty for all those who had participated in the rebellion; the only exceptions were those under indictment—which meant that only Jefferson Davis was excluded. Like the vetoes, this gesture had no practical effect. But it was calculated to appeal to Southern delegates at the convention.

Despite the effectiveness of the appeal, however, Southerners were not going to select the Democratic candidate. Prior to the convention their leaders agreed that the choice should be left to the Northern Democrats. They, presumably, would be best qualified to nominate someone who could carry the North and so win the election; afterwards the president could proceed to dismantle military Reconstruction, which to the South was the all-important objective.

Thus if Johnson was to win the nomination, he would have to secure the backing of the Northern Democrats—above all, of the New York organization. Knowing this, two weeks before the convention he sent several political agents to New York City in quest of support, but they accomplished nothing. The New York Democratic leaders refused even to consider Johnson as a candidate unless he first dumped both Seward and McCulloch. And as always they demanded patronage, particularly in the Treasury Department. "Your friends here have an awful load to carry in the Treasury," reported one of the agents. "Can't you confidentially give some of us here either the news of a bold stroke at the Cabinet or something to say in explanation?" asked another one.[4]

More than likely, Johnson seriously considered giving the Democrats one of the things they wanted—the dismissal of McCulloch. As described earlier, by the fall of 1867 the president had become annoyed with the treasury secretary. During the impeachment Johnson's annoyance increased. He believed that McCulloch had failed to exert himself to influence certain senators to vote for acquittal. "Mr. McCulloch won't do," he remarked to Moore on May 17. "He won't do." Also Johnson suspected McCulloch, wrongly probably, of corrupt currency manipulations; and he realized that McCulloch's fiscal policies were highly objectionable to the Greenback Democrats of the Midwest. But the worst of McCulloch's offenses in Johnson's eyes remained the larger number of Republicans ("Radicals") in the Treasury Department, occupying key posts and working against the administration politically. He shared the Democratic resentment over this state of affairs—a feeling he made manifest when, on June 8, he sarcastically told McCulloch that "we might take a loaded swivel [cannon] and fire it into your Department without fear of injuring any of our adherents."[5]

Yet despite everything, Johnson decided to keep McCulloch in the cabinet. His personal loyalty could not be reasonably doubted, and his administration of the Treasury Department was politically as much an asset as it was a liability. For every Democrat who denounced McCulloch's policies, there was at least one Democrat or Conservative who praised them. In addition, Johnson probably understood that McCulloch's retention of antiadministration office-holders was the price that had to be paid to appease the Republicans, who would have reacted strongly had the Treasury's potent patronage been turned over exclusively to the Democrats.[6]

As for Seward, by the summer of 1868 Johnson was less inclined to dismiss him than at any time previously. Seward had raised the money to pay for Johnson's legal expenses during the impeachment trial. He had selected Evarts and probably was behind the Schofield deal. When told by an emissary from Wade that "bluff Ben," after becoming president, would keep him in the cabinet, Seward replied, "I'll see you damned first. The impeachment of the President is the impeachment of his cabinet"—a declaration which was duly reported to Johnson. Moreover, Seward backed his words with action. Two days before the first impeachment vote, he handed Johnson a letter of resignation to take effect if Johnson was found guilty. Following that vote Johnson said to Moore, "Mr. Seward has shown more interest in this matter than any other of my cabinet and I believe him to be sincere."[7]

Nor was that all. For a brief time after Stanton "relinquished" the War Department, the Senate balked at confirming Schofield. Seward thereupon not only agreed to serve as acting secretary of war but he also contacted Senator Roscoe Conkling of New York; Seward astutely noted that "no mischief can go on without him" and through Conkling brought about Schofield's confirmation. Furthermore, when the Senate rejected Stanbery's reappointment as attorney general out of resentment for his crippling interpretation of the military Reconstruction acts, Johnson at Seward's suggestion named Evarts, whom the Senate quickly approved. As Welles ruefully remarked in his diary, Evarts's presence in the cabinet made Seward "potent beyond what he has hitherto been with the President."[8]

Thus by insisting that Seward and McCulloch be dropped, the Democrats asked Johnson to pay a price he was unwilling—and, in the case of Seward, psychologically unable—to pay. So, if he were to obtain the Democratic nomination, it would have to be on his terms, not theirs. On the evening of July 3, after Moore expressed hope that the Democrats would pick Johnson, he commented: "Why should they not take me up? They profess to accept my measures; they say I have stood by the Constitution and made a noble struggle. It is true I am asked, why don't I join the Democratic party. Why don't they join me?"[9]

The Democrats spent the first three days of their convention adopting a platform which denounced military Reconstruction as "unconstitutional" and "revolutionary," called for state control of suffrage (which, of course, meant no votes for Negroes), and advocated the Greenback position on the national debt and the currency issues. Then on July 7, the day on which Johnson's letter announcing his availability appeared in the press, the Democrats began balloting for a candidate. George H. Pendleton, the Ohio Copperhead and Greenback leader, topped the first count with 105 votes and Johnson was second with 65—all of them from the South and Border states. After that, Johnson's total rapidly dwindled until only the Tennessee delegation continued to support him. Still, neither Pendleton nor the other two leading aspirants, Hendricks and Hancock, could get the needed two-thirds majority. Chase, who covertly but actively sought the nomination, gained virtually no backing at all; to most of the delegates he remained an abolitionist and a Radical. Finally, on July 9, after twenty-one ballots, Horatio Seymour, the former governor of New York and a lukewarm Copperhead, received the nomination despite having repeatedly declined it and despite his being an anti-Greenbacker. As his running mate the Democrats chose Frank Blair, Jr., who had recently aroused Southern enthusiasm by publishing a letter to Representative James O. Brodhead of Missouri declaring that it would be both the right and the duty of a Democratic president to restore white rule in the South by dispersing the Republican carpetbag governments.

The outcome of the first ballot on July 7 pleased Johnson and caused him to feel hopeful, but as the day went on, he began falling farther behind. Also that day Stevens, perhaps with an eye to influencing affairs in New York, introduced in Congress five more proposed articles of impeachment; at the same time he warned the House that unless Johnson was removed, the only escape from his "tyranny" might have to be "found in the dagger of Brutus." By July 8 Johnson seemed to Moore to be "worried and nervous"—indeed, "much more anxious as to the result of the New York convention than he was as to the result of the Impeachment proceedings." Seizing on Stevens's proposal and words, Johnson telegraphed one of his agents in New York, Edmund Cooper, that his nomination was demanded by this latest Radical attack: "How is it possible for me to maintain my position against a vindictive and powerful majority," Johnson asked, "if [I am] abandoned by those who profess to agree in principle with and to be supporters of the policies of the administration?"[10]

Cooper asked permission to publish this statement. He also hinted that Johnson could revive his prospects by removing Seward and other cabinet members. Johnson replied that Cooper could follow his own judgment about publication, but as to the removals, the president asked, "Are we not doing well in carrying seven Cabinet officers who were Republicans in favor of all the measures that Democrats profess to support? Accessions of strength from some quarter," he continued, are "indispensable to the overthrow of the Radical order." Also, had he not convicted Grant of "deception and falsehood" with respect to Stanton's regaining the War Department, and had he not driven the Republican nominee back "in shame and disgrace" in the impeachment? Hence, Johnson told Cooper, it was "not time to change front, and while the enemy is in the field, to select some new leader to fight the last battle." These were words of desperation and they had no effect. At noontime, July 9, a telegram arrived at the White House announcing Seymour's nomination. "The President," recorded Welles, "was calm and exhibited very little emotion, but I could see he was disturbed and disappointed." Twenty-four hours later, however, Moore found him "in bright spirits, the suspense being over."[11]

Actually, Johnson was guilty of self-deception (the occupational disease of presidents) in thinking he had a chance of winning the Democratic nomination. He was popular in the South, where his acquittal on the impeachment charges had been hailed joyfully. But the Northern Democratic leaders considered him weak, inept, and untrustworthy. They had no use for him personally, only for the influence and patronage of his office, and they resented his refusal to let them have as much as they desired. Perhaps Welles was not entirely wrong in suspecting the Democratic leaders of secretly wanting the impeachment effort to succeed, in the belief that Johnson's conviction would turn public opinion against the Republicans and thus aid them in the forthcoming election.[12] Certainly throughout the impeachment proceedings, Democratic spokesmen made it a point to declare they they were defending the president out of principle and not because they backed him politically.

On the other hand, Johnson expressed more than mere bitterness when he told Welles that "the Democratic Party had for twelve years acted as if demented, and seemed determined to continue in error." He stated the truth. By embracing Greenbackism, Democrats lost more potential supporters than they gained. Contrary to the Greenback mythology, not all bondholders were bloated Eastern financiers; instead they came from nearly all classes and were numerous in the West as well. In contrast to the Democrat's fiscal plank, the Republican platform, by calling for payment of the national debt "not only according to the letter, but the spirit of the laws," was sufficiently ambiguous to satisfy both pro- and anti-Greenbackers. More importantly, Seymour himself was a poor choice. His dubious wartime record frightened off many Conservative Republicans and War Democrats who otherwise might have voted for him; he lacked personal magnetism; and during the campaign he made only a few ineffectual speeches. A better candidate would have been Hancock, who looked magnificent, had a fine war record, and had hardly any political record. But the Democratic strategists (if such they can be called) wanted to be able to oppose Grant on the grounds that he was a military man—as if that somehow was supposed to bother American voters. The only nominee worse than Seymour would have been Pendleton or Johnson himself: The prospect of another four years of Johnson would have been intolerable to the mass of Northerners. Grant, on the other hand, struck a resounding chord when, on accepting his nomination, he declared, "Let us have peace." For this reason the Democrats' selection of Blair as their vice-presidential candidate compounded their mistakes: What Blair proposed in his letter to Brodhead was tantamount to starting another civil war.[13]

So Johnson's dream of succeeding himself as president, once so promising, came to an end. Still, he had eight months left in office, eight more months of power. And there remained things he could do, things he needed and wanted to do.

The most pressing of these was completing the acquisition of Alaska. Although the Senate had ratified Seward's treaty, the House so far had refused to appropriate the money required for the purchase. The reason was spite: The Republicans were determined to frustrate the hated Johnson administration in every way possible. Late in March, just before the start of the impeachment trial, the House voted to postpone consideration of the Alaska appropriation for two months, confident that by then Johnson no longer would be in the White House. By so doing, however, it violated the treaty which called for payment no later than April 20. Johnson was disgusted. "We are in a very singular attitude," he remarked to Moore.

Here we have made a treaty with one of the principal powers of the world—perhaps the greatest power in the world. The treaty has been ratified. We have taken possession of the territory and hoisted our flag there, and yet we stand as a nation refusing to pay the money. Such a proceeding might produce war between the two nations.[14]

There was, however, no danger of war. The Russians preferred money—none of them more so than Baron Stoeckl, who stood to receive from his government a slice of the $7.2 million the United States had agreed to pay under the terms of the treaty he and Seward had negotiated. Following Johnson's acquittal, Stoeckl and Seward mounted a campaign to obtain the appropriation; they hired lobbyists and circulated pro-Alaska propaganda. Seward asked Johnson to use his influence—such as it was—with the Democratic congressmen. Stoeckl, knowing where the real power lay, bribed key Republican congressmen. Among them, according to Seward's subsequent testimony, were Nathaniel P. Banks, chairman of the House Foreign Affairs Committee, John W. Forney, editor of the Radical *Washington Chronicle*, and Thad Stevens. Stoeckl also paid off one of Ben Butler's clients who had a dubious claim against the Russian government, with the result that Butler, whose cut was $30,000, suddenly stopped calling Alaska worthless. On July 14—by which time it was obvious that Johnson could derive no political benefit therefrom—the House passed the appropriation by a vote of 114 to 43. All but two of the nays came from Republicans.[15]

The summer of 1868 also saw Johnson's administration achieve another diplomatic success. Late in May a delegation of Chinese, led by Anson Burlingame, the former United States envoy to China, arrived in Washington on what was the first official mission ever from the Celestial Empire to a Western nation. Johnson received and dined the Chinese at the White House, where he called on them "to take an active part in the general progress of civilization." Subsequently, on July 4, Seward and Burlingame signed a treaty (drafted by the former) which defined the legal status of Chinese in the United States and of Americans in China, authorized the stationing of Chinese consuls in American ports, and allowed unrestricted immigration by Chinese into the United States. Seward's purpose was to secure cheap "coolie" labor for the Western states and to foster American trade with China. The Senate did not take immediate action on the treaty—again, the Republicans opposed anything that would redound to the credit of Johnson and Seward—but eventually it was approved after Grant became president.

Another Seward treaty did not fare so well. Late in 1867, after prolonged and complex negotiations, the secretary had signed an agreement whereby the United States was to purchase the Virgin Islands of St. John and St. Thomas from Denmark for $7.5 million. Seward claimed that they would make excellent naval bases; Welles did not think they were needed. Nevertheless, in his 1867 message to Congress Johnson declared that their acquisition was "immediately desirable." But Republican hostility to the administration, a hurricane which devastated the islands and beached an American warship on one of them, and opposition from Sumner and Grant combined to kill the treaty. Likewise, schemes by Seward to buy ports in Santo Domingo and Haiti, to acquire Cuba and Puerto Rico, and to bring Hawaii into the American orbit withered in the chilly climate of Congress. "How sadly domestic disturbances of ours," he wrote John Bigelow in October 1868, "demoralize the national ambition." The basic problem, however, was that overseas expansion at this time was not a national ambition but mainly a Seward ambition. He was thirty years premature—or a prophet, if you prefer.[16]

For Seward, diplomacy was a pleasure—one might even say an addiction. To Johnson it was merely a duty which, for the most part, he gladly left to the New Yorker. As ever Johnson's primary concern, during the fall and summer of 1868 remained events at home—in particular and above all, the presidential election. He hoped very much that it would result in the defeat of Grant and of the Republicans: That would at least be indirect vengeance and vindication. Hence, despite his resentment at being passed over by the Democrats, Johnson did everything prudently possible to help them and Seymour win.

To that end, on July 20 he vetoed a bill which excluded from the electoral college (and so from Seymour's column) the three unreconstructed states of Virginia, Mississippi, and Texas. Congress, needless to say, promptly repassed the bill, but at least in his veto message he could again call attention to the way in which the Republicans trampled over the Constitution in order to cling to power.[17] For the same reason Johnson had Seward word the July 20 announcement that the requisite number of states had ratified the Fourteenth Amendment in such a way as to cast doubt on the legality of the ratifying process. Six of the ratifications, it read, came from "newly-constituted and newly-established bodies avowing themselves to be, and acting as, the legislatures, respectively, of the States of Arkansas, Florida, North Carolina, Louisiana, South Carolina, and Alabama," and two other ratifications were valid only if "the resolutions of the legislatures of Ohio and New Jersey ratifying the aforesaid amendment are to be deemed as remaining in full force and effect, notwithstanding the subsequent resolutions of the legislatures of those States which purport to withdraw the consent of said States from such ratification. . . ." Congress, of course, quickly declared the amendment a part of the Constitution and directed Seward to so proclaim; this he did on July 28.[18] Thus the Fourteenth Amendment became a legal fact, but the stark historical fact is that less than three-fourths of the states had expressed the will of a majority of their inhabitants in ratifying it.

Another opportunity for Johnson to strike at the Republicans came on July 25, two days before Congress adjourned, when he received a bill refunding the national debt. Sponsored by Senator Sherman, it was a compromise measure designed to appease the pro- without offending the anti-Greenback forces. Johnson pocket-vetoed it, however, thereby preventing the Republicans from eluding the financial issue—an issue on which many Democrats were counting for victory. Unfortunately for their campaign plans, an economic upswing began that summer, lessening the appeal of Greenbackism.[19]

Finally, Johnson sought to assist the Democratic cause by taking advantage of an opening that Congress itself had given him. The readmission of North Carolina, South Carolina, Georgia, Florida, Alabama, Arkansas, and Louisiana meant that Johnson as commander in chief regained control of the army in those states, for the military Reconstruction acts now no longer applied to them. Therefore late in July he placed the conservative Meade in command of Georgia, Florida, Alabama, and the Carolinas and Major General Lowell Rousseau, a Democrat, in charge of Arkansas and Louisiana. As at least a partial consequence, both Georgia and Louisiana went to Seymour in the election.

Thus Johnson loosened some of the restrictions placed on him by Congress. He remained tightly bound, however, by the Tenure of Office Act. This became irritatingly evident when, near the end of July, he asked E. A. Rollins to resign as collector of internal revenue, a politically potent post which was being used to benefit the Republicans. Rollins did so, but made his resignation contingent on the Senate's confirmation of a successor. Moreover McCulloch and Evarts warned Johnson against dismissing Rollins—it might lead to a new impeachment, they said, a risk doubly dangerous now that fourteen rabid Radicals from the South sat in the Senate.

Reluctantly heeding their advice, Johnson then had Rollins indicted on charges of corruption involving the New York "whiskey ring," a group of distillers who were bribing federal officials in return for illegal favors. But this too failed to dislodge Rollins; the federal district attorney for New York (whom Doolittle reported to Johnson was himself in the pay of the "whiskey ring") sabotaged the prosecution, with the result that Rollins gained an acquittal. Earlier that summer Johnson did succeed in forcing another Republican incumbent, Assistant Secretary of the Treasury William E. Chandler, to resign. The Senate, however, understandably enough and at McCulloch's secret behest, rejected the man Johnson nominated to replace him—a political crony, Edmund Cooper. In sum, Johnson was unable to wield the patronage sword on behalf of the Democrats even to the limited extent he tried. In fact, the Republicans practically wrested it from him, assessing federal officeholders for political contributions during the campaign.[20]

After Congress adjourned Johnson relaxed a little. Moore found him one Saturday afternoon in his bedroom with a basket of flour from a mill near Greeneville. Johnson pointed to some nibble marks on the basket and said that one night while getting ready for bed he saw a little mouse, whereupon he put the basket on the hearth and let the mice get their fill. "I am now," he explained, "filling it for them tonight." Several days later Moore asked him if he were still feeding the Executive Mansion rodents. Yes, he replied, "The little fellows give me their confidence and I give them their basket and pour upon the hearth some water that they might quench their thirst."[21]

On August 11 Thad Stevens died. For a brief time circumstances had made him a powerful influence; that brief time had ended in May with the failure of impeachment. His death, declared James G. Blaine, "is an emancipation for the Republican party." Shortly before his own death Johnson remarked that "Old Thad Stevens was the most honest man among them [Republicans]."[22]

In September Vermont and Maine voted, overwhelmingly, for the Republican ticket. The Democrats had expected the result but not the margin; it was a bad sign. Then in October Pennsylvania, Ohio, and Indiana went for Grant, spelling disaster for Seymour. The *New York World* pleaded with him to step aside for a better candidate. Some Democrats favored Chase, others Johnson. Although the proposal flattered Johnson and it is possible that he would have accepted a draft, he telegraphed Seymour urging him to intensify the battle against "the despotic power now ready to enter the very gates of the citadel."[23] Seymour responded by making a few more speeches. They did little, if any, good. On November 3 the final totals came in: Grant received 3,013,421 popular and 214 electoral votes to 2,706,829 and 80, respectively, for Seymour. Every state in the North went for Grant except New York, New Jersey, and Oregon. Apart from these three Seymour carried only Delaware, Maryland, Kentucky, Georgia, and Louisiana.

On close inspection, however, the election returns were not altogether discouraging from an anti-Republican standpoint. Grant's victory margin in several Northern states was quite narrow—in Indiana less than 10,000, in California a mere 514. This was scarcely a brilliant performance by the North's number one hero running against a reluctant and lacklustre civilian. Furthermore, the Democrats gained 24 seats in the House, while the Republicans, despite their rotten boroughs in the South, won only 6. But most significant of all, Seymour received more white votes than Grant did. Grant owed his 300,000 popular majority to the Negro votes in the South. Coupled with the disfranchisement of former Confederates in Tennessee, West Virginia, and Missouri, Negro voters also gave him 67 of his 214 electoral votes. Had Seymour been able to add those 67 to his own 80 electoral votes, the election would have ended in a tie! Obviously, therefore, the Republican victory had been a precarious one. Should the Negro vote in the South be eliminated or substantially reduced, the Democrats stood an excellent chance of winning in 1872.[24]

The Republicans recognized this danger. In addition they realized that Negro votes could help them win closely contested Northern states. Hence in February 1869 they pushed through Congress the Fifteenth Amendment, affirming that "the right of citizens of the United States to vote shall not be denied or abridged by the United States or by any state on account of race, color, or previous condition of servitude." At the same time the Republicans required that Virginia, Mississippi, and Texas ratify it as an added condition for readmission.

Sumner and a few other Radicals wanted simply to pass a congressional act giving Negroes the vote—"anything for human rights," he declared, anticipating certain modern judges, "is Constitutional." Also the Radicals criticized the amendment's negative phraseology. They desired a positive assertion of the Negro's right to vote. But the Moderate majority feared that a mere law might be replaced or declared unconstitutional; furthermore, they wished to avoid too flagrant a violation of the party's implied campaign promise to confine black suffrage to the South and not to impose it on the North, where since 1865 only two states, Iowa and Minnesota, had voluntarily established it. During 1869 the Republicans, by taking advantage of their control of most Northern legislatures and nearly all of the Southern ones, secured ratification of the amendment; it went into effect on March 30, 1870, in plenty of time for the congressional elections of that year and the presidential campaign of 1872. It would be too cynical to say that the Republicans were devoid of idealism in thus conferring the vote on the Negro. On the other hand it is naive to claim that their main motive was anything other than political self-preservation.[25]

Overall, the election of 1868 signified the triumph of the Republican Reconstruction program. Before the election most Southerners still hoped that the North, via the Democratic party, would rescue them. Now they could only accept the new order of things as an unpleasant but undeniable fact. Their determination, however, to restore "home rule" and "white supremacy" in no way decreased. On the contrary they resolved to gain twin goals by whatever means proved necessary—political organizations and agitation, economic coercion of Negroes, and deliberate terrorism. The latter, carried out by the Ku Klux Klan and similar outfits, already had proved effective in Georgia and Louisiana, where Seymour won, and in South Carolina and Tennessee, where the Negro vote (and so the Republican majorities) had been substantially reduced. In the future terrorism would be used on a larger scale and with greater success. For the present the Republicans were in the saddle in the South, but they were in for a very rough ride.[26]

To Johnson the election was a bitter disappointment. Moore noted on November 4 that the president "seemed disheartened that the people of the country should have voted to continue Radical." Nonetheless he remained confident of ultimate vindication for both himself and his policies. That was evident in the message he sent to Congress when it convened on December 9.[27]

As he had done so often before, Johnson blasted the Reconstruction acts. They had, he said, "substantially failed and proved pernicious" and should be repealed along with the tenure act and all of the other "unnecessary and unconstitutional" measures which had been adopted during the past two years "under the influence of party passion and sectional prejudice." In addition, for the first time Johnson specifically and publicly criticized the fiscal policy of Congress—and of McCulloch. The federal debt, he asserted, had imposed a new slavery on the nation. The way to abolish it was to make an arrangement with the bondholders whereby the payment of interest would be applied to the principal. In this way, at the end of sixteen years and eight months, bondholders would receive a sum equivalent to one-and-one-half times their original investment measured in gold—"and with this they should be satisfied." Johnson concluded by proposing four constitutional amendments: first, the direct popular election of the president and vice-president, limiting them to one four-year term; second, a "distinct designation" of the successor to the president in the event of the death, resignation, or removal of both the president and the vice-president; third, the popular election of senators; and fourth, "the limitation to a period of years of the terms of federal judges."

The message so incensed Senate Republicans that they ordered the reading of it stopped half-way through. The next day, however, they changed their minds and consented to listen to the rest of it. They then pounced on the fiscal section to condemn Johnson as an advocate of repudiation. In the House, Republicans did the same. Obviously Johnson was seeking to brand them as the servants of "big business" in exploiting "the people."

As for the proposed constitutional changes, they were, in Welles's words, "a favored bantling" of Johnson.[28] He had no expectation of their being adopted at the time but was looking to the future. Two of them, the popular election of senators and a detailed provision for presidential succession, eventually were added to the Constitution. A third, fixed terms for federal judges, perhaps should be adopted, given the dominant role that the judiciary now plays in determining national policy.[29] But in advocating the direct popular election of the president. Johnson proposed something which, fortunately, still stands little chance of being put into effect: the electoral vote helps preserve the two-party system and practically guarantees the election of a president.

Johnson observed Christmas by issuing the last in his long series of amnesty proclamations. This one covered all former rebels without exception—even Jefferson Davis was included. On Evarts's advice, Johnson had abandoned the long and futile attempt to bring the Confederate president to trial. Later Johnson would declare that the greatest disappointment of his presidency was the failure to hang Davis for treason.[30]

On December 29 Johnson celebrated his sixtieth birthday by giving a children's party at the White House, and a few days later he held his final New Year's reception. Many Republicans attended, including Ben Butler. Johnson received them all, even Butler, with his customary courtesy.[31]

But once the holidays ended, he and Congress resumed their squabbling. On January 15 he sent to the Senate a treaty with Britain. This had been negotiated by Reverdy Johnson, who during the summer had replaced Charles Francis Adams as minister to London. (McClellan's nomination to that post back in February 1867 had been quietly buried.) The treaty dealt with the claims that the United States had against Britain arising from the depredations committed on American shipping during the Civil War by the *Alabama* and other British-built Confederate raiders. Instead of providing compensation for the damages inflicted by these ships, however, the treaty merely stipulated that claims by citizens of both nations would be settled on an equal basis, and it contained no apology or expression of regret from the British government. Despite these defects Johnson believed it was as good a treaty as could be hoped for, and he was naive enough to think it could be passed. Instead, Sumner opposed it, Grant denounced it, and the Senate ignored it until April 13 when it was rejected by a vote of 54 to 1. Two years later the United States obtained a much better settlement of the *Alabama* claims.[32]

Throughout January and February the Senate also systematically rejected or ignored practically all of the nominations for office made by the lame duck president. Johnson in turn retaliated with two more vetoes. One was of a bill pertaining to the administration of the District of Columbia's Negro schools, the other blocked a tariff raising duties on copper. Of course Congress overrode both vetoes. Johnson, however, was able to get in a parting blow by pocket-vetoing the Republicans' reply to the fiscal proposal he had made in his message, namely a resolution which declared that "the faith of the United States is solemnly pledged to the payment in coin or its equivalent" of the national debt.[33]

At last March 4, the day of Grant's inauguration, arrived. Grant had let it be known that he had no intention of riding up Pennsylvania Avenue in the same carriage with his predecessor, as was customary. This suited Johnson fine. He spent the morning at the White House, from which his family and all personal property had been moved, signing bills and talking to members of his cabinet. When Seward asked if they should not go to the Capitol for the swearing in ceremonies, Johnson answered, "I am inclined to think that we will finish up our work here by ourselves." At a few minutes past twelve, he announced that the time had come to depart. He shook hands with each cabinet member, then walked down the stairs to the portico, entered his carriage, and drove away.[34] The presidency which had begun three years, ten months, and eleven days before in the parlor of the Kirkwood House had ended.

12

★★★★★

JOHNSON BEFORE THE BAR
OF HISTORY

From the White House Johnson went to the residence of John Coyle, proprietor of the *National Intelligencer* (a circumstance that makes it all the more unlikely that anything of political importance had appeared in that paper without Johnson's prior approval). Except for a brief trip to Baltimore to attend a banquet in his honor, he stayed there until March 18. Then he and his family boarded the train that took them back to Greeneville, Tennessee, where they arrived two days later. His second oldest daughter, Mrs. Mary Stover, had gone to the village earlier and readied his home which had been vandalized by both Confederate and federal soldiers.[1] At the end of March a Knoxville reporter found Johnson in a "neatly furnished parlor, containing a piano [and] two or three small tables," and with pictures of Lincoln, Jackson, Washington, and himself on the walls. The former president's chief complaint, according to the reporter, was that "Rebel troops" had made off with his books.

> I regret the loss of my books. They were not valuable, in one sense of the word, but dollars and cents cannot replace them. There was one in particular that I believe formed a turning point in my life; that is, it caused my thoughts to take a channel which they might not and probably would not have otherwise taken. This book was a volume of extracts from the speeches of Pitt, Fox, Burke and other English orators. When I was learning my trade at Raleigh,

North Carolina, a gentleman used to come into the shop and read aloud, and seeing that we tailors enjoyed it so much, he used frequently to come, and finally gave me the book which was the first property I ever owned. How many times I have read the book I am unable to say, but I am satisfied it caused my life to take a different turn from what it otherwise would.[2]

On June 23 Johnson wrote the former Confederate general, James Longstreet, whose army had occupied Greeneville early in 1864, asking his aid in recovering the books and also his personal papers. However, Longstreet (who had become a "scalawag"—that is, a Southern Republican) replied that he knew nothing of the matter.[3]

During the nearly eight years since he had left Greeneville, Johnson had experienced several lifetimes of excitement, strife, and tribulation. Furthermore, soon after his return his son, Robert Johnson, gave up his losing battle with alcohol and committed suicide. Yet in spite of everything—or perhaps because of it all—Andrew Johnson had no desire for a peaceful retirement in what he called the "lifeless village" of Greeneville.[4] Politics was not only his profession, it was his passion. Moreover he was just sixty, and although his hair was now grey, there was, in that Knoxville reporter's words, "nothing about him that would indicate his being over forty-five." But above all Johnson burned with a determination to achieve what had eluded him as president: vindication for his policies and himself, vengeance against his enemies and betrayers. Consequently, less than a month after leaving Washington, he launched a campaign to return there once again as a senator from Tennessee.

His prospects for success were good. Early in 1869 Tennessee Republicans split into Radical and Conservative factions; the state supreme court restored the ballot to some thirty thousand whites; and the Klan continued to curtail the black vote. As a result, Democrats captured the legislature in the August election, and Tennessee, the first Confederate state to come under Republican domination, was the first to overthrow it. Johnson, who spoke to large and enthusiastic audiences throughout the state, contributed to this outcome.

When the legislature met in October to choose a senator (to replace, incidentally, Fowler, one of the seven "recusants"), Johnson led the early balloting—in fact, he came within one vote of victory. However, enough Confederate Democrats, who could not forgive

Johnson for his wartime stand, joined with Republicans, who could not forgive him for his peacetime record, to prevent him from obtaining a majority. Then the Republicans, employing a nice little bit of skulduggery, nominated Henry Cooper, the brother of Edmund Cooper, who was Johnson's spokesman in the legislature and who had represented the former president at the Democratic convention in New York. Edmund Cooper thereupon deserted Johnson in favor of his own brother, who won by 54 votes to Johnson's 51. Understandably Johnson felt frustrated and bitter.[5]

For the next three years Johnson bided his time, waiting for another opportunity to make a political comeback. Becoming governor or an ordinary House member would not do—he wanted to return to Washington, and he wanted to do it with the endorsement, so to speak, of all of Tennessee. Then, in 1872, a special election for congressman-at-large took place. Johnson sought the Democratic nomination, but when he perceived that it would go instead to Benjamin F. Cheatham, a renowned Confederate general, he decided to play the role of spoiler by running as an independent. In this he was successful. Although he finished a poor third, he drew enough Democratic votes away from Cheatham to enable the Republican candidate, his old Unionist ally, Horace Maynard, to win. He had, Johnson boasted, "reduced the rebel brigadiers to the ranks."

Even so, it appeared that the former president, *persona non grata* to the dominant elements of both parties, was finished politically. Perhaps Johnson himself thought so too. According to the testimony of several men who observed him during this period, he began—or resumed—drinking heavily. One of them, John S. Wise, later described him as being so drunk on one occasion that when a Nashville crowd called on him to speak, he could only stand swaying on a balcony, unable to utter a word—something that borders on the incredible in view of Johnson's fondness for oratory![6]

In June 1873 a cholera epidemic swept East Tennessee and Johnson was stricken. Believing that he was about to die, he penned the following:

All seems gloom and dispair [sic].

I have performed my duty to my God, my country and my family—I have nothing to fear—approaching death to me is the mere shadow of God's protecting wing—beneath it I almost feel sacred—here I know can no evil come—here I will rest in quiet and peace beyond the reach of calumny's poisened [sic] shaft—the influence of envy and jealous enemies, where Treason and Traitors in state, backsliders and hypocrites in church can have no place—where the great fact will be realized *that God is* truth and gratitude, the *highest* atribute [sic] of *men.*

—Sic iter astra is the way to the stars or immortality—[7]

But he survived. Furthermore, a newspaper debate later that summer with John Holt over the case of Mrs. Surratt and the clemency petition revived his spirits, as a good fight always did. By 1874 he was ready to make another bid for the Senate: The term of Parson Brownlow, who had been elected senator in 1869, supplanting Johnson's son-in-law, Patterson, was about to expire. If Johnson could succeed Brownlow, that would be vengeance indeed.

So once more Johnson stumped Tennessee. As ever, the popular response was favorable, but what counted was the legislature. Early in January 1875 it assembled—ninety-two Democrats and eight Republicans (outside of the towns, few Negroes were now voting in the state). At first Johnson forged ahead. Then he dropped behind William Bate, a Confederate "brigadier." Bate, however, was unable to get a majority, and on the forty-fourth ballot he withdrew. Then the third major aspirant, Governor Neil Brown, faltered. Finally, on the fifty-fourth ballot, Johnson was elected by one vote—a most appropriate margin of victory.

News of Johnson's election created a sensation in both the North and the South. It was, declared the *St. Louis Republican,* "the most magnificent personal triumph which the history of American politics can show." Thurlow Weed, in a public letter, asserted that "no common man could have dug himself out of a pit so deep and so dark as that into which he had fallen." *The Nation,* now a stern critic of Grant, stated that Johnson's "personal integrity was beyond question" and that his "respect for the law and the Constitution [had] made his Administration a remarkable contrast to that which succeeded it." Welles and Stanbery sent Johnson letters of congratulation, as did Edmund G. Ross, who wrote, "Your vindication from the slanders born of the hatred & malice of the impeachers of 1868 is now well nigh complete."[8]

Late in February Johnson traveled to Washington to attend a special session of the Senate that Grant had called for the purpose of ratifying a treaty with Hawaii. During the six years since Johnson had left the city, much had happened and much had changed. Of the nineteen senators who had voted for his acquittal, just one remained; only thirteen of the thirty-five who had declared him guilty were still present. Sumner was not among them—he had died the year before. And Stanton had died in 1869, shortly after Grant appointed him to the Supreme Court. As for Grant, although he had won reelection, he too had come to know what it was like to have his favorite projects rejected by Congress, to have friends turn into enemies, and to be scourged by the press. Moreover, the laurels of Appomattox were now badly withered by the series of scandals that had occurred during his administration, some of them involving his closest associates. Finally, all but four of the former Confederate states had thrown off Republican rule, and in 1874 the Democrats, for the first time since 1856, had gained control of the House of Representatives.

On March 5 Johnson took his seat in the Senate—the first and to this day the only former president to do so. Vice-president Henry Wilson, who as a senator had voted to disqualify Johnson from ever holding a federal office, administered the oath to him. Johnson took it in company with Hannibal Hamlin, who had sworn him in as Lincoln's vice-president on that unfortunate occasion ten years before. Some of the Republicans studiously ignored the Tennessean. Others, notably Sherman and Morton, shook his hand. Throughout the proceedings he wore a "kindly smile."[9]

That smile was gone when he arose on March 22 to deliver a speech. Its object was Grant; its subject, fittingly enough, was Louisiana, where Grant recently had used troops to prop up the tottering Carpetbag government. Grant, Johnson proclaimed, was guilty of usurpation, he had trampled the Constitution under his foot. His purpose, Johnson charged, was to raise the "war cry" so that he could "triumphantly ride" into a third term. Should that happen, Johnson asked, "How far off is military despotism?" He concluded by saying that the only hope for preserving liberty and restoring the Union was to respect the Constitution: "May God bless this people and God save the Constitution."[10]

Nothing Johnson said was new and his speech changed nothing; still, it made him feel good to say it. When the special session ended and he headed back home, the former president had every intention of returning to Washington in December and saying the same things again—and much more besides.

But it was not to be. On July 28 he boarded the train at Greeneville to go to Carter's Station, near where his daughter, Mary Stover, lived. During the trip he sat with Captain David Jenkins, a former Union officer, and Captain W. E. McElwee, formerly of the Confederate army. According to McElwee's recollection, written many years later, Johnson stated that he planned to go soon to Ohio and make several speeches. (Was he thinking of the Democratic presidential nomination in 1876?) He described Stanton as the "Marat of American politics," blamed him for causing Lincoln's assassination and suppressing the clemency petition for Mrs. Surratt, and asserted that Stanton had "cut his throat from ear to ear" because his reason had been "dethroned by vindictive anger and disappointment."[11]

From Carter's Station, Johnson took a wagon to his daughter's farm. On the way he complained to the driver of feeling a "fullness" in the head. Shortly after lunch Mrs. Stover heard a thud in her father's bedroom: Johnson had fallen to the floor with a paralytic stroke. He lingered two days, then suffered another stroke; at 2:30 A.M., July 31, he died.[12]

While talking to Jenkins and McElwee on the train, Johnson had stated that on the night of Lincoln's assassination, "I walked the floor, feeling a responsibility I never felt heretofore. More than a hundred times I said to myself, what will the calm and correct historian say to my acts and administration one hundred years from now?" As might be suspected, the immediate verdict, particularly in the North, was unfavorable.[13] Thus Henry Wilson in *History of the Rise and Fall of the Slave Power in America*, published in 1877, and James G. Blaine in *Twenty Years of Congress*, published in 1884, portrayed Johnson as an obstinate, boorish character who arrogantly defied Congress in a vain effort to carry out a pro-Southern Reconstruction policy. The only Northerners of note to defend him in print were Gideon Welles and Hugh McCulloch, and even they admitted that he suffered from serious personal flaws.

Not until the turn of the century did some truly historical evaluations of Johnson appear. The most influential of these was written by James Ford Rhodes in the sixth volume of his *History of the United States from the Compromise of 1850*, published in 1906. Rhodes, who had been a young Ohio businessman and a Republican during Reconstruction, found no reason to dissent from the prevailing view of Johnson's character: "Of all men in public life, it is difficult to conceive of one so ill-fitted for this delicate work [of Reconstruction] as was Andrew Johnson." In his opinion, Johnson's main defects were obstinacy and conceit; and although he admitted that Johnson possessed "intellectual force" and "strict integrity," Rhodes declared that these qualities were cancelled out by his inflexibility and "lack of political sense." Also Rhodes strongly criticized Johnson's vetoes of the Freedmen's Bureau Bill and the Civil Rights Act and the president's opposition to the Fourteenth Amendment. Not only did he thereby destroy any chance of co-operation between the executive and legislative branches, Rhodes argued, Johnson thus opened the way for Radical domination. This was unfortunate in Rhodes's view because it led to an immoral, unconstitutional, and impractical attempt to reconstruct the South on the basis of military force and Negro suffrage. In general, Rhodes concluded that "no one else was so instrumental in defeating John-son's own aims as was Johnson himself."

Rhodes's interpretation was supplemented by the work of John Burgess, Woodrow Wilson, and William Dunning, all of whom wrote about Reconstruction at roughly the same time and all of whom were Southerners. Burgess declared that "Mr. Johnson was an unfit person to be President of the United States" and that "he was low-born and low-bred, violent in temper, obstinate, coarse, vindictive, and lacking in the sense of propriety. . . ." Wilson characterized Johnson as "self-willed, imperious, implacable," a man who "saw to it . . . that nobody should relish or trust him whom bad temper could alienate." Only Dunning tended towards a sym-pathetic view of Johnson personally, describing him as a man of "integrity of purpose, force of will, and rude intellectual force." But Dunning followed Rhodes in describing the Freedman's Bureau and civil rights vetoes (both of which he criticized) as being polit-ically inept, and he believed that the "swing around the circle" "again demonstrated that Andrew Johnson was not a statesman of national size in such a crisis as existed in 1866."[14]

On the other hand Rhodes, Burgess, Wilson, and Dunning all more or less agreed that Johnson tried to put into effect the essence of Lincoln's Reconstruction plan and that, in Burgess's words, John-son was "nearer right" than the Radicals. They also denounced the Tenure of Office Act, Stanton's conduct, and the House impeach-ment. Indeed, their main complaint against Johnson was not what he attempted but how he went about it.

But even as they wrote and published, a trend towards what might be termed the total historical rehabilitation of Johnson had gotten underway. It began in 1903 with David Miller DeWitt's *The Impeachment and Trial of President Andrew Johnson.* DeWitt was the first scholar to use Johnson's private papers and Moore's diary— materials which Martha Patterson furnished him prior to her death in 1901. Although DeWitt's book focused on the subject indicated by its title, it did present a general account of Johnson's policies and activities before and after his impeachment. The portrait that emerged was of a man who not only labored to do good, but who also was good himself—a noble giant pulled down by vicious Lilliputians.[15]

Ten years later, in 1913, James Schouler attempted a full-scale revision of Johnson's reputation in his *History of the Reconstruction Period*. Schouler based his book on the Johnson Papers, which the Library of Congress had acquired in 1904. He was also the first historian to utilize fully Welles's diary, published in 1911. Schouler criticized Rhodes for having been "quite unjust to Johnson," exonerated Johnson of having been influenced by liquor while in the White House, and, like DeWitt, asserted that Johnson had been the victim of slanderous propaganda. Schouler's account of Johnson's struggle with Congress was highly sympathetic and assigned the greater share of the blame for what Schouler considered to be the failure of Reconstruction to the Radicals, whom he characterized as "vengeful and visionary." Yet his overall assessment of Johnson was actually much the same as Rhodes's: "This President created difficulties for himself at every step, while trying to carry out ideas often of themselves sound and useful."[16]

Both DeWitt and Schouler made an impression. Nevertheless through World War I and the decade immediately following most historians continued to file a negative report on Johnson, even though they considered his policies fundamentally correct. Thus E. P. Oberholtzer in the first two volumes of his *History of the United States since the Civil War*, published in 1917, was just as critical of Johnson as Rhodes had been; and Walter L. Fleming in his *Sequel to Appomattox*, published in 1919, described the seventeenth president as an "ill-educated, narrow, vindictive . . . stubborn, irascible, and undignified man" who "never sloughed off his backwoods crudeness."[17]

But then, at the end of the 1920s, an historiographical revolution took place. In the span of three years five widely read books appeared, all highly pro-Johnson. First, in 1928, came Robert W. Winston's *Andrew Johnson: Plebian and Patriot*. Next, in 1929, was Lloyd Paul Stryker's *Andrew Johnson: A Study in Courage* and Claude G. Bowers's *The Tragic Era: The Revolution after Lincoln*. Finally, in 1930, Howard K. Beale published *The Critical Year: A Study of Andrew Johnson and Reconstruction* and George Fort Milton, *The Age of Hate: Andrew Johnson and the Radicals*. Not all of these works were of equal merit; some were more influential than others. They differed in general approach and specific interpretations, but they all glorified Johnson and condemned his enemies. According to these writers, Johnson was a humane, enlightened, and liberal statesman who waged a courageous battle for the Constitution and democracy against scheming and unscrupulous Radicals, who were motivated by a vindictive hatred of the South, partisanship, and a desire to establish the supremacy of Northern "big business." In short, rather than a boor, Johnson was a martyr; instead of a villain, a hero.

From the standpoint of its influence on professional historians the most significant of these books was Beale's *The Critical Year.* Beale was a disciple of Charles Beard's quasi-Marxist economic determinism; and his book presented an elaboration of Beard's "second American Revolution" thesis, contending (with only the skimpiest basis in fact) that Reconstruction was a conspiracy by the "capitalistic" North to confirm politically and economically the military victory it had gained over the "agrarian" South during the Civil War. In addition Beale openly proclaimed that his purpose was to dethrone Rhodes as the standard authority on Reconstruction. Rhodes, Beale charged, had failed to see "the larger economic and social aspects." In his opinion "the future had vindicated" Johnson on "reconstruction and constitutional interpretation." The main reason Johnson lost to the Radicals, Beale argued, was his failure to exploit economic issues during the 1866 elections. The Radicals, on the other hand, triumphed through a clever combination of villification and demagogic "claptrap." On the whole, Beale believed that "in spite of obvious mistakes and shortcomings, Johnson becomes more worthy of respect."[18]

This pro-Johnson historiographical revolution was enormously successful. It even led to the 1942 Hollywood film, *Tennessee Johnson,* in which Van Heflin portrayed Johnson as a heroic fighter for democracy and justice. Moreover, in 1948 the prominent historian Arthur M. Schlesinger, Sr., conducted a poll of fifty-five fellow historians which resulted in Johnson being rated as an "average" president; in 1956 Clinton L. Rossiter in *The American Presidency* classified Johnson as one of the "near great" presidents.[19] By then it seemed that the tailor-statesman had not hoped in vain that his performance as president would be approved by "calm and correct" future historians.

But also in 1956 David Donald, one of the most influential and innovative Civil War historians, published an article entitled "Why They Impeached Andrew Johnson." Donald wrote of Johnson in terms reminiscent of Rhodes. Johnson, he contended, suffered from "chronic lack of discretion"; "he lacked political sagacity"; and "his mind was immovably closed, and he defended his course with all the obstinacy of a weak man." Donald also arrived at almost the same basic conclusion as had Rhodes: Johnson, who "played into his enemies' hands" by his crude personal conduct, had "sacrificed all influence with the party which had elected him and . . . turned over its control to the Radicals. . . ." As a consequence, Donald wrote, "he threw away a magnificent opportunity" to achieve a reconstruction that would have been fair to North and South, black and white.[20]

Donald's article was the opening shot in what turned out to be a titantic historical barrage directed against Johnson. Within the next seven years no less than five major works appeared, all highly critical of Johnson and of his policies: Fawn M. Brodie, *Thaddeus Stevens: Scourge of the South* (1959); Eric L. McKitrick, *Andrew Johnson and Reconstruction* (1960); Benjamin Thomas and Harold M. Hyman, *Stanton: The Life and Times of Lincoln's Secretary of War* (1962); LaWanda Cox and John Cox, *Politics, Principle and Prejudice* (1962); and William Brock, *An American Crisis: Congress and Reconstruction, 1865–67* (1963).

Of these works, McKitrick's made the strongest impact on the historical profession. In it he explicitly set out to do to Beale what Beale had supposedly done to Rhodes—that is, render his interpretation obsolete. Indeed, McKitrick frankly admitted "an unusual rapport" not only with Rhodes but even with James G. Blaine. Beale, McKitrick declared, was dead wrong in claiming that the "real" issue of Reconstruction was economic and that Johnson's great blunder was failing to exploit it. The true issue, McKitrick argued, was the status of the Negro in American society. Futhermore, he wrote that Johnson lost in his struggle with Congress because of his defects in character and his ineptitude as a politician. McKitrick, however, differed from the Rhodes tradition in one very important respect, arguing that the Moderate Republicans (as exemplified by Fessenden and Sherman) generally controlled Congress, not the Radicals (led by Sumner and Stevens), and that the Reconstruction program of the Republicans, although not ideal, was on the whole necessary and, given the circumstances, just.

Brodie, Thomas and Hyman, the Coxes, and Brock all presented basically the same interpretation of Johnson; the only differences were that Thomas and Hyman pictured him as unscrupulous as well as incompetent and that the Coxes emphasized his racism.

By the time these historians got through, Johnson's historical reputation once more was quite low—in fact, it was even lower than it had been at the turn of the century. At least Rhodes and Dunning had approved of Johnson's Reconstruction policy while criticizing what they deemed to be the excesses of Congress. This new school of revisionist historians, however, considered the president's Reconstruction program inadequate at best and vicious at worst; and about the only thing they found wrong with the congressional program was that after a while the North and the Republicans ceased to enforce it, thereby betraying the Negro and the cause of equal rights.

Throughout the 1960s this revisionist version of Johnson dominated the historical profession, as can be seen in Kenneth M. Stampp's *The Era of Reconstruction* (1965) and a host of other writings which argued that Johnson was wrong in opposing (happily in vain) the essentially moderate and idealistic Republicans. The only scholar to take a significantly different approach during this period was David Donald in *The Politics of Reconstruction, 1863–1867*, published in 1965. Contending that the traditional methods of historical research had reached a dead end when it came to analyzing motivation during Reconstruction, Donald applied some of the techniques of quantitative history to examining the early phases of the conflict between the president and Congress over Reconstruction policy. Donald's findings led him to suggest, first, that objective political factors left Johnson with little choice except to follow the course he did and, second, that practical considerations arising from the political situation within their constituencies possibly had more to do with the attitudes of Republican congressmen than did their personal ideologies.

So far only a few scholars have followed Donald's lead in using quantitative methods to study Reconstruction history.[21] Instead the most spectacular recent development in Reconstruction historiography has been the emergence of a neo-Radical school. Its leading exponents are Hans L. Trefousse, author of *The Radical Republicans: Lincoln's Vanguard for Racial Justice* (1969) and *The Impeachment of a President: Andrew Johnson, the Blacks, and Reconstruction* (1975); Michael Perman, who wrote *Reunion without Compromise: The South and Reconstruction, 1865–1868* (1973); and Michael Les Benedict, whose principal book is *A Compromise of Principle: Congressional Republicans and Reconstruction, 1863–1869* (1974).

These historians agree that Johnson misused and abused the

powers of his office, that he was both evil and cunning, and that although he made mistakes in implementing it, his basic strategy of uncompromising resistance to congressional Reconstruction ultimately proved successful, for in combination with the adamant opposition of the Southern whites and the conservatism of the Republican Moderates, it prevented the achievement of a true reconstruction of the South. That, these neo-Radicals contend, required much more than the military Reconstruction acts and the Fourteenth and Fifteenth amendments. What Congress should have done, they believe, was to do what Sumner and Stevens wanted: keep the South under total and indefinite military rule, confiscate the "rebels'" lands, and distribute them among the Negroes. In this way, these writers argue, the South's "political and economic elite" would have been removed from power and "racial equality" established in America. The failure to do this, they conclude, meant the failure of Reconstruction—and the triumph of Johnson and racism.

The neo-Radicals, however, have not been the only historians to publish important books pertaining to Johnson and Reconstruction during the late 1960s and early 1970s. Distinguished for their balance and scholarship are the following: William C. Harris, *Presidential Reconstruction in Mississippi* (1967); James E. Sefton, *The United States Army and Reconstruction, 1865–1877* (1967); David Donald, *Charles Sumner and the Rights of Man* (1970); John Niven, *Gideon Welles: Lincoln's Secretary of the Navy* (1973); and Martin E. Mantell, *Johnson, Grant, and the Politics of Reconstruction* (1973). None can be termed pro-Johnson, but each work eschews moralistic interpretations and demonstrates that there was more behind Johnson's actions and those of Southerners than a benighted racism. If a label has to be pinned on these works, perhaps "conservative revisionist" would be appropriate.

A variety of factors account for the oscillations in Johnson's historical reputation, but probably the main one is the influence on historians of their own times and their resultant intellectual outlook. Thus nearly every historian who wrote about Johnson between 1895 and 1945 assumed, as did the majority of his fellow white Americans, first, that the top priority of Reconstruction should have been reconciliation between North and South and, second, that the Negro, because of nature, nurture, or both, was an inferior being. Consequently these historians praised Johnson for endeavoring to restore the South to the Union as quickly as possible and condemned the "Radicals" for delaying this reconciliation by imposing "Negro rule" on the South. By the same token, to the degree that they criticized Johnson, it was because they believed that his weaknesses and mistakes had enabled the "Radicals" to open up the ballot box to the unqualified black voters.

Of course Beale and the other historians of the Beard school, although pro-Johnson, were not anti-Negro. Writing during the "Big Boom" of the 1920s and the "Big Bust" of the 1930s, convinced that economics was the mainspring of history, they were, in effect, simply blind to the Negro. To them the real story and the real tragedy of Reconstruction was the ascendancy gained by "Eastern industrial capitalism." Accordingly they considered Johnson a hero for trying however ineptly to prevent this from happening, and they looked upon the Radicals as villains for causing it to happen. As for civil and political rights for the Negro, in the opinion of the Beardians, these issues were mere Radical propaganda.

The revisionists of the late 1950s and early 1960s, on the other hand, regarded the Negro as central to Reconstruction, and they rejected out-of-hand the concept of racial inferiority. Hence they sympathized with the efforts of the Radicals on behalf of Negro rights and condemned Johnson for his callousness towards them. In so doing these historians undoubtedly reflected the emotions generated by the civil rights movement. They perceived the Negro almost one hundred years after adoption of the Fourteenth and Fifteenth amendments as still being oppressed and suppressed. Therefore, they wrote about the "first Reconstruction" of the 1860s with the purpose, sometimes frankly avowed, of advancing the cause of the "second Reconstruction" of the 1960s. They were both determined and optimistic that this time, there would be no failure.

The second Reconstruction, however, although it accomplished much, fell far short of the hopes and expectations of liberals—which is to say most intellectuals. Chronic unemployment, educational backwardness, and social demoralization remained endemic among the black population. This unpleasant but undeniable fact coupled with the Vietnam conflict caused some intellectuals to conclude that American society suffered from an inherent corruption which could not be remedied by reform and required a revolutionary solution. Possibly the neo-Radical historians of Reconstruction are, to some degree, a product of this reaction. If so, then this might help explain their contention that what was needed after the Civil War was a truly radical Reconstruction.

On the other hand, other intellectuals concluded from the events of the 1960s and after that it was unrealistic to expect a quick solution, or even (in a sense) any solution at all, to the "American dilemma" of race. They were disillusioned by the minimal or nonexistent success of various highly ambitious and expensive governmental programs allegedly designed to eliminate poverty and uplift the minorities, and they were disgusted by the excesses of self-styled revolutionaries whose main concrete achievement was to make possible the election of Richard Nixon. Perhaps, therefore, the more sober outlook on Reconstruction by the conservative revisionists is, at least to some degree, an outcome of this reaction: Are the leaders of the 1860s, including even Johnson, to be condemned for a failure to accomplish something that has proved to be difficult—if not impossible—to achieve a hundred years later?

The quantity and quality of research done by the neo-Radicals is impressive and I personally have benefited greatly from it. Nevertheless, I believe that they are guilty of treating the past as present politics and of ignoring the warning made by Thomas J. Pressly in 1966. In demonstrating the close link between racial attitudes and Reconstruction scholarship, he asked, "Should not historians today caution themselves that, since they believe in racial equality, they should examine with particular vigor those findings which coincide with their convictions?"[22] On the other hand I find the approach and, as a rule, the evaluations of the conservative revisionists more congenial and satisfactory. This, presumably, has been made evident by the foregoing pages in which I have presented my own specific views on Johnson and Reconstruction.

Concerning Johnson, the man, the judgment of those sympathetic but perceptive contemporaries who had personal contact with him is, on the whole, sound. He "possessed great natural capacity," although in no sense was he a great man; he held "few ideas" and was "narrow-minded"; and although not "utterly deficient" in tact, he often was insufficiently adroit. Furthermore, he was "naturally distrustful," had "few constant friends," was "always impatient of advice" (but like any president got plenty of it anyway), and "resented dictation from any quarter." Courage, of course, he had in abundance, and (to quote McCulloch) he was "a combatant by temperament" who enjoyed controversy even if he did not invariably court it. But as Benjamin Curtis observed shortly after coming to Washington to serve as one of the president's defense lawyers, Johnson lacked "discretion and forecast," with the result, in McCulloch's words, that he "ran against snags which he might easily have avoided."[23] In addition, as Welles repeatedly commented in his diary, the president frequently was indecisive and hesitant, with a tendency, when he did act, to do so hastily and without proper preparation. These traits cost him dearly in the case of Stanton.

Johnson was more an ideologue than a politician in the usual sense of the word. More important to him than the success of any political party was the upholding and triumph of those "correct principles" of Jacksonian democracy and constitutionalism of which, no doubt quite sincerely, he considered himself to be the embodiment. This attitude explains his unshakable belief in his own rectitude, his unwillingness to compromise, and his lone-wolf approach to politics. As noted by a modern political analyst, "persons attached to politics by ideology do not identify themselves with organizations but with a point of view, and their commitment to organizations is therefore weak, instrumental, [and] conditional. . . ." Moreover, such persons "tend to hold relatively extreme and intense views, and to . . . see particular questions as part of larger wholes." Consequently they regard "virtually any policy or issue" as involving "fundamental questions" which cannot be compromised without a sacrifice of "principle."[24]

Most likely Welles was correct in his assessment that Johnson committed a "fatal error" in seeking to prolong his presidency another four years.[25] On entering the White House, had he dedicated himself to completing the term and work of Lincoln, kept the Democrats at a distance, and above all not embarked on a campaign to create a new party, he would have greatly strengthened his position with respect to Congress and the North and would have avoided arousing Republicans' fears that he was conniving with the Democrats and the South to oust them. And most certainly David Donald was correct in criticizing Johnson for trying as president to act like Andrew Jackson when "common sense" dictated that, given the manner in which he became president, Johnson should have proceeded with caution and restraint.[26] Johnson was driven by an incessant urge for power. His previous experience first as the embattled governor and then as the nearly omnipotent military governor of Tennessee probably influenced him; Andrew Jackson was his hero and model; and he inherited from Lincoln what in some respects was an almost dictatorial presidency. Hence, although unfortunate, perhaps it was inevitable that he made Welles's' "fatal error" and failed to display Donald's "common sense."

The basic reason for the defeat of Johnson's Reconstruction policy was his inability to comprehend the postwar mood of the North and to yield to it sufficiently and in time. For him, the war had achieved its sole legitimate goals with the suppression of the rebellion and the destruction of slavery. As a Southerner, a Jacksonian Democrat, and a believer in white supremacy, he simply could not believe that the North would support the imposition on the South, by means of military rule and unconstitutional legislation, of civil and political equality for blacks.

Johnson's anti-Negro prejudice, which so many modern historians deplore, was indeed deplorable. It rarely—if ever—was decisive, however, in determining his policies and conduct. Furthermore his attitude on race did not differ substantially from that of Jefferson, Jackson, or Lincoln. Given Johnson's background, it would have been incredible had he held the same views as Charles Sumner or Wendell Phillips; yet during the past twenty years he has been denounced for not possessing them. Also it should be kept in mind that during Johnson's time the majority of white Americans, Northerners as well as Southerners, despised blacks. Only a temporary and fragile combination of unique circumstances made possible ratification of the Fourteenth and Fifteenth amendments. Idealism and humanitarianism were a part of that combination, but the main ingredient was the desire of the North and of the Republicans to preserve the "fruits of victory." When, during the 1870s, it became politically impossible and unnecessary to enforce the Fourteenth and Fifteenth amendments in the South, the North and the Republicans abandoned any serious effort to do so. By then, too, most Northern leaders had come to recognize that continued federal intervention in the South was counterproductive for the Negro and that it prevented a true restoration of national unity.

The neo-Radical contention that Johnson by his wrong-headed and bull-headed resistance to Congress frustrated the achievement of "democracy" in the South and consequently became the ultimate victor in the battle over Reconstruction is, to put it bluntly, nonsense. By establishing "democracy" these neo-Radicals mean specifically the confiscation of land from Southern whites and its distribution among the blacks, thereby supposedly providing Negroes with the economic basis for political power. There was never, however, the slightest chance of this taking place, Johnson or no Johnson. Only a handful of ultra Radicals, notably Stevens, advocated it (and his motive was more hatred of Southerners than love of Negroes). The vast majority of Republican congressmen and of Northern people strongly opposed it; not only did it run counter to their belief in the sacredness of property rights, but they realized rightly that it would create, in the words of Henry Wilson, "an Ireland or Poland in America." Had such a redistribution of land been attempted, the outcome would have been large-scale guerrilla war in the South. The North could not have suppressed Southern resistance of this type except by means intolerable to the majority of Northerners and fatal to the Negroes.[27]

Johnson's vetoes of the Freedmen's Bureau Bill and the Civil Rights Act and his opposition to the Fourteenth Amendment were bad policy as well as bad politics. These measures were needed and they were right. (The framers of the Fourteenth Amendment neither foresaw nor desired that the Supreme Court would pervert it, first to promote capitalism and then egalitarianism.) On the other hand, Johnson was correct in asserting that ultimately the blacks in the South would have to come to terms with the whites and that it would be the whites who would set the terms; despite everything the whites remained socially, economically, and intellectually dominant, and it was only a matter of time before they prevailed politically. As McCulloch predicted to Sumner in August 1865, the enfranchisement of the Negro in the South could not be "secured without a strong military force in every county."[28] Less than ten years after passage of the First Military Reconstruction Act practically the entire South was under white Democratic control and the Negro was in the process of being reduced to a condition that was in some ways worse than slavery. Indeed, until recently the main legacy of congressional Reconstruction in the South was an intensification of anti-Negro prejudice and oppression. Not until the middle of the twentieth century did the Southern Negroes' lot substantially improve, and even then, progress was as much the product of industrialization, urbanization, and massive migration to the North as it was of governmental action.

It was unfortunate that Johnson was not a wiser, abler, and nobler man. But seldom do nations have the leaders they need. In Johnson's case his blunders repeatedly played into the hands of the Republicans, and particularly the Radicals. As a paradoxical consequence the process of Reconstruction in the South, for which he had much sympathy, was prolonged and embittered, whereas the Negroes, for whom he had little sympathy, achieved civil and political rights (at least on paper) sooner and in fuller measure than they otherwise would have. In contrast, had Lincoln lived, and had he pursued (as he probably would have) the same basic Reconstruction policy as did Johnson, his greater political skill and strength would, in all likelihood, have resulted in the speedier restoration of the Southern states, some essential but limited gains for the Negro, and the general frustration of the Radicals. Hence, the Radicals were right, although for the wrong reasons, to hail Johnson's accession to power; and later they had good reason to join Wendell Phillips in praying "that the President may continue to make mistakes."

Johnson can be respected for his courage, for his unwavering adherence to his "correct principles," and for upholding the integrity, if not always the dignity, of the presidency. For these reasons, despite being impeached and having all of his major vetoes overridden, he was a strong president in the personal sense. Johnson had, thought Henry Adams, a "self-assurance" that not only gave him "the look of a true President, but actually made him one."[29] On the other hand, because of his blunders and obstinacy, the presidency in an institutional sense plummeted to the lowest point of power and prestige in its history. Yet this drop was not permanent nor even long-lasting. Moreover, if America had, as Woodrow Wilson called it, "congressional government" during the remainder of the nineteenth century, it was more the result of historical circumstance than of any legacy of Johnson's.

Finally, Johnson was far from being altogether wrong about Reconstruction, and the Republicans were far from being altogether right. Yet the dominant fact of his presidency is this: His policies were defeated, those of his enemies triumphed. In large part this was because of factors beyond his control, but in larger part it was because of his ineptness in using the power he so suddenly and unexpectedly inherited. For that reason he must be judged as being, on the whole, a failure as president.

Andrew Johnson was buried on a hill near his home. His body was wrapped in the United States flag, and beneath his head lay his well-thumbed copy of the Constitution.

Notes

CHAPTER 1

1. Lately Thomas, *The First President Johnson* (New York: William Morrow & Co., 1968), pp. 3–4, 314–316; Milton Lomask, *Andrew Johnson: President on Trial* (New York: Farrar, Straus & Co., 1960), pp. 3–9.

2. The following account of Johnson's prepresidential career is based, except where otherwise indicated, on Thomas, *President Johnson*, pp. 7–309, and on Robert W. Winston, *Andrew Johnson: Plebian and Patriot* (New York: Henry Holt, 1928), pp. 3–263.

3. Ralph W. Haskins, "Andrew Johnson and the Preservation of the Union," *East Tennessee Historical Society Publications* 33 (1961): 45.

4. Leroy P. Graf and Ralph W. Haskins, eds., *The Papers of Andrew Johnson* (Knoxville: University of Tennessee Press, 1967 – [hereafter cited as *Johnson Papers*]), 2:xv–xxix; W. M. Caskey, "First Administration of Governor Andrew Johnson," *East Tennessee Historical Society Publications* 1 (1929): 43–59; W. M. Caskey, "The Second Administration of Governor Andrew Johnson," ibid. 2 (1930): 34–54; Robert G. Russell, "Prelude to the Presidency: The Election of Andrew Johnson to the Senate," *Tennessee Historical Quarterly* 26 (Summer, 1967): 152, 171–172.

5. Russell, "Prelude to the Presidency," p. 154 n. 27; *Johnson Papers*, 2:xxx.

6. *Johnson Papers*, 2:xviii; Thomas, *President Johnson*, p. 86.

7. Thomas, *President Johnson*, p. 123.

8. Oliver P. Temple, *Notable Men of Tennessee* (New York: Cosmopolitan Press, 1912), pp. 373–382, 451–467.

9. Thomas, *President Johnson*, pp. 70, 91, 229.

10. Temple, *Notable Men*, pp. 368–369; Thomas B. Alexander, "Strange Bedfellows: The Interlocking Careers of T. A. R. Nelson, Andrew Johnson and W. G. (Parson) Brownlow," *East Tennessee Historical Society Publications* 24 (1952):69.

11. *Johnson Papers*, 3:xvii–xxi, 638–639.

12. Lloyd Paul Stryker, *Andrew Johnson: A Profile in Courage* (New York: Macmillan Co., 1929), p. 837.

13. John M. Palmer, *Personal Recollections of John M. Palmer: The Story of an Earnest Life* (Cincinnati: Robert Clarke Co., 1909), p. 127.

14. George Fort Milton, *The Age of Hate: Andrew Johnson and the Radicals* (New York: Coward, McCann, 1930), p. 145.

15. William E. Smith, *The Francis Preston Blair Family in Politics* (New York: Macmillan Co., 1933), pp. 327–328; Thomas, *President Johnson*, pp. 196–197.

16. Hugh McCulloch, *Men and Measures of Half a Century: Sketches and Comments* (New York: Charles Scribner's Sons, 1888), 373–374.

17. Allan Nevins, *The War for the Union* (New York: Charles Scribner's Sons, 1971), 4:323.

18. Except where otherwise indicated, the data presented in the following description of America at the

end of the Civil War is derived from: E. B. Long, *The Civil War Day by Day* (Garden City, N.Y.: Doubleday & Co., 1971), pp. 700–728; J. G. Randall and David Donald, *The Civil War and Reconstruction*, 2d ed. (Boston: D. C. Heath and Co., 1961), pp. 529–532; and Ellis Paxson Oberholtzer, *A History of the United States since the Civil War* (New York: Macmillan Co., 1917), 1: 50–114, 189–267.

19. Thomas C. Cochran, "Did the Civil War Retard Industrialism?" *Mississippi Valley Historical Review* 58 (Sept. 1961):197–210.

20. Albert Castel, *A Frontier State at War: Kansas, 1861–1865* (Ithaca, N.Y.: Cornell University Press, 1958), p. 232.

CHAPTER 2

1. McCulloch, *Men and Measures*, p. 376.
2. Ibid.
3. Eric L. McKitrick, *Andrew Johnson and Reconstruction* (Chicago: University of Chicago Press, 1960), pp. 43–48, 53–84.
4. Nevins, *War for the Union*, 4:342.
5. Ibid., pp. 342–343.
6. Wade to Lewis D. Campbell, May 6, 1865, Lewis D. Campbell Papers, Ohio Historical Society, Columbus; David Donald, *Charles Sumner and the Rights of Man* (New York: Alfred A. Knopf, 1970), pp. 219–223.
7. Nevins, *War for the Union*, 4: 341–345; McKitrick, *Johnson and Reconstruction*, pp. 47, 67–68; LaWanda Cox and John Cox, *Politics, Principle and Prejudice, 1865–1866* (New York: Free Press of Glencoe, 1963), pp. 50–52.
8. Michael Perman, *Reunion without Compromise: The South and Reconstruction, 1865–1868* (Cambridge: Cambridge University Press, 1973), pp. 49–52.
9. Howard K. Beale, ed., *Diary of Gideon Welles* (New York: W. W. Norton & Co., 1960 [hereafter cited as Welles, *Diary*]) 2:291; Benjamin P. Thomas and Harold M. Hyman, *Stanton: The Life and Times of Lincoln's Secretary of War* (New York: Alfred A. Knopf, 1962), pp. 402–404.
10. Thomas and Hyman, *Stanton*, pp. 405–417; Raoul S. Naroll, "Lincoln and the Sherman Peace Fiasco—Another Fable?" *Journal of Southern History* 20 (Nov. 1954): 459–483.
11. Thomas and Hyman, *Stanton*, pp. 419–424, 443–444.
12. Welles, *Diary*, 2:301–302.
13. Thomas and Hyman, *Stanton*, pp. 445–446; Milton, *Age of Hate*, pp. 186–189; Glyndon G. Van Deusen, *William Henry Seward* (New York: Oxford University Press, 1967), p. 415.
14. Edward McPherson, ed., *The Political History of the United States of America during the Period of Reconstruction* (Washington, D.C.: Solomons & Chapman, 1875), pp. 9–12; Milton, *Age of Hate*, pp. 187–189.
15. McKitrick, *Johnson and Reconstruction*, pp. 69–70.
16. Ibid., pp. 61–65; Hans L. Trefousse, *Impeachment of a President: Andrew Johnson, the Blacks, and Reconstruction* (Knoxville: University of Tennessee Press, 1975), pp. 8–9; Thomas, *President Johnson*, p. 359; Donald, *Sumner*, pp. 224–225.
17. Donald, *Sumner*, pp. 223–225.
18. James G. Blaine, *Twenty Years of Congress* (Norwich, Conn.: Henry Bill Publishing Co., 1884), 2:66–68; Howard P. Nash, *Andrew Johnson: Congress and Reconstruction* (Rutherford, N.J.: Farleigh Dickinson University Press, 1972), pp. 27–31; John Niven, *Gideon Welles: Lincoln's Secretary of the Navy* (New York: Oxford University Press, 1973),

pp. 502–504; Cox, *Politics, Principles and Prejudice,* p. 46.

19. See, for example, Milton, *Age of Hate,* p. 89; Nevins, *War for the Union,* 4:345–346; Stryker, *Johnson: Profile in Courage,* pp. 214–228.

20. McPherson, *Political History,* p. 49.

21. Cox, *Politics, Principle and Prejudice,* pp. 32–33, 40–42, 95–105; McKitrick, *Johnson and Reconstruction,* p. 47; Van Deusen, *Seward,* pp. 421–422.

22. Trefousse, *Impeachment of a President,* pp. 4–5; Cox, *Politics, Principle and Prejudice,* pp. 152–153; David W. Bowen, "Andrew Johnson and the Negro," *East Tennes-*

see *Historical Society Publications* 40 (1968):28–49.

23. See Avery Craven, *Reconstruction: The Ending of the Civil War* (New York: Holt, Rinehart and Winston, 1969), p. 94; Martin E. Mantell, *Johnson, Grant, and the Politics of Reconstruction* (New York: Columbia University Press, 1973), pp. 14–15; Trefousse, *Impeachment of a President,* pp. 3–11.

24. James E. Sefton, *The United States Army and Reconstruction, 1865–1877* (Baton Rouge: Louisiana State University Press, 1967), p. 19; Cox, *Politics, Principle and Prejudice,* p. 53.

CHAPTER 3

1. McCulloch, *Men and Measures,* pp. 373–374.

2. Diary of Col. William G. Moore, May 7, 1868, typescript, Andrew Johnson Papers, Manuscripts Division, Library of Congress, Washington, D.C. (hereafter cited as Moore Diary; the abbreviation A. J. Papers will be used for all citations of the Andrew Johnson Papers at the Library of Congress).

3. Thomas and Hyman, *Stanton,* pp. 428–434; Milton, *Age of Hate,* pp. 204–212.

4. Welles, *Diary,* 2:479, 491, 494; Milton, *Age of Hate,* p. 325; Fawn M. Brodie, *Thaddeus Stevens: Scourge of the South* (New York: W. W. Norton, 1959), p. 325; Howard K. Beale, *The Critical Year: A Study of Andrew Johnson and Reconstruction* (New York: Harcourt, Brace, 1930), p. 17.

5. Beale, *Critical Year,* pp. 20–22; Milton, *Age of Hate,* p. 233.

6. McCulloch, *Men and Measures,* p. 386.

7. U.S. Bureau of the Census, *Historical Statistics of the United States: Colonial Times to 1970* (Washington, D.C.: GPO, 1975),

p. 1103; U.S. Congress, Senate, S. Exec. Docs. 83, 86, 87, 89, 91, 92, 44th Cong., 1st Sess., 1875.

8. Herbert S. Schell, "Hugh McCulloch and the Treasury Department, 1865–1869," *Mississippi Valley Historical Review* 17 (Dec. 1930):404–406; Robert P. Sharkey, *Money, Class, and Party: An Economic Study of Civil War and Reconstruction* (Baltimore: Johns Hopkins University Press, 1959), pp. 64, 118; Walter T. K. Nugent, *Money and American Society, 1865–1880* (New York: W. W. Norton, 1968), pp. 26–28; Beale, *Critical Year,* pp. 225–298.

9. William B. Hesseltine, *Ulysses S. Grant, Politician* (New York: Dodd, Mead & Co., 1935), pp. 52–53; Dexter Perkins, *The Monroe Doctrine, 1826–1867* (Baltimore: Johns Hopkins University Press, 1933), p. 471.

10. Van Deusen, *Seward,* pp. 400, 422–423, 432; Cox, *Politics, Principle and Prejudice,* pp. 1–49.

11. Van Deusen, *Seward,* pp. 434–435, 487–490.

12. Ibid., pp. 486–493; Frederic Bancroft, *The Life of William H. Seward* (New York and London:

Harper & Bros., 1900), 2:436–441.
13. Cox, *Politics, Principle and Prejudice*, pp. 45–46; Van Deusen, *Seward*, pp. 433–434.
14. Cox, *Politics, Principle and Prejudice*, p. 60.
15. Ibid., pp. 61–66, 101.
16. Ibid., pp. 66, 100–101.
17. Ibid., pp. 68–69, 101–104.
18. McKitrick, *Johnson and Reconstruction*, pp. 28–31.
19. Perman, *Reunion without Compromise*, pp. 73–78.
20. William C. Harris, *Presidential Reconstruction in Mississippi*, (Baton Rouge: Louisiana State University Press, 1967), p. 52.
21. Ibid.
22. Trefousse, *Impeachment of a President*, pp. 10–11.
23. Donald, *Sumner*, p. 235; Perman, *Reunion without Compromise*, pp. 81–82.
24. McPherson, *Political History*, pp. 48–49.
25. McKitrick, *Johnson and Reconstruction*, pp. 171–172.
26. Perman, *Reunion without Compromise*, pp. 71–72.
27. McPherson, *Political History*, pp. 29–32, 34–36; Joel Williamson, *After Slavery: The Negro in South Carolina during Reconstruction* (Chapel Hill: University of North Carolina Press, 1965), pp. 72–73, 75–76, 93–94; Harris, *Reconstruction in Mississippi*, pp. 128–129.
28. Harris, *Reconstruction in Mississippi*, p. 141; Williamson, *After Slavery*, pp. 76–77; McKitrick, *Johnson and Reconstruction*, pp. 36–41; Thomas and Hyman, *Stan-*

ton, pp. 448–450; Harold M. Hyman, ed., *The Radical Republicans and Reconstruction, 1861–1870* (Indianapolis: Bobbs-Merrill, 1967), pp. 298–299.
29. Perman, *Reunion without Compromise*, p. 105.
30. Ibid., pp. 105–107.
31. McKitrick, *Johnson and Reconstruction*, p. 146.
32. Blaine, *Twenty Years*, 2:69–70; Mantell, *Johnson, Grant*, p. 15; McKitrick, *Johnson and Reconstruction*, pp. 144–150; Perman, *Reunion without Compromise*, p. 98–102.
33. Beale, *Critical Year*, p. 233.
34. Oberholtzer, *United States since the Civil War*, 1:103.
35. Harris, *Reconstruction in Mississippi*, pp. 68–75; McKitrick, *Johnson and Reconstruction*, pp. 192–195; Sefton, *Army and Reconstruction*, pp. 26–29; Oberholtzer, *United States since the Civil War*, 1:135. Harris and McKitrick give conflicting accounts of this affair.
36. Perman, *Reunion without Compromise*, pp. 170–177.
37. Ibid., pp. 106–107, 153; McKitrick, *Johnson and Reconstruction*, pp. 205–206.
38. Bancroft to Johnson, Dec. 1, 1865, A. J. Papers.
39. Quoted in Charles Fairman, *Reconstruction and Reunion, 1864–88: Part One* (New York: Macmillan Co., 1971), p. 105.
40. Donald, *Sumner*, pp. 225–237; Brodie, *Stevens*, pp. 228–233.
41. Milton, *Age of Hate*, pp. 259–260.
42. Donald, *Sumner*, pp. 237–238.

CHAPTER 4

1. Welles, *Diary*, 2:387; Perman, *Reunion without Compromise*, pp. 104–105; Cox, *Politics, Principle and Prejudice*, p. 141.
2. McPherson, *Political History*, pp. 143–146.
3. James D. Richardson, ed., *A Compilation of the Messages and*

Papers of the Presidents, 1789–1897 (Washington, D.C.: GPO, 1896–99), 6:354–358.
4. Milton, *Age of Hate*, pp. 273–274.
5. Donald, *Politics of Reconstruction*, pp. 23–24.
6. McKitrick, *Johnson and Recon-*

struction, pp. 5–6, 60, 73–80.

7. LaWanda Cox and John Cox, "Negro Suffrage and Republican Politics: The Problem of Motivation in Reconstruction Historiography," *Journal of Southern History* 33 (Aug. 1967):330; Glenn M. Linden, "A Note on Negro Suffrage and Republican Politics," *Journal of Southern History* 36 (Aug. 1970):419.

8. John Richard Dennett, *The South As It Is, 1865–1866*, ed. Henry M. Christman (New York: Viking Press, 1965), p. 348. This book consists of articles written by Dennett for *The Nation* between July 1865 and April 1866.

9. Milton, *Age of Hate*, pp. 214, 218–219, 239–242; Donald, *Sumner*, pp. 228–229; McKitrick, *Johnson and Reconstruction*, pp. 162–164; W. R. Brock, *An American Crisis: Congress and Reconstruction, 1865–1867* (New York: St. Martin's Press, 1963), pp. 39–42.

10. McPherson, *Political History*, pp. 66–68; Oberholtzer, *United States since the Civil War*, 1:157.

11. Hesseltine, *Grant*, pp. 59–61.

12. Donald, *Politics of Reconstruction*, p. 24; Perman, *Reunion without Compromise*, pp. 176–180, 185–187; Cox, *Politics, Principle and Prejudice*, pp. 174–175; Welles, *Diary*, 2:421.

13. McPherson, *Political History*, p. 115; Donald, *Politics of Reconstruction*, pp. 24–25; Brodie, *Stevens*, pp. 249–250; Cox, "Negro Suffrage," pp. 329–330.

14. McPherson, *Political History*, pp. 51–52.

15. Donald, *Sumner*, pp. 244–245; McKitrick, *Johnson and Reconstruction*, p. 283; Cox, *Politics, Principle and Prejudice*, pp. 160–161.

16. McPherson, *Political History*, pp. 52–55; Cox, *Politics, Principle and Prejudice*, p. 163; Trefousse, *Impeachment of a President*, p. 15.

17. Welles, *Diary*, 2:432.

18. Brock, *American Crisis*, pp. 136–137; McKitrick, *Johnson and Reconstruction*, pp. 274–84, 317–318.

19. Welles, *Diary*, 2:434–435; Cox, *Politics, Principle and Prejudice*, pp. 172–184; LaWanda Cox and John Cox, "Andrew Johnson and His Ghost Writers: An Analysis of the Freedmen's Bureau and Civil Rights Veto Messages," *Mississippi Valley Historical Review* 47 (Dec. 1961):460–473.

20. McPherson, *Political History*, pp. 68–71.

21. Ibid., pp. 71–72.

22. Cox, *Politics, Principle and Prejudice*, pp. 190–193; McKitrick, *Johnson and Reconstruction*, pp. 292–295; Michael Les Benedict, *A Compromise of Principle: Congressional Republicans and Reconstruction, 1863–1869* (New York: W. W. Norton, 1974), pp. 158–159.

23. McPherson, *Political History*, p. 60.

24. Ibid., p. 61.

25. Ibid.

26. Ibid., p. 62.

27. Welles, *Diary*, 2:439; McCulloch, *Men and Measures*, p. 393; Jacob Cox to Lewis D. Campbell, Apr. 28, 1866, Campbell Papers; Oberholtzer, *United States since the Civil War*, 1:172–173; McKitrick, *Johnson and Reconstruction*, pp. 292–296; Milton, *Age of Hate*, pp. 290–292; Donald, *Sumner*, pp. 256–258.

28. Albert Castel and Scott L. Gibson, *The Yeas and Nays: Key Congressional Decisions, 1774–1945* (Kalamazoo, Mich.: New Issues Press, 1975), pp. 84–85; Cox, *Politics, Principle and Prejudice*, pp. 200–201; McKitrick, *Johnson and Reconstruction*, pp. 316–317.

29. Richardson, *Messages and Papers of the Presidents*, 6:405–413; Cox, "Johnson and His Ghost Writers," pp. 474–476.

30. Oberholtzer, *United States since the Civil War*, 1:179–180; Mc-

Kitrick, *Johnson and Reconstruction*, pp. 314–319; Cox, *Politics, Principles and Prejudice*, pp. 196–197, 202–206; Benedict, *Compromise*, pp. 162–167.
31. Castel and Gibson, *Yeas and Nays*, pp. 84–85.
32. Milton, *Age of Hate*, p. 310; Oberholtzer, *United States since the Civil War*, 1:178–179.
33. Brock, *American Crisis*, pp. 111–121; Cox, *Politics, Principle and Prejudice*, pp. 195–202; Perman, *Reunion without Compromise*, pp. 188–189.
34. McKitrick, *Johnson and Reconstruction*, p. 324; Welles, *Diary*, 2:463–465.

35. Castel and Gibson, *Yeas and Nays*, p. 85.
36. Benedict, *Compromise*, pp. 150–169.
37. McKitrick, *Johnson and Reconstruction*, pp. 361–363.
38. Richardson, *Messages and Papers of the Presidents*, 6:391–392.
39. Oberholtzer, *United States since the Civil War*, 1:187; Eugene Feistman, "Racial Disfranchisement and the Restoration of Tennessee, 1865–1866," *Tennessee Historical Quarterly* 12 (June 1953):145–147; McKitrick, *Johnson and Reconstruction*, pp. 361–363.

CHAPTER 5

1. McKitrick, *Johnson and Reconstruction*, pp. 309–310.
2. Milton, *Age of Hate*, pp. 337–340.
3. Ibid., pp. 338–340.
4. Thomas Wagstaff, "The Arm-in-Arm Convention," *Civil War History* 14 (June 1968):102–104; Benedict, *Compromise*, pp. 191–192; Perman, *Reunion without Compromise*, pp. 189–211.
5. Van Deusen, *Seward*, pp. 385–389, 429–430; Ernest N. Paolino, *The Foundations of the American Empire: William Henry Seward and U.S. Foreign Policy* (Ithaca: Cornell University Press, 1973), pp. 206–207; Cox, *Politics, Principle and Prejudice*, pp. 204–205, 220–221.
6. Niven, *Welles*, pp. 529–530.
7. Thomas and Hyman, *Stanton*, pp. 469–470, 475–476, 481–485, 491–494.
8. Ibid., pp. 489–490; Feistman, "Racial Disfranchisement," p. 146; Sefton, *Army and Reconstruction*, p. 101.
9. Sefton, *Army and Reconstruction*, p. 85.
10. Donald E. Reynolds, "The New Orleans Riot of 1866 Reconsidered," *Louisiana History* 5 (Winter 1964):6–13; Sefton, *Army and*

Reconstruction, pp. 84–87; Brodie, *Stevens*, pp. 277–278.
11. Reynolds, "New Orleans Riot," pp. 14–15, 26–27; Brodie, *Stevens*, p. 278; Thomas and Hyman, *Stanton*, pp. 494–496.
12. Richardson, *Messages and Papers of the Presidents*, 6:590.
13. Wagstaff, "Arm-in-Arm Convention," pp. 107–117.
14. Adam Badeau, *Grant in Peace from Appomattox to Mount McGregor* (Hartford, Conn.: S. S. Scranton & Co., 1887), pp. 38, 47; McKitrick, *Johnson and Reconstruction*, pp. 410–416; Mantell, *Johnson, Grant*, p. 20.
15. McPherson, *Political History*, pp. 127–129.
16. Perman, *Reunion without Compromise*, p. 229; W. S. Neidhardt, *Fenianism in North America* (University Park: Pennsylvania State University Press, 1975), pp. 51–108; Van Deusen, *Seward*, pp. 501–503.
17. Beale, *Critical Year*, pp. 225–299.
18. McKitrick, *Johnson and Reconstruction*, pp. 367–377; Brock, *American Crisis*, pp. 237–238.
19. Brock, *American Crisis*, pp. 61–62, 160–166, 256–257; James C. Mohr, ed., *Radical Republicans in the North: State Politics during*

Reconstruction (Baltimore: Johns Hopkins University Press, 1976), pp. 152–153; McKitrick, *Johnson and Reconstruction*, pp. 377–391; Cox, *Politics, Principle and Prejudice*, pp. 126–128; Brodie, *Stevens*, p. 290.

20. Cox, *Politics, Principle and Prejudice*, p. 117.
21. William Gray to McCulloch, Aug. 9, 1866, Hugh McCulloch Papers, Manuscript Division, Library of Congress, Washington, D.C.
22. Nivens, *Welles*, p. 530.
23. Moore Diary, Mar. 18, 1868; Perman, *Reunion without Compromise*, p. 230; Bowen, "Johnson and the Negro," p. 41. Originally the invitation was to Seward; see Van Deusen, *Seward*, p. 460.
24. Milton, *Age of Hate*, pp. 357–358; Hesseltine, *Grant*, pp. 71–73; McKitrick, *Johnson and Grant*, pp. 428–429; Mantell, *Johnson, Grant*, pp. 28–29.
25. Milton, *Age of Hate*, pp. 359–360.
26. McPherson, *Political History*, p. 135.
27. McKitrick, *Johnson and Reconstruction*, p. 432.
28. Ibid., pp. 437–438; Oberholtzer, *United States since the Civil War*, 1:411–412; Gregg Phifer, "Andrew Johnson Versus the Press in 1866," *East Tennessee Historical Society Publications* 25 (1953): 15, 21.
29. For Grant getting drunk, see Milton, *Age of Hate*, p. 367; the *New York Post* quote appears in Oberholtzer, *United States since the Civil War*, 1:411.
30. McKitrick, *Johnson and Reconstruction*, pp. 429–435.
31. Quoted in Brodie, *Stevens*, p. 285.

32. Thomas Schoonover, "Mexican Affairs and the Impeachment of President Andrew Johnson," *East Tennessee Historical Society Publications* 46 (1974):80.
33. Oberholtzer, *United States since the Civil War*, 1:408–409.
34. Lomask, *President on Trial*, p. 205.
35. McKitrick, *Johnson and Reconstruction*, pp. 420, 439–442; Oberholtzer, *United States since the Civil War*, 1:419; Phifer, "Johnson Versus the Press," pp. 10–11. The Fessenden quote is from Fessenden to McCulloch, Sept. 11, 1866, McCulloch Papers.
36. Badeau, *Grant in Peace*, p. 51.
37. Ibid.; Oberholtzer, *United States since the Civil War*, 1:417–418.
38. William T. Sherman Diary, Oct. 20, 25, 29, 1866, Sherman Family Papers, University of Notre Dame Archives, South Bend, Ind.; William T. Sherman, *Memoirs of Gen. W. T. Sherman* (New York: Charles L. Webster & Co., 1891), 2:414–420; M. A. DeWolfe Howe, ed., *Home Letters of General Sherman* (New York: Charles Scribner's Sons, 1909), p. 361; St. George L. Sioussat, ed., "Notes of Colonel W. G. Moore, Private Secretary to President Johnson, 1866–68," *American Historical Review* 19 (Oct. 1913):99–102; Hesseltine, *Grant*, pp. 77–79; Badeau, *Grant in Peace*, pp. 49–55; Thomas and Hyman, *Stanton*, pp. 498–504.
39. Brock, *American Crisis*, p. 168.
40. Quoted in Benedict, *Compromise*, pp. 208–209.
41. Quoted in Beale, *Critical Year*, p. 403.

CHAPTER 6

1. Niven, *Welles*, p. 531.
2. Quoted in Oberholtzer, *United States since the Civil War*, 1:419–420.
3. Van Deusen, *Seward*, p. 469.
4. Cox, *Politics, Principle and Prejudices*, pp. 228–229.

5. McPherson, *Political History*, pp. 143–147.
6. Milton, *Age of Hate*, p. 378.
7. Benedict, *Compromise*, pp. 210–211; Perman, *Reunion without Compromise*, pp. 234–238; Joseph B. James, "Southern Reaction to

the Proposal of the Fourteenth Amendment," *Journal of Southern History* 22 (Nov. 1956):478–479; *Johnson and Reconstruction,* McKitrick, *Johnson and Reconstruction,* pp. 449–453.

8. McPherson, *Political History,* pp. 352–353.

9. Ibid.; James, "Southern Reaction," pp. 468–472; Perman, *Reunion without Compromise,* pp. 250–259.

10. Perman, *Reunion without Compromise,* pp. 234–249; McKitrick, *Johnson and Reconstruction,* pp. 460–468.

11. McKitrick, *Johnson and Reconstruction,* p. 476.

12. McPherson, *Political History,* pp. 160–166, 183–184.

13. McKitrick, *Johnson and Reconstruction,* pp. 474–484; Brock, *American Crisis,* pp. 175–198; Benedict, *Compromise,* pp. 220–240; Donald, *Sumner,* pp. 287–288.

14. Perman, *Reunion without Compromise,* pp. 260–263; Benedict, *Compromise,* pp. 231–232.

15. Sioussat, "Notes of Colonel Moore," p. 105.

16. Blair to Johnson, Feb. 24, 1867; Este to Johnson, Feb. ?, 1867, A. J. Papers.

17. Sioussat, "Notes of Colonel Moore," p. 106; Benedict, *Compromise,* p. 239.

18. Milton, *Age of Hate,* p. 396.

19. Benedict, *Compromise,* pp. 239–240.

20. McPherson, *Political History,* pp. 166–173.

21. Hesseltine, *Grant,* p. 83; Brock, *American Crisis,* pp. 199–200; Milton, *Age of Hate,* pp. 399–400.

22. Brock, *American Crisis,* pp. 257–258.

23. Welles, *Diary,* 3:49.

24. Thomas and Hyman, *Stanton,* pp. 525–526; Van Deusen, *Seward,* p. 472.

25. Hesseltine, *Grant,* pp. 81–83; Thomas and Hyman, *Stanton,* pp. 514–515, 524; Sefton, *Army and Reconstruction,* pp. 111–112.

26. Sioussat, "Notes of Colonel Moore," p. 106; Thomas and Hyman, *Stanton,* pp. 529–530; Niven, *Welles,* p. 541.

27. James G. Randall and Theodore C. Pease, eds., *The Diary of Orville Hickman Browning* (Springfield: Illinois State Historical Library, 1933 [hereafter cited as Browning, *Diary*]), 2:134–135.

28. Welles, *Diary,* 3:64.

29. McPherson, *Political History,* pp. 178–181; Oberholtzer, *United States since the Civil War,* 1:453; Perman, *Reunion without Compromise,* pp. 268–273; Mantell, *Johnson, Grant,* pp. 25–26.

30. Diary of John Bigelow, Mar. 1, 1867, John Bigelow Papers, New York Public Library.

CHAPTER 7

1. McPherson, *Political History,* pp. 141–143.

2. Beale, *Critical Year,* pp. 297–298; Sharkey, *Money, Class, and Party,* pp. 82–88; Irwin Unger, *The Greenback Era: A Social and Political History of American Finance, 1865–1879* (Princeton: Princeton University Press, 1964), pp. 78–79.

3. Mantell, *Johnson, Grant,* pp. 58–60; Oberholtzer, *United States since the Civil War,* 2:297–298.

4. Van Deusen, *Seward,* pp. 463–464; Paolino, *American Empire,* pp. 106–107.

5. Ellen M. Perry, "Glimpses of an Excursion with the Diplomatic Corps," MSS in possession of Mrs. Ann Paulson, Kalamazoo, Michigan; copy in Regional History Collection, Waldo Library, Western Michigan University, Kalamazoo.

6. Van Deusen, *Seward,* p. 541.

7. Ibid., pp. 535–544; Donald, *Sumner,* pp. 303–309; Bancroft, *Seward,* 2:477–479.

8. Samuel J. Crawford to Johnson, Aug. 22, 1868, A. J. Papers; Robert M. Utley, *Frontier Regulars: The United States Army and the Indians, 1866–1891* (New York: Macmillan Co., 1973), pp. 93–159; Francis Paul Prucha, *American Indian Policy in Crisis: Christian Reformers and the Indian, 1865–1900* (Norman: University of Oklahoma Press, 1976), pp. 3–29.

9. Benedict, *Compromise*, pp. 240–246.

10. Welles, *Diary*, 3:77–78; Milton, *Age of Hate*, p. 434.

11. Sefton, *Army and Reconstruction*, p. 140; Thomas and Hyman, *Stanton*, pp. 534–535.

12. Welles, *Diary*, 3:93–98; Thomas and Hyman, *Stanton*, pp. 539–540; Benedict, *Compromise*, p. 252.

13. Trefousse, *Impeachment of a President*, pp. 68–72; Milton, *Age of Hate*, pp. 405–421, 434–437.

14. Sefton, *Army and Reconstruction*, pp. 132–133.

15. Oberholtzer, *United States since the Civil War*, 1:478; Thomas, *President Johnson*, pp. 536–537.

16. Welles, *Diary*, 3:80–81; Milton, *Age of Hate*, pp. 437–439; Perman, *Reunion without Compromise*, pp. 293–296.

17. Perman, *Reunion without Compromise*, pp. 270–303; Mantell, *Johnson, Grant*, pp. 39–43; Harris, *Reconstruction in Mississippi*, pp. 238–244.

18. McPherson, *Political History*, p. 323; Welles, *Diary*, 3:104–105; Sefton, *Army and Reconstruction*, pp. 140–141; Thomas and Hyman, *Stanton*, p. 541.

19. Welles, *Diary*, 3:105–114; George C. Gorham, *Life and Public Services of Edwin M. Stanton* (Boston and New York: Houghton Mifflin Co., 1899), 2:360–371; Thomas and Hyman, *Stanton*, pp. 542–545; Milton, *Age of Hate*, pp. 442–444.

20. Sefton, *Army and Reconstruction*, p. 134; Thomas and Hyman, *Stanton*, p. 545; Welles, *Diary*, 3:114.

21. Welles, *Diary*, 3:117, 125–126; Thomas and Hyman, *Stanton*, p. 546.

22. Thomas and Hyman, *Stanton*, pp. 545–546; Sefton, *Army and Reconstruction*, pp. 134–135.

23. Sefton, *Army and Reconstruction*, p. 134.

24. Welles, *Diary*, 3:104–114.

25. Benedict, *Compromise*, pp. 252–253; Castel and Gibson, *Yeas and Nays*, p. 87; McPherson, *Political History*, pp. 335–336.

26. Thomas and Hyman, *Stanton*, p. 546; Benedict, *Compromise*, pp. 253–255; Niven, *Welles*, pp. 546–548.

27. Niven, *Welles*, pp. 549–550; Mantell, *Johnson, Grant*, pp. 34–35; Sefton, *Army and Reconstruction*, p. 155; Thomas and Hyman, *Stanton*, p. 547; Trefousse, *Impeachment of a President*, pp. 99–100.

28. Grant to Johnson, Aug. 1, 1867, A. J. Papers.

29. Welles, *Diary*, 3:151.

30. Ibid., pp. 152–154.

31. Ibid., pp. 154–157.

32. Milton, *Age of Hate*, pp. 451–452; there had been earlier newspaper reports that Johnson had not seen the clemency petition.

33. Ibid., p. 448.

34. Ibid., p. 453.

35. Sioussat, "Notes of Colonel Moore," pp. 107–108; Welles, *Diary*, 3:149–162; Milton, *Age of Hate*, pp. 447–454; Thomas and Hyman, *Stanton*, pp. 547–549.

36. Welles, *Diary*, 3:162–166.

37. Moore Diary, Aug. 11, 1867.

38. Ibid., Aug. 12, 1867; Welles, *Diary*, 3:162–169; Thomas and Hyman, *Stanton*, pp. 549–552; *Army and Reconstruction*, p. 155.

CHAPTER 8

1. Milton, *Age of Hate*, pp. 458–459.
2. Sioussat, "Notes of Colonel Moore," pp. 110–112; Hesseltine, *Grant*, pp. 93–94.
3. Milton, *Age of Hate*, p. 459.
4. Welles, *Diary*, 3:170; Milton, *Age of Hate*, pp. 460–461.
5. Welles, *Diary*, 3:174–176, 182–183.
6. Welles, *Diary*, 3:187–188.
7. Badeau, *Grant in Peace*, pp. 566–567.
8. Ibid., pp. 185–189; Sioussat, "Notes of Colonel Moore," pp. 111–113; Moore Diary, Aug. 26, 27, 28, 1867.
9. Ewing to Hugh Ewing, Sept. 16, 1867, Hugh Ewing MSS, Ohio Historical Society, Columbus; Fessenden to McCulloch, Sept. 2, 1867, McCulloch Papers.
10. Welles, *Diary*, 3:176–181, 184–185, 196; Badeau, *Grant in Peace*, pp. 73–74, 90, 104–105, 142–143, 371; Mantell, *Johnson, Grant*, pp. 67–70; Hesseltine, *Grant*, pp. 98–101.
11. Welles, *Diary*, 3:189.
12. Thomas and Hyman, *Stanton*, pp. 558–559.
13. Moore Diary, Aug. 14, 1867.
14. Van Deusen, *Seward*, pp. 474–475, 526–534; Paolino, *American Empire*, pp. 23–24, 101–102, 127; Albert Castel and Andrew C. Nahm, "Our Little War with the Heathen," *American Heritage* 19 (Apr. 1968):19–20; Welles, *Diary*, 3:106–107, 124–125.
15. Moore Diary, Aug. 14, 1867; Sioussat, "Notes of Colonel Moore," p. 110.
16. McCulloch to Johnson, Aug. 19, 1867, A. J. Papers; Moore Diary, Aug. 14, 1867; Sioussat, "Notes of Colonel Moore," p. 110; Benedict, *Compromise*, pp. 264–265; Milton, *Age of Hate*, pp. 465–466.
17. Milton, *Age of Hate*, pp. 468–470; Benedict, *Compromise*, pp. 272–273; Mantell, *Johnson, Grant*, pp. 90–91; Oberholtzer, *United States since the Civil War*, 1:479.
18. Mantell, *Johnson, Grant*, pp. 56–57, 63–65; Benedict, *Compromise*, pp. 272–274; Trefousse, *Impeachment of a President*, pp. 90–93.
19. *New York Times*, November 14, 1867.
20. Mantell, *Johnson, Grant*, pp. 65–66.
21. Ibid., pp. 45–49; Perman, *Reunion without Compromise*, pp. 270–286, 307–337.
22. Benedict, *Compromise*, pp. 273–274; Trefousse, *Impeachment of a President*, pp. 94–95.
23. Fairman, *Reconstruction and Reunion*, pp. 402–403; Perman, *Reunion without Compromise*, pp. 288–290.
24. Trefousse, *Impeachment of a President*, pp. 94–95; Mantell, *Johnson, Grant*, pp. 68–70.
25. Benedict, *Compromise*, p. 274; Donald, *Sumner*, p. 331.
26. Welles, *Diary*, 3:231–232; Browning, *Diary*, 2:162–163.
27. Sherman Diary, Oct. 2, 4, 6, 7, 11, 1867, Sherman Family Papers; Welles, *Diary*, 3:234.
28. Moore, "Small Diary" (typescript, A. J. Papers), pp. 61–62.
29. Welles, *Diary*, pp. 238–239.
30. Moore Diary, Nov. 30, 1868; Welles, *Diary*, 3:237–239; Browning, *Diary*, 2:168–169.
31. Richardson, *Messages and Papers of the Presidents*, 6:558–569.
32. Ibid.
33. Ibid., p. 569.
34. Benedict, *Compromise*, pp. 283–287.
35. Trefousse, *Impeachment of a President*, pp. 112–114.
36. Richardson, *Messages and Papers of the Presidents*, 6:583–594.
37. Ibid., pp. 595–596; Moore Diary, Nov. 30, Dec. 15, 1867; McKitrick, *Johnson and Reconstruction*, pp. 499–500.
38. Forsyth to Johnson, Dec. 12, 1867, A. J. Papers; Welles, *Diary*, 3:242–243; Sefton, *Army and Reconstruction*, pp. 165–169; Milton, *Age of Hate*, pp. 477–480.

39. Benedict, *Compromise*, p. 290.
40. Fairman, *Reconstruction and Reunion*, pp. 437–440, 449–50.
41. Benedict, *Compromise*, pp. 288–293.
42. Moore Diary, Jan. 7, 1868.
43. Sherman, *Memoirs*, 2:421–422; McPherson, *Political History*, pp. 283–288; Badeau, *Grant in Peace*, pp. 110–112; Welles, *Diary*, 3:259–261.
44. Ewing to Johnson, Jan. 12, 1868, A. J. Papers; Sherman, *Memoirs*, 2:422; Howe, *Home Letters of Sherman*, pp. 364–365.
45. E. D. Townsend, *Anecdotes of the Civil War in the United States* (New York: Appleton, 1884), p. 124; Thomas and Hyman, *Stanton*, pp. 569–570.
46. W. S. Hillyer to Johnson, Jan. 14, 1868, A. J. Papers; in this letter Hillyer vouches for Grant's good intentions—but this is not, of course, proof.
47. Moore Diary, Jan. 14, Feb. 4, 1868; Welles, *Diary*, 3:259–262; Browning, *Diary*, 2:173–175.
48. Sherman, *Memoirs*, 2:423; Moore Diary, Jan. 15, 1868; Welles, *Diary*, 3:262.

49. Howe, *Home Letters of Sherman*, pp. 366–367; Sherman, *Memoirs*, 2:423–424; Moore Diary, January 26, 1868.
50. Grant to Sherman, Jan. 19, 1868, Sherman Family Papers; Welles, *Diary*, 3:267.
51. Sioussat, "Notes of Colonel Moore," p. 117.
52. Richardson, *Messages and Papers of the Presidents*, 6:615.
53. Ibid.
54. Ibid., p. 619.
55. Ibid., pp. 603–610.
56. Milton, *Age of Hate*, p. 500; see also Sefton, *Army and Reconstruction*, p. 180 n. 42.
57. Badeau, *Grant in Peace*, pp. 84–85, 106–109, 112–115, 126–127.
58. Milton, *Age of Hate*, pp. 496–497.
59. Benjamin C. Truman, "Anecdotes of Andrew Johnson," *Century Magazine* 85 (Jan. 1913):439. The authenticity of this letter is however, open to doubt. If authentic, then someone drafted it for Johnson; it is too literate for him to have composed it personally. (Truman, a journalist, served for a while as one of Johnson's private secretaries.)

CHAPTER 9

1. Sherman, *Memoirs*, 2:425–428; Howe, *Home Letters of Sherman*, pp. 366–370.
2. Sherman, *Memoirs*, 2:426–428; Welles, *Diary*, 3:272. Moore Diary, Feb. 6, 1868.
3. Sherman, *Memoirs*, 2:428–433; Howe, *Home Letters of Sherman*, pp. 370–373.
4. DeWitt, *Impeachment and Trial of Johnson*, pp. 335–336; Milton, *Age of Hate*, pp. 499–500.
5. Moore Diary, Feb. 16, 1868.
6. Ibid., Feb. 17, 1868.
7. Welles, *Diary*, 3:279.
8. Moore Diary, Feb. 19, 1868.
9. Ibid., Feb. 20, 1868.
10. *Trial of Andrew Johnson, President of the United States, Before the Senate of the United States, on Impeachment by the House of Representatives for High Crimes and Misdemeanors* (Washington, D.C.: G.P.O., 1868 [hereafter cited as *Trial of Johnson*]), 1:418–420, 426–427, 433; Townsend, *Anecdotes*, pp. 125–126; Thomas and Hyman, *Stanton*, pp. 583–584.
11. Welles, *Diary*, 3:284–285.
12. DeWitt, *Impeachment and Trial of Johnson*, pp. 345–350; McKitrick, *Johnson and Reconstruction*, pp. 500–501; Michael Les Benedict, *The Impeachment and Trial of Andrew Johnson* (New York: W. W. Norton & Co., 1973), pp. 103–110; Trefousse, *Impeachment of a President*, pp. 134–144; Donald, *Sumner*, pp. 323–334.
13. *Trial of Johnson*, 1:431–432;

Townsend, *Anecdotes*, p. 129; DeWitt, *Impeachment and Trial of Johnson*, pp. 351–352; Thomas and Hyman, *Stanton*, pp. 586–587.

14. *Trial of Johnson*, 1:427–428.
15. Moore Diary, Feb. 22, 1868.
16. *Trial of Johnson*, 1:2, 232–233, 428–429; Townsend, *Anecdotes*, pp. 126–128; DeWitt, *Impeachment and Trial of Johnson*, pp. 359–373.
17. *Trial of Johnson*, 1:235–236; Welles, *Diary*, 3:289; Niven, *Welles*, p. 561.
18. Milton, *Age of Hate*, pp. 509–510; Welles, *Diary*, 3:337–338; Thomas and Hyman, *Stanton*, p. 594; Logan to "Dear General," Feb. 22, 1868, John A. Logan Papers, Manuscripts Division, Library of Congress.

19. *Trial of Johnson*, 1:2, 232–233, 428–429; DeWitt, *Impeachment and Trial of Johnson*, pp. 359–373; Brodie, *Stevens*, p. 336.
20. *Trial of Johnson*, 1:5.
21. DeWitt, *Impeachment and Trial of Johnson*, p. 376. Thomas and Hyman's contention that "Stanton's concern was not with a possible court test of the tenure law, but a criminal action against himself" (*Stanton*, p. 597) is illogical and not supported by the sources cited. Also the argument they and other anti-Johnson historians make that Johnson's attempt to get the Tenure of Office Act before the Supreme Court was an afterthought is contrary to the evidence.
22. Welles, *Diary*, 3:315.
23. Moore Diary, Feb. 22, 24, 1868.

CHAPTER 10

1. Ben Perley Poore to W. W. Clapp, May 27, 1868, William Warland Clapp Papers, Manuscripts Division, Library of Congress.
2. DeWitt, *Impeachment and Trial of Johnson*, pp. 397–400; William Norwood Brigance, "Jeremiah Black and Andrew Johnson," *Mississippi Valley Historical Review* 19 (Sept. 1932):205–218.
3. Lomask, *President on Trial*, pp. 309–310; Castel and Gibson, *Yeas and Nays*, p. 87; Benedict, *Compromise*, pp. 290–291.
4. Sefton, *Army and Reconstruction*, pp. 177–178.
5. The following exchange appeared in the *New York World*, March 10, 1868, clipping, Andrew Johnson Project, University of Tennessee, Knoxville.
6. Fairman, *Reconstruction and Reunion*, pp. 464–465.
7. Ibid., pp. 3–4, 467–478; Stanley I. Kutler, *The Supreme Court and Reconstruction: Politics and Judicial Power* (Chicago: University of Chicago Press, 1968), pp. 77–80, 112–113. Kutler is correct in arguing that the Supreme Court as an institution did not decline during Reconstruction. Nevertheless it did wisely avoid a direct clash with Congress in the McCardle case, and it is probably safe to assume that most of the justices were glad that Johnson failed to get the Tenure of Office Act before the Court.
8. Benedict, *Compromise*, p. 299.
9. Chester L. Barrows, *William M. Evarts: Lawyer, Diplomat, Statesman* (Chapel Hill: University of North Carolina Press, 1941), pp. 145–161; DeWitt, *Impeachment and Trial of Johnson*, pp. 404–514; Trefousse, *Impeachment of a President*, pp. 149–150, 177–179; Benedict, *Impeachment*, pp. 145–148.
10. Barrows, *Evarts*, pp. 150–151; Welles, *Diary*, 3:378–379, 410; Moore Diary, Apr. 23, 24, 1868; Benedict, *Impeachment*, pp. 133–138; James L. McDonough and William T. Alderson, eds., "Republican Politics and the Impeachment of Andrew Johnson," *Tennessee Historical Quarterly* 26

(Summer 1967):178–183.
11. Browning, *Diary*, 2:195.
12. Pomeroy to James Legate, Apr. 6, 1867, copy in A. J. Papers.
13. Moore Diary, Feb. 29, Mar. 17, 18, 27; Apr. 29, 30; May 1, 2, 1868. See also Niven, *Welles*, pp. 636–637; and DeWitt, *Impeachment and Trial of Johnson*, pp. 569–570.
14. Ben Perley Poore to W. W. Clapp, April 10, 1868, Clapp Papers; Benedict, *Impeachment*, p. 139.
15. Moore Diary, Apr. 24, May 2, 1868.
16. Browning, *Diary*, 2:196; Welles, *Diary*, 3:350.
17. Welles, *Diary*, 3:351–352.
18. Ibid., pp. 352–353; Browning, *Diary*, 2:196–197.
19. DeWitt, *Impeachment and Trial of Johnson*, pp. 522–545; Welles, *Diary*, 3:353–357; Edmund G. Ross, "Historical Moments: The Impeachment Trial," *Scribner's Magazine* 11 (Apr. 1892):520–521; Hesseltine, *Grant*, pp. 114–115.
20. Welles, *Diary*, 3:355–357; Moore Diary, May 16, 1868; DeWitt, *Impeachment and Trial of Johnson*, pp. 549–554; Trefousse, *Impeachment of a President*, pp. 165–167.
21. Ibid., pp. 168–170; DeWitt, *Impeachment and Trial of Johnson*, pp. 573–574; Welles, *Diary*, 3:359, 362; Donald, *Sumner*, p. 337; *White Cloud* (Kansas) *Chief*, May 21, 1868; Mark A. Plummer, *Frontier Governor: Samuel J. Crawford of Kansas* (Lawrence: University Press of Kansas, 1971), pp. 107–110.
22. Mantell, *Johnson, Grant*, pp. 97–99.
23. Browning, *Diary*, 2:199; Welles, *Diary*, 3:368.
24. Truman, "Anecdotes of Johnson," p. 438.

25. William A. Dunning, *Reconstruction: Political and Economic, 1865–1877* (New York: Harper & Bros., 1907), p. 107; Horace White, *The Life of Lyman Trumbull* (Boston: Houghton Mifflin Co., 1913), p. 321.
26. John B. Henderson, "Emancipation and Impeachment," *Century Magazine* 85 (Dec. 1912):207.
27. Thomas and Hyman, *Stanton*, p. 364; Welles, *Diary*, 3:349.
28. Bigelow Diary, Sept. 23, 1868, Bigelow Papers.
29. Benedict, *Compromise*, p. 310.
30. Charles A. Jellison, "The Ross Impeachment Vote: A Need for Reappraisal," *Southwestern Social Science Quarterly* 41 (Sept. 1960): 150–155; Larry Massie, "Edmund G. Ross, Hero?" MS, Regional History Collection, Waldo Library, Western Michigan University, Kalamazoo.
31. Trefousse, *Impeachment of a President*, p. 175; William A. Dunning, *Essays on the Civil War and Reconstruction* (New York: Harper Torchbooks, 1965), pp. 272–303.
32. Benedict, *Impeachment*, pp. 107–112, 139–167, 173–180. Thomas and Hyman's *Stanton* also holds Johnson guilty. Trefousse (*Impeachment of a President*, pp. 172–175) parts company with his fellow neo-Radicals on this issue. The essence of Benedict's thesis is expounded and then refuted in William A. Dunning, *Essays on the Civil War and Reconstruction*, pp. 296–297, 302–303; and in DeWitt, *Impeachment and Trial of Johnson*, pp. 576–590.
33. For example, Blaine, *Twenty Years*, 2:376–383.
34. Moore Diary, May 26, 1868; Townsend, *Anecdotes*, pp. 132–136.

CHAPTER 11

1. McKitrick, *Johnson and Reconstruction*, pp. 506–509; Benedict, *Compromise*, p. 314.
2. Mantell, *Johnson, Grant*, pp. 100–

101, 113–114.

3. Trefousse, *Impeachment of a President*, p. 182.

4. Ibid., p. 122; Milton, *Age of Hate*, pp. 636–637.

5. Moore Diary, May 17, June 8, 1868.

6. Schell, "McCulloch," pp. 418–419.

7. Moore Diary, Mar. 8, May 16, 1868.

8. Van Deusen, *Seward*, pp. 480–482; Welles, *Diary*, 3:409.

9. Moore Diary, July 3, 1868.

10. Johnson to Cooper, July 8, 1868, A. J. Papers; Moore Diary, July 7, 8, 1868.

11. Moore Diary, July 9, 1868; Welles, *Diary*, 3:396–398; Cooper to Johnson, July 8, 1868, A. J. Papers.

12. Welles, *Diary*, 3:320, 328.

13. Ibid., p. 403; Mantell, *Johnson, Grant*, pp. 110–111, 114–128.

14. Moore Diary, Sept. 6, 1868.

15. Van Deusen, *Seward*, pp. 545–548.

16. Ibid., pp. 524–534; Paolino, *American Empire*, pp. 118–128, 154–161.

17. Richardson, *Messages and Papers of the Presidents*, 6:651–654.

18. McPherson, *Political History*, pp. 379–380.

19. Mantell, *Johnson, Grant*, pp. 111–112.

20. Ibid., pp. 134, 138; Milton, *Age of Hate*, pp. 641–642.

21. Moore Diary, Aug. 1, 3, 1868.

22. Brodie, *Stevens*, p. 366; W. E. McElwee, "The Last Political Conversation of Andrew Johnson," copy of typescript provided by Mr. August Lehe of the *Sylacauga* (Alabama) *News*; original in possession of Mrs. Permelia Dunn of Sylacauga, Alabama, a descendant of McElwee's.

23. Oberholtzer, *United States since the Civil War*, 2:191-194.

24. McPherson, *Political History*, p. 499; Mantell, *Johnson, Grant*, pp. 147–148.

25. Benedict, *Compromise*, pp. 325–336; Donald, *Sumner*, pp. 352–

353; C. Vann Woodward, "Seeds of Failure in Radical Race Policy," in *New Frontiers of the American Reconstruction*, ed. Harold M. Hyman (Urbana: University of Illinois Press, 1966), pp. 140–142. William Gillette (*The Right to Vote: Politics and the Passage of the Fifteenth Amendment* [Baltimore: Johns Hopkins University Press, 1965], pp. 34–53), considers the Republican desire for Negro votes in the North to be the main motive behind the Fifteenth Amendment; Benedict (*Compromise*, pp. 446–447) takes issue with Gillette, but Gillette is upheld as regards the Republican leaders in Connecticut, New York, Ohio, Michigan, and Wisconsin—all states with strong Democratic parties—by the material presented by Mohr in *Radical Republicans in the North*, pp. 28, 38, 44–45, 68–69, 71–73, 88–92, 100, 130–131, 141, 149–150. As with most debates concerning the motivation of large groups of people, the issue here is more philosophical than historical.

26. Mantell, *Johnson, Grant*, pp. 148–149.

27. Richardson, *Messages and Papers of the Presidents*, 6:672–691.

28. Welles, *Diary*, 3:406.

29. See Raoul Berger, *Government by Judiciary: The Transformation of the Fourteenth Amendment* (Cambridge, Mass.: Harvard University Press, 1977).

30. Moore Diary, Oct. 13, 1868; Barrows, *Evarts*, pp. 171–172.

31. Milton, *Age of Hate*, pp. 647–649.

32. Van Deusen, *Seward*, pp. 507–510.

33. Milton, *Age of Hate*, p. 649; Richardson, *Messages and Papers of the Presidents*, 6:705–707.

34. Welles, *Diary*, 3:541–542. Previously John Adams and John Quincy Adams did not participate in the inauguration of their successors.

CHAPTER 12

1. Hugh A. Lawing, "Andrew Johnson National Monument," *Tennessee Historical Quarterly* 20 (June 1961):113. My account of Johnson's postpresidential career is based mainly on Milton, *Age of Hate*, pp. 654–675.

2. *Knoxville Daily Press and Herald*, Apr. 1, 1869, typescript, Andrew Johnson Project, University of Tennessee.

3. Johnson to Longstreet, June 23, 1869; Longstreet to Johnson, June 28, 1869, A. J. Papers.

4. Johnson to "dear son" [Andrew, Jr.], May 11, 1869, typescript, Andrew Johnson Project, University of Tennessee.

5. James C. Parker, "Tennessee Gubernatorial Elections, I: 1869—The Victory of the Conservatives," *Tennessee Historical Quarterly* 33 (Spring 1974):34–48.

6. John S. Wise, *Recollections of Thirteen Presidents* (New York: Doubleday, Page & Co., 1906), pp. 111–112; see also Milton, *Age of Hate*, pp. 664, 753.

7. Typescript, Andrew Johnson Project, University of Tennessee.

8. Ross to Johnson, Jan. 26, 1875, A. J. Papers; Milton, *Age of Hate*, p. 669.

9. Milton, *Age of Hate*, pp. 670–671.

10. Ibid., pp. 671–672.

11. McElwee, "Last Political Conversation of Johnson."

12. Milton, *Age of Hate*, p. 673; Fay Warrington Brabson, *Andrew Johnson: A Life in Pursuit of the Right Course* (Durham, N.C.: Seeman Printery, 1972), p. 266.

13. The following discussion of the historiography of Johnson is adapted from Albert Castel, "Andrew Johnson: His Historiographical Rise and Fall," *Mid-America* 45 (July 1963):175–184; full bibliographical references and citations will be found in that article.

14. Dunning, *Reconstruction*, pp. 19, 72, 82.

15. Carmen Anthony Notaro, "History of the Biographic Treatment of Andrew Johnson in the Twentieth Century," *Tennessee Historical Quarterly* 24 (Summer 1965):144, labels DeWitt as an anti-Johnson historian! Obviously Notaro misread DeWitt.

16. James Schouler, *History of the Reconstruction Period, 1865–1877* (New York: Dodd, Mead, 1913), p. 142.

17. Walter L. Fleming, *The Sequel of Appomattox* (New Haven: Yale University Press, 1919), pp. 71–72, 137.

18. Beale, *Critical Year*, pp. 4–29, 398–399.

19. Clinton L. Rossiter, *The American Presidency* (New York: Harcourt, Brace, 1956), p. 79.

20. David Donald, "Why They Impeached Andrew Johnson," *American Heritage* 8 (Dec. 1956):21–25, 102–103.

21. See, for example, Glenn M. Linden, *Politics or Principle: Congressional Voting on the Civil War Amendments and Pro-Negro Measures, 1838–69* (Seattle: University of Washington Press, 1976).

22. Thomas J. Pressly, "Racial Attitudes, Scholarship, and Reconstruction: A Review Essay," *Journal of Southern History* 32 (Fall 1966):92–93.

23. Palmer, *Personal Recollections*, p. 127; Curtis in Milton, *Age of Hate*, p. 527; McCulloch, *Men and Measures*, pp. 403–407.

24. Jeanne Kirkpatrick, "Why the New Right Lost," *Commentary*, Feb. 1977, p. 39.

25. Undated memorandum, Gideon Welles Papers, New York Public Library.

26. Donald, "Why They Impeached Johnson," p. 23.

27. David M. Potter, *Division and the Stresses of Reunion* (Glenview, Ill.: Scott, Foresman & Co., 1973), p. 186; C. Vann Woodward, "Seeds of Failure in Radical

Race Policy," in *New Frontiers of the American Reconstruction*, ed. Harold M. Hyman (Urbana: University of Illinois Press, 1966), pp. 144–146; Williamson, *After Slavery*, pp. 80–87, 143–144. In fact, a considerable amount of land was made available to Negroes in a number of Southern states under carpetbag rule, but as with many modern welfare programs about the only ones to benefit were politicians and bureaucrats. For what happened in South Carolina, see the splendid monograph by Carol K. Rothrock Bleser, *The Promised Land: The History of the South Carolina Land Commission, 1869–1890* (Columbia: University of South Carolina Press for the South Carolina Tricentennial Commission, 1969).

28. McCulloch Papers, Library of Congress.

29. Thomas, *President Johnson*, p. 612.

Bibliographical Essay

The quantity of primary and secondary sources pertaining directly or indirectly to Johnson's presidency is enormous because his term coincided with one of most crucial and controversial periods in American history. No vain attempt will be made here to list all the sources but only the most important. Those desiring a discussion of the main works and trends in the field of Reconstruction history should consult: B. P. Gallaway, "Economic Determinism in Reconstruction Historiography," *Southwestern Social Science Quarterly* 46 (Dec. 1965):244–254; Thomas J. Pressly, "Racial Attitudes, Scholarship, and Reconstruction: A Review Essay," *Journal of Southern History* 33 (Feb. 1966):88–93; Larry Kincaid, "Victims of Circumstances: An Interpretation of Changing Attitudes Toward Republican Policy Makers and Reconstruction," *Journal of American History* 47 (June 1970):48–66; and Richard O. Curry, "The Civil War and Reconstruction, 1861–1877: A Critical Overview of Recent Trends and Interpretations," *Civil War History* 20 (Sept. 1974):215–238.

The principal general histories of Reconstruction recently published are: John Hope Franklin, *Reconstruction: After the Civil War* (Chicago: University of Chicago Press, 1961); Kenneth M. Stampp, *The Era of Reconstruction: 1865–1877* (New York: Alfred A. Knopf, 1965); Rembert W. Patrick, *The Reconstruction of the Nation* (New York: Oxford University Press, 1967); and Avery Craven, *Reconstruction: The Ending of the Civil War* (New York: Holt, Rinehart and Winston, 1969). The latter is the most balanced in its treatment. In addition, despite their age, there is much that remains sound in William A. Dunning's *Essays on the Civil War and Reconstruction* (New York: Macmillan, 1898), which was republished in 1965 by Harper & Row with an introduction by David Donald, and in Dunning's *Reconstruction: Political and Economic: 1865–1877* (New York: Harper & Bros., 1907). In fact, on some topics Dunning has never been bettered.

The highlights of the historiography of Andrew Johnson have been surveyed in Chapter 12. In addition to the articles by Castel and Notaro cited there, the following are useful: Willard Hays,

"Andrew Johnson's Reputation," *East Tennessee Historical Society Publications* 31 (1959):1–31; 32 (1960):18–50; and James E. Sefton, "The Impeachment of Andrew Johnson: A Century of Writing," *Civil War History* 14 (June 1968):120–147.

The main primary source on Johnson's presidency is, of course, the Andrew Johnson Papers in the Manuscripts Division of the Library of Congress; the diary of William G. Moore, his private secretary, is by far the most valuable item in the collection. These papers are available at most university libraries on microfilm. Unfortunately they consist almost entirely of correspondence received by Johnson and contain few letters of consequence written by him. All of the important official documents of Johnson's presidency are in Volume 6 of James D. Richardson, ed., *A Compilation of the Messages and Papers of the Presidents, 1789–1897*, 10 vols. (Washington, D.C.: G.P.O., 1896–1899). Edward McPherson, ed., *The Political History of the United States of America during the Period of Reconstruction* (Washington, D.C.: Solomons & Chapman, 1875; reprinted in 1967 by the Negro Universities Press, A Division of Greenwood Publishing Co., New York) contains, along with many official papers of Johnson's, a number of newspaper interviews and reports of his speeches. Indispensable both for official documents and firsthand testimony covering the events surrounding the impeachment is *The Trial of Andrew Johnson . . . on Impeachment . . .*, 3 vols. (Washington, D.C.: G.P.O., 1868; reprinted in 1970 by the De Capo Press, New York).

Ultimately Leroy P. Graf and Ralph W. Haskins, eds., *The Papers of Andrew Johnson* (Knoxville: University of Tennessee Press, 1967–) will be an extremely valuable source on Johnson's presidency. So far four volumes of this collection have been published, covering Johnson's career to the beginning of the Civil War. Although the editors are handicapped by the dearth of significant letters written by Johnson, they have brought together much useful material which otherwise would be difficult to use. Moreover, their prefaces to each volume combine to make the best account ever written of Johnson's life prior to 1861. The facilities of the Andrew Johnson Project at the University of Tennessee, which is sponsoring this work, are open to scholars.

In some respects an even more useful source on Johnson's presidency than his own papers is the *Diary of Gideon Welles*. First published in 1911, then reprinted in 1960 by W. W. Norton of New York and edited by Howard K. Beale, who indicated the changes and additions made by Welles in his diary, it is one of the great political diaries of all time. Welles, of course, was intensely anti-Radical, anti-Seward, anti-Stanton, and anti-Grant and must be read accordingly. Nevertheless he supplies an unsurpassed close-up view of Johnson and his administration. *The Diary of Orville H. Browning*, edited by James G. Randall and Theodore C. Pease (published in 1933 by the Illinois State Historical Library, Springfield), is occasionally very useful but on the whole, scant and fragmentary. Hugh McCulloch's *Men and Measures of Half a Century: Sketches and Comments* (New York: Charles Scribner's Sons, 1888) provides a good general view of Johnson's presidency but is disappointingly deficient when it comes to specifics. McCulloch's papers at the Library of Congress furnish some insights into Johnson's administration and policies, as do those of Thomas Ewing, Sr., and Lewis D. Campbell at the Ohio Historical Society. Unfortunately, Seward, who could have told so much, chose to say very little about Johnson in his private letters and wrote no memoirs. Others who were closely associated in one way or another with Johnson during his presidency likewise left nothing behind, or else just some odds and ends useful only for certain episodes.

Every biographer of Johnson, from the first, James S. Jones, *Life of Andrew Johnson, Seventeenth President of the United States* (Greeneville, Tenn., 1901), to the latest, Fay Warrington Brabson, *Andrew Johnson: A Life in the Pursuit of the Right Course* (Durham, N.C.: Seeman Printery, 1972) has been very favorable to him—which may or may not have some significance. Of them all, the best from a scholarly and literary standpoint is George Fort Milton, *The Age of Hate: Andrew Johnson and the Radicals* (New York: Coward, McCann, 1930). Next in line is Robert W. Winston, *Andrew Johnson: Plebian and President* (New York: Henry Holt, 1928), which was the first work to give a full account of his pre-presidential career. Lately Thomas's *The First President Johnson* (New York: William Morrow & Co., 1968) is well written and contains some material not to be found in earlier biographies, but it represents no interpretative advance over Milton, Winston, or Lloyd Paul Stryker's *Andrew Johnson: A Profile in Courage* (New York: Macmillan Co., 1929). Thomas, in effect, simply ignores everything written about Johnson and Reconstruction since 1930. Margaret Shaw Royall's *Andrew Johnson—Presidential Scapegoat: A Biographical Re-evaluation* (New York: Exposition Press, 1958) did not reevaluate anything; Milton Lomask's *Andrew Johnson: President on Trial* (New York: Farrar, Straus & Co., 1960) contains some useful tidbits but is the same old story retold; John N. Dickinson, ed., *Andrew Johnson, 1808–1875* (Dobbs Ferry, N.Y.: Oceana Publications, 1970), is merely a chronology with a few documents and some bibliographical aids; and the attitude of Brabson's *Andrew Johnson: A Life in the Pursuit of the Right Course* is conveyed by its title. There is, in short, a need for a full-length biography of Johnson that takes into account modern scholarship on the Civil War and Reconstruction era.

By far the best book focusing on Johnson's presidency is Eric L. McKitrick's *Andrew Johnson and Reconstruction* (Chicago: University of Chicago Press, 1960). It achieved a revolution in Reconstruction historiography and almost totally demolished Claude G. Bowers's *The Tragic Era: The Revolution after Lincoln* (Boston: Houghton Mifflin Co., 1929), which portrayed the Radicals as fiends, and Howard K. Beale's *The Critical Year: A Study of Andrew Johnson and Reconstruction* (New York: Harcourt, Brace, 1930), which depicted them as the stooges of Wall Street. Although some parts of McKitrick's work possibly require modification in the light of subsequent scholarship, on the whole nothing published since supplants it—instead, recent work merely supplements it. Certainly Howard P. Nash's *Andrew Johnson: Congress and Reconstruction* (Rutherford, N.J.: Farleigh Dickinson University Press, 1972) offers no competition.

Naturally Johnson's impeachment—one of the most dramatic episodes in all of American history—has stimulated the writing of a number of books, all of which, of necessity, present an overview of his presidency. The best is the first: David Miller DeWitt's *The Impeachment and Trial of Andrew Johnson* (originally published by Macmillan in 1903 and reprinted in 1967 by Russell & Russell, New York). Although some of DeWitt's interpretations are obsolete or dubious, no other subsequent work contains so much information, and his analysis of the impeachment proceedings as such remains basically sound. Michael Les Benedict's *The Impeachment and Trial of Andrew Johnson* (New York: W. W. Norton, 1973) and Hans L. Trefousse's *Impeachment of a President: Andrew Johnson, the Blacks, and Reconstruction* (Knoxville: University of Tennessee Press, 1975) are both well researched and offer the neo-Radical viewpoint of the impeachment—the former more so than the latter. Gene Smith's *High Crimes and Misdemeanors: The Impeachment and Trial of Andrew Johnson* (New York: William Morrow & Co., 1977), is a lively but superficial account which offers nothing of scholarly value.

For Johnson's relations with Grant, the best book (although I differ with some of its conclusions on that subject) is Martin E. Mantell's *Johnson, Grant, and the Politics of Reconstruction* (New York: Columbia University Press, 1973). Originally a Ph.D. dissertation written under the direction of McKitrick, it is also an excellent general political history of Johnson's presidency. William B. Hesseltine's *Ulysses S. Grant, Politician* (New York: Dodd, Mead & Co., 1935) is still useful and often perceptive, but its scholarship is outmoded and it is flawed by a Beardian "second American Revolution" concept of Reconstruction. Adam Badeau's *Grant in Peace from Appomattox to Mount McGregor* (Hartford, Conn.: S. S. Scranton & Co., 1887) is of course totally pro-Grant, Badeau having been Grant's private secretary, but it provides material not to be found anywhere else, as does William T. Sherman, *Memoirs of Gen. W. T. Sherman*, 2 vols. (New York: Charles L. Webster & Co., 1891). Presumably T. Harry Williams will fill the long-standing need for a modern, scholarly, and detailed account of Grant's post-Appomattox career in his forthcoming biography of that phase of the general's life.

Benjamin P. Thomas and Harold M. Hyman's *Stanton: The Life and Times of Lincoln's Secretary of War* (New York: Alfred A. Knopf, 1962) contains a great deal about Grant as well as about Stanton during Johnson's presidency. Heavily researched and detailed, it is, however, marred by an extreme anti-Johnson bias and by major factual errors. Many of the latter are corrected in James E. Sefton's *The United States Army and Reconstruction, 1865–1877* (Baton Rouge: Louisiana State University Press, 1967), which also provides a much more balanced view of the role of Stanton, Grant, and the army in Reconstruction than appears either in Thomas and Hyman or in Hyman's article, "Johnson, Stanton, and Grant: A Reconsideration of the Army's Role in the Events Leading to Impeachment," *American Historical Review* 56 (Oct. 1960):85–100.

John Niven's *Gideon Welles: Lincoln's Secretary of the Navy* (New York: Oxford University Press, 1973) is a definitive biography which both supplements and corrects Welles's diary-picture of the Johnson administration. Seward receives perceptive treatment in Glyndon G. Van Deusen's *William Henry Seward* (New York: Oxford University Press, 1967). Seward's career, however, had many facets more important than either Johnson or Reconstruction; hence, although Van Deusen provides useful information on both, his main emphasis quite properly is Seward's diplomatic activities. Ernst N. Paolino's *The Foundation of the American Empire: William Henry Seward and U.S. Foreign Policy* (Ithaca, N.Y.: Cornell

University Press, 1973) is a revealing work despite the overstating of its thesis. Frederic Bancroft's *The Life of William H. Seward,* 2 vols. (New York: Harper & Bros., 1900) can still be consulted with profit.

The best insight into Seward's part in the Johnson presidency is to be found in LaWanda Cox and John Cox, *Politics, Principle and Prejudice, 1865–1866* (New York: Free Press of Glencoe, 1963). This book is also highly valuable for information on Johnson's relations with the Democrats and his attempt to form a new party. Likewise the Coxes' article, "Andrew Johnson and His Ghost Writers: An Analysis of the Freedmen's Bureau and Civil Rights Veto Messages," *Mississippi Valley Historical Review* 47 (Dec. 1961):460–479, is revealing and insightful.

The essential books on Congress and the Republicans during Reconstruction are: William R. Brock, *An American Crisis: Congress and Reconstruction, 1865–1867* (New York: St. Martin's Press, 1963); David Donald, *The Politics of Reconstruction, 1863–1867* (Baton Rouge: Louisiana State University Press, 1965); and Michael Les Benedict, *A Compromise of Principle: Congressional Republicans and Reconstruction, 1863–1869* (New York: W. W. Norton, 1974). Brock's book is the most readable and the best general analysis. Donald's work is the most stimulating from a scholarly standpoint as it seeks to apply a new approach, involving quantitative history, to explaining Republican policies. Benedict's monograph endeavors to refute both Brock and Donald on certain key issues through a combination of awesome archival research and a computer-based analysis of roll-call votes. For firsthand views of Congress during the Johnson years by top Republican leaders, the standard works are: James G. Blaine, *Twenty Years of Congress,* 2 vols. (Norwick, Conn.: Henry Bill Publishing Co., 1884); and John Sherman, *Recollections of Forty Years in the House, Senate, and Cabinet: An Autobiography,* 2 vols. (New York: The Warner Co., 1895). The Democratic viewpoint is to be found in Samuel S. Cox, *Three Decades of Federal Legislation, 1855–1885* (Providence: J. A. & R. A. Reid, 1885).

On the controversial issue of Republican motives during Reconstruction, Stanley Coben in "Northeastern Business and Radical Reconstruction: A Re-examination," *Mississippi Valley Historical Review* 46 (June 1959):69–90, smashed Beard's "second American Revolution" thesis, which he had presented in Volume 2 of *The Rise of American Civilization* (New York: Macmillan Co., 1927). On the other hand, the Coxes, in "Negro Suffrage and Republican

Politics: The Problem of Motivation in Reconstruction Historiography," *Journal of Southern History* 33 (Aug. 1967):303–330, argue that the Republican support of Negro voting was prompted as much, if not more, by idealistic conviction as it was by a desire for political power. Contending the same thing and also discounting economic influences on the Radicals is Glenn M. Linden in " 'Radicals' and Economic Policies: The Senate, 1861–1873," *Journal of Southern History* 32 (May 1966):189–199; " 'Radicals' and Economic Policies: The House of Representatives, 1861–1873," *Civil War History* 13 (March 1967):51–65; and "A Note on Negro Suffrage and Republican Politics," *Journal of Southern History* 36 (Aug. 1970):411–420. I agree with the Coxes and Linden in their downplaying of economic motives, but I believe that they attribute too much idealism to the Republicans as a group. Hans L. Trefousse's *The Radical Republicans: Lincoln's Vanguard for Racial Justice* (New York: Alfred A. Knopf, 1968) is as extreme in glorifying the Republicans as is Bowers's *The Tragic Era* in glorifying the Democrats.

There is no comprehensive study of the Democrats during Johnson's presidency. The closest is Joel H. Sibley's *A Respectable Minority: The Democratic Party in the Civil War Era, 1860–1868* (New York: W. W. Norton, 1977); it is longer on analysis, however, than it is on narrative, with the result that one has to be already familiar with the history of the Democratic party during this period in order to appreciate the analysis, which on the whole is excellent. Charles H. Coleman's *The Election of 1868: The Democratic Effort to Regain Control* (New York: Columbia University Press, 1933) contains much valuable information but is somewhat dated from a scholarly standpoint. Bowers's *The Tragic Era* depicts the Democrats as heroic defenders of the Constitution, whereas Forrest G. Wood's *Black Scare: The Racist Response to Emancipation and Reconstruction* (Berkeley: University of California Press, 1968) portrays them as villainous racists. Useful data on and good interpretations of the Democrats appear in the works of McKitrick, Mantell, and LaWanda and John Cox previously mentioned.

The best biographies of Johnson's two arch antagonists are: Fawn M. Brodie, *Thaddeus Stevens: Scourge of the South* (New York: W. W. Norton, 1959); and David Donald, *Charles Sumner and the Rights of Man* (New York: Alfred A. Knopf, 1970). Brodie, although favorable to Stevens, does not conceal his faults. Donald successfully accomplishes the difficult task of being both sympathetic and critical towards Sumner, which is one of the reasons he won a Pulitzer Prize for this book. Hans L. Trefousse has written good, but perhaps excessively favorable, biographies: *Ben Butler: The South Called Him Beast* (New York: Twayne Publishers, 1957); and *Benjamin Franklin Wade: Radical Republican from Ohio* (New York: Twayne Publishers, 1963). Charles A. Jellison, *Fessenden of Maine: Civil War Senator* (Syracuse: University of Syracuse Press, 1962) and Mark Krug, *Lyman Trumbull: Conservative Radical* (New York: A. S. Barnes & Co., 1965) have provided all that most people will want to know about these two leading Moderate Republicans. There is a need for good, modern studies of John Sherman, James G. Blaine, and, above all, John A. Bingham.

In relation to Johnson, the most useful studies of Democratic leaders are: William E. Smith, *The Francis Preston Blair Family in Politics*, 2 vols. (New York, Macmillan Co., 1933); Stewart Mitchell, *Horatio Seymour of New York* (Cambridge, Mass.: Harvard University Press, 1938); David Lindsey, *"Sunset" Cox, Irrepressible Democrat* (Detroit: Wayne State University Press, 1959); Irving Katz, *August Belmont: A Political Biography* (New York: Columbia University Press, 1968); and George T. McJimsey, *Genteel Partisan: Manton Marble, 1834–1917* (Ames: Iowa State University Press, 1971).

Books and articles dealing with the impact of Reconstruction on the South and on the Negro are legion. Among the most useful in connection with Johnson's presidency are: George R. Bentley, *A History of the Freedmen's Bureau* (Philadelphia: University of Pennsylvania Press, 1955); Joel Williamson, *After Slavery: The Negro in South Carolina during Reconstruction, 1861–1877* (Chapel Hill: University of North Carolina Press, 1965); William C. Harris, *Presidential Reconstruction in Mississippi* (Baton Rouge: Louisiana State University Press, 1967); Elizabeth Studley Nathans, *Losing the Peace: Georgia Republicans and Reconstruction, 1865–1871* (Baton Rouge: Louisiana State University Press, 1968); and James L. Roark, *Masters without Slaves: Southern Planters in the Civil War and Reconstruction* (New York: W. W. Norton, 1971). Of special value with respect to Johnson and the South is Jonathan T. Dorris, *Pardon and Amnesty under Lincoln and Johnson: The Restoration of the Confederates to their Rights and Privileges* (Chapel Hill: University of North Carolina Press, 1953). Michael Perman's pro-Radical *Reunion without Compromise: The South and Reconstruction, 1865–1868* (Cambridge: Cambridge University Press, 1973) is the most thorough published study of the response of the white South to Reconstruction while Johnson was president.

Allen W. Trelease, *White Terror: The Ku Klux Klan Conspiracy and Southern Reconstruction* (New York: Harper & Row, 1971) performs a service in highlighting the violent aspects of Southern resistance to congressional Reconstruction, but the book tends to be exaggerated and one-sided in its approach.

For the Supreme Court, particularly as its actions and non-actions related to Johnson, by far the best work is Charles Fairman's massive and magisterial *Reconstruction and Reunion, 1864–88: Part One* (New York: Macmillan Co., 1971). Stanley I. Kutler's *The Supreme Court and Reconstruction: Politics and Judicial Power* (Chicago: University of Chicago Press, 1968) is a good general history, but it is impaired by its preoccupation with demonstrating the thesis that the Court preserved and even enhanced its power during Reconstruction and showing that the Republicans were not hostile to the Court as an institution. The standard monographs on their subjects are: Joseph B. James, *The Framing of the Fourteenth Amendment* (Urbana: University of Illinois Press, 1956); and William Gillette, *The Right to Vote: Politics and the Passage of the Fifteenth Amendment* (Baltimore: Johns Hopkins University Press, 1965). Raoul Berger's *Government by Judiciary: The Transformation of the Fourteenth Amendment* (Cambridge, Mass.: Harvard University Press, 1977) reveals the moderate and limited intentions of the framers of the Fourteenth Amendment.

The economic issues of politics during the Johnson years are covered in greater or lesser detail in: Robert P. Sharkey, *Money, Class, and Party: An Economic Study of Civil War and Reconstruction* (Baltimore: Johns Hopkins University Press, 1959); Irwin Unger, *The Greenback Era: A Social and Political History of American Finance, 1865–1879* (Princeton: Princeton University Press, 1964); and Walter T. K. Nugent, *Money and American Society, 1865–1880* (New York: W. W. Norton, 1968).

There is no end to books dealing with United States Indian policy and the Indian wars of the late 1860s. The best places to begin are: Francis Paul Prucha, *American Indian Policy in Crisis: Christian Reformers and the Indian, 1865–1900* (Norman: University of Oklahoma Press, 1976); and Robert M. Utley, *Frontier Regulars: The United States Army and the Indian, 1866–1891* (New York: Macmillan Co., 1973).

Index